THE PARTY THAT LOST ITS HEAD

The
PARTY
That Lost
Its HEAD

George·F·Gilder AND
Bruce·K·Chapman

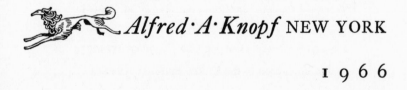 *Alfred·A·Knopf* NEW YORK

1 9 6 6

THIS IS A BORZOI BOOK
PUBLISHED BY ALFRED A. KNOPF, INC.

◇◇

First Edition
Copyright © 1966 by Bruce K. Chapman and
George F. Gilder

Library of Congress Catalog Card Number: 65-18754

Manufactured in the United States of America

To John L. Loeb, Jr.

ACKNOWLEDGMENTS

THIS BOOK does not seek to vindicate a magazine most of our readers never heard of. Nonetheless we do wish to acknowledge with gratitude the sustaining inspiration and encouragement of our former colleagues on *Advance*: Robert Beal, Joel M. Fisher, Emil Frankel, Alice Kepler, Michael M. Laurence, Jr., J. Eugene Marans, Virginia May, John McClaughry, Bruce Rabb, and Dr. John S. Saloma, Jr.

To Miss Kepler we owe an additional debt for her selfless gift of countless hours in preparation of the manuscript. Devoted assistance similarly was rendered by Susan Arensberg, Constance Carden, Ann Cunningham, Carrie Johnson, Mario Del Pilar and Ann Thayer. Mr. McClaughry gave especially valuable help on the book's research. Finally, our editor and friend at Knopf, Ashbel Green, bore our problems with patience, insight, and uncommon good sense.

Scores of participants and commentators on the Republican scene gave information and editorial advice, usually in confidence. We do not list them here, but they have our deepest thanks.

CONTENTS

Part One

‹◊◊›

THE STATE OF
THE PARTY

PROLOGUE

◇◇◇

A Testament
of Bias

W E ARE Republicans. Because we believe in the importance of responsible partisanship, because we prefer,
on balance, the long Republican heritage and its potentialities,
we are even willing to give our party the benefit of the doubt
whenever reason and conscience permit. Though we are young,
we have been Republicans years longer than many of those who
controlled the party in the 1964 campaign and we expect to remain
loyal to the party long after many of them leave it.

We do not believe, however, that party loyalty consists in
the denial of unpleasant realities or in the evasion of difficult
political challenges. We reject both the kind of party loyalty
exhibited by the right-wing supporters of Barry Goldwater who
betrayed the party's heritage for tactical advantage in the South
in 1964, and the kind of party loyalty exhibited by those progressive Republicans whose reticence and inertia allowed that
betrayal. We reject, too, the view of those "organizational men"
who put "unity" first among all partisan values. We believe the

party is best served by an honest appraisal of its condition. This is the prerequisite of reform and regeneration, the prime concerns of this book.

The truth is that the party is compounding its drift to disaster of 1960–64 by drifting again. Its response to the catastrophe has been not change, but repression of its traumatic experience and resumption of its former pattern of self-destructive behavior. Like the Germans after World War I, some Republicans seem to have persuaded themselves that they did not really lose at all. Others fully recognize the defeat, but misinterpret its causes. Many lack the courage or the imagination to advocate more than the most marginal changes. Hence the future is allowed to take the shape of the past; and with new elections bearing down, the party is already back on the collision course of 1964.

In that year, when the Goldwater forces seized control of the Republican National Committee, they dismantled the already weakened Minorities Division whose cause was winning votes among Negroes. More than a year after the election and its unmistakable lesson on this matter, the Minorities Division still had not been restored by the new National Chairman, Ray Bliss. Indeed, the most prominent Negro at Republican headquarters was a leftover from the old Dean Burch regime, a man implicated in a fraudulent election-eve appeal to New Jersey Negroes to write in the name of the Reverend Martin Luther King for President (to draw votes away from Johnson).

The leading candidate for chairman of the Republican Women's Federation was none other than Mrs. Phyllis Schafly, the John Birch[1] author of *A Choice Not An Echo* in 1964. The Young Republicans, with a post-Goldwater chairman easily as right-wing and jingoist as his predecessor, continued with programs fervidly irrelevant to the interests and views of American youth. Ray Bliss's sponsorship of a right-wing delegation to an international youth conference in July, 1965, provided further evidence of

[1] Mrs. Schlafly recently denied that she has been a member of the John Birch Society. However, in his *White Book* of March, 1960, Robert Welch described her as "a very loyal member."

the chairman's disposition to appease the right. The conference brought together in Oxford, England, young political leaders from throughout the Atlantic Community, and the Republicans were represented by a collection of arch-right functionaries with no discernible knowledge of the world outside their hometowns. Their incongruous presence seemed to confirm all that had been reported abroad in 1964 about the party's irresponsibility.

In Washington, the progressive GOP gubernatorial candidate, Daniel J. Evans, survived the overall Democratic crush in 1964. Yet a year later, the Republican National Committeewoman, Mrs. Francis Cooper, rather than resigning for her part in foisting Goldwater on the state's Republicans, declared her regret that the "Conservative Republican Party" had so generously acquiesced in Evans's candidacy. "Evans is supported by the Ripon Society," she reported, "which everybody knows is Communist dominated."[2] (The Ripon Society is a Republican research organization.)

As before the election, the party is most deeply and bitterly split in California, the nation's largest state, where Republicanism takes its most exotic and colorful shapes. Here the far right has retained most of its former strength and most of its former illusions. Reality is to be shut out altogether as the GOP eschews the problematical and mentally taxing world of politics for the more glamorous, exhilarating, free-floating world of entertainment. This is the home of the pop-politician, ruggedly handsome, blond, alliterative, Ronald Reagan—the party's hope to usurp reality with the fading world of the class-B movie. With his more moderate colleague George Murphy victorious before him both in show biz and pol-biz; with John Wayne eager to aid in the right-wing cause; with Roy Rogers and Dale Evans ready for one last right-wing roundup; and with Air Force Brigadier General James Stewart as Sky King—the Republican party in California is becoming a Hollywood retirement home, where the stars of the past re-create in politics the fictitious glories of their antic youths. Its center, appropriately, is Knott's Berry Farm outside Los

[2] Seattle *Argus* (September 3, 1965), p. 1.

Angeles, the site of a scrupulously reconstructed Western frontier town. It is a world of good guys versus bad guys (patriots versus Leftists) as easy to tell apart as cowboys and Indians, and political reality always wears a black hat.

Thus the Republican Assembly of California, the largest amateur Republican group in the state, invited a Birch Society spokesman to keynote its convention in April, 1965, and wildly applauded his assertion that if Goldwater were to run again he would win overwhelmingly. Condemning extremist groups, the assembly could think of just four: the American Communist party, the American Nazi party, the Ku Klux Klan, and . . . the Council on Foreign Relations, the eminently respectable and nonpartisan institution in New York, regarded by the lunatic right as a center of Communist subversion. The state's John Birch Society is richer and stronger than ever, and with some 10,000 fanatic members is the most effective political-action group on the California right.[3]

This pop-pol Republicanism is, of course, a special variant, and it is still possible that the moderates can hold it at bay even in California. However, the repression of the trauma of 1964 and the recurrence of the syndrome which led to it is endemic in the party across the country. In short, the Republican party is still in civil war, still cursed with the incubus of extremism and undermined by the incompetence of a timid national headquarters. Most of the supposed moderate leaders, such as Richard Nixon, who failed the party from 1960 to 1964, fail it still and the right wing is eager for the party to perform yet another self-immolation.

We believe that major reform is urgent. We believe that the Republican party must be regained by the Republican majority from which it was seized during the last few years. The right wing represents a small minority of Republicans; a national poll by Louis H. Bean and Roscoe Drummond suggests that there are not more than three million strongly committed to it.[4] But the evident strength of this minority is greatly inflated by the im-

[3] Raymond R. Coffey, "Birchers Bouncing Back Strong," *Chicago Daily News* (February 1, 1965)
[4] *Look* magazine (March 23, 1965).

potence of the moderate and progressive Republican majority. At the grass roots in many areas moderate Republicans are even withdrawing from active Republican politics, and many of them seem likely to remain withdrawn until the party produces a new leadership with a program of party reform and an ideology responsive to the times and clearly distinguishable from the Great Society. Since the right wing is completely incapable of such initiative, it is clear that the new leadership must come from the more progressive wing.

The progressive Republican leaders today, however, are just another facet of the party's decline. Many of them cannot even answer convincingly and relevantly the simple, indispensable questions: "Why are you a Republican?" "How does your position differ from that of the moderate Democrats who currently control *their* party?" The questions are not impertinent and they are not adequately answered by erecting a few splendid rhetorical pillars of principle, or citing some doomed outpost of legislation marginally different from the Democratic proposal. The fact is that the progressives are not offering a coherent or constructive opposition on either domestic or foreign issues. Some of them seem to regard the 1964 election results not as a mandate for creativity but as a rationale for me-tooism. They are ideologically bereft. Their potentialities and opportunities are great; these men are the hope of the party; but their intellectual contribution to the opposition to Johnson has been insignificant, and with a very few exceptions they have shown little appreciation of their own potential strength and necessary mission.

Such is our bias. We do not offer apologetics for the conduct of the progressive Republicans over the last years and we do not have much respect for the far right. We spent the years between 1960 and 1964 fighting against its takeover of the party and we do not think it is very capable or very strong. We reject emphatically the view, still maintained even by Arthur Krock of *The New York Times*, that the Goldwater nomination was either a true or a legitimate expression of majority sentiment in the Republican party. We believe it was the product of the fanaticism and duplicity of a minority so small as to be literally negligible, since it alienates far more than its own numbers. We believe that the triumph of this minority was made possible by the ideological and political abdication and ineptitude of the progressive and moderate Republicans. We believe that a history of the right-wing takeover—if it is not fettered by a false "objectivity" or neutrality —will corroborate our bias. We do not believe that a history so "balanced" that Barry Goldwater approves it could have fully reported the origins, methods, and purposes of the movement he led, or that a history which pleases the progressive Republicans could have accounted fully their ineptitude.

So this will be a history without heroes. But not without hope. For we believe that the present impotence and paralysis of the Republican party is completely unnecessary. It is completely unnecessary because the Democratic dominance is largely a function of right-wing control of the Republican party, because the potential strength of the progressives is overwhelmingly greater than that of the right wing, and because a progressive Republican ideology can be propounded that could substantially unify the party and give hope for future victories.

CHAPTER 1

The Obstacle
of the Past

THE REPUBLICAN party today is both much weaker and
much stronger than it appears.

It appears weak because it is split, because only a quarter of
the electorate will identify itself as Republican, and because Republicans control less than a third of the Congress and Senate, less
than a quarter of the governorships, and less than a third of the
state legislatures. But the party is in fact much weaker than that,
because a substantial portion of its currently evident strength
consists of parvenu Republicans on the extreme right who entered
the party during the right-wing ascendancy and will not support it
in any campaign which can appeal to a national majority; and it
is much weaker because Republican statistical weakness is compounded by intellectual bankruptcy, by ideological banality, and
by political illusion.

In another sense, however, the party is much stronger than it
appears. Its strength is in potential and in opportunity, and is the
converse of Democratic weakness, currently disguised by its
Goldwater-inflated majorities. For an analysis of the Democratic

domestic programs, passed with ceremony and celebration during the Kennedy and Johnson Administrations, will show weaknesses as grave as those which are already impairing Democratic foreign policies. If the Republican party can conceive a convincing critique of the Democrats and an inviting program for the future —a new and responsible ideology, based on Republican traditions but not petrified by them—the voters will be responsive. The electorate is changing rapidly and radically and will not be bound to those ethnic and economic voting patterns which have favored the Democrats in the past. The election of John V. Lindsay as mayor of New York on the Republican and Liberal tickets is an indication of the change in one of the most intensely Democratic cities. An ideologically revived Republican party will discover, too, that it is split not between two substantial segments of its membership, but between an expendable extremist fringe and an overwhelming majority ready to accept responsible and progressive leadership. If it can produce such leadership, the party may return to national power.

The ostensible balance of strengths and weaknesses between the two parties since 1964 is deceptive. It reflects the capture of the Republican party organization by an unpopular and unrepresentative but militant and well-financed minority. If the party had been controlled by its moderate majority over the last few years, if its internal democratic processes had not suffered the unprecedented breakdown which culminated at the convention in San Francisco, the party would be much stronger today. If it is not captured again by the arch-right, it seems certain to regain some of its lost strength, if not its lost time.

However, without major reforms, the increase in party strength will be completely insufficient to bring victory in a national election. Although the party is potentially stronger than the statistics indicate today, it is still weaker than it was in 1960. The party's weaknesses were both exploited and exacerbated by Goldwater and his following. But these weaknesses originated many years before and were evident in the diminishing congressional and gubernatorial strength during the Eisenhower Administration and in Nixon's defeat in 1960. Even after the party recognizes the expendability of its far-right "strength" and cashiers its extremists—something it shows little sign of willingness to do; even after it reforms its organizational structure, it still will have to face its deeper problems: the exhaustion of its ideology and the estrangement of almost the entire intellectual community.

The election was not simply a rejection of Goldwater himself; it was a rejection of right-wing positions on the issues. Goldwater himself was universally conceded to have been a more attractive personality than Lyndon Johnson. It was his ideology which was rejected: his vote on the civil-rights bill, his skepticism toward public-welfare and social-security programs, his animus for the Supreme Court, his hostility toward the Eastern megalopolis, and his hopes for summary victories in the cold war which could only be achieved by the reckless brandishing of nuclear weapons. His most provocative remarks—so exploited by both his Democratic and Republican opponents—were only chips of this unpopular ideology falling where they may.

Furthermore, contrary to the propaganda of the Americans for Constitutional Action,[1] right-wing congressmen suffered more than any other group in 1964. All across the country, including much of the South, they were selectively defeated or their margins were reduced—in some cases by over 15 percent. Of the sixty-four congressmen, most from hitherto safe districts, who endorsed Goldwater before the California primary, nineteen were defeated in 1964 and almost all suffered sharp reductions in their vote. Meanwhile progressive Republicans, generally from more competitive districts, usually managed to win, often by increased pluralities.

Yet most of the party officialdom refuses to accept the ideological explanation for the defeat. According to most of the 1,395 county chairmen questioned by the Gallup poll after the election, there was nothing wrong with the party that a little "unity" and

---

[1] A right-wing congressional lobby patterned after the liberal Americans for Democratic Action and including among its officers several endorsers and members of the John Birch Society.

"organization" would not cure. There was, of course, the question of ten million Negro votes. There were those "two biggest lies in the history of American politics"—that Goldwater was against social security and survival. There was the matter of campaign ineptitude (as usual, "We failed to get our message across"). There were those incompetent "people around Goldwater" (or "Why didn't he take *my* advice?"). And there was the problem that only a quarter of the American people consider themselves Republicans. But the party itself, according to its victim leadership, is fine, thank you, and its adoption of a new "conservative" philosophy was barely connected with its electoral failures. As F. Clifton White, director of Citizens for Goldwater-Miller, asserted: "I do not really feel that conservatism versus liberalism ever got to be an issue in the campaign."[2]

The issue, as defined by John Grenier of Alabama, executive director of the Republican National Committee during the campaign and one of the most powerful men in the Goldwater movement, was: "What are you willing to pay for the South?" And that question is still unresolved, though both Grenier and former National Chairman Dean Burch regarded 1964 as a good down payment ("absolutely necessary," said Burch). In 1964 the party sacrificed Robert A. Taft, Jr., and Charles H. Percy (who laid down their coattails for Goldwater and were pulled over backward), perhaps 40 congressmen, almost 600 state legislators, over 12 million dollars, almost the entire Negro vote North and South, and its traditional principles, and still won fewer electoral votes in the South than in 1952, 1956, or 1960, and fewer popular votes than in 1952 or 1956.

The South seems to become more expensive every year. Grenier was not satisfied with the price paid in 1964 because some "ambitious" Northerners "out for themselves," notably George W. Romney, refused to walk the Goldwater civil-rights and extremism planks. The Alabaman, an able and ambitious man himself, has announced that he will run for governor, and he may be more difficult to please in the future. But perhaps

[2] St. Louis *Post-Dispatch*, December 7, 1964.

between now and 1968 a suitable price can be arranged to be "paid for the South." In fact, many Republican leaders are already working on it, while others—many of them prospective victims—are fatuously calling for "unity" and "organization" as politicians do instead of talking about the weather when they have nothing to say.

The embodiment of "unity" and "organization" is, of course, Ray C. Bliss, the National Chairman, chosen with the support of the progressives and the expressed appproval of Goldwater. Bliss is an excellent organizer, but his own career is resounding testimony to the insufficiency of these two Republican shibboleths. Ohio a decade ago was one of the most solidly Republican states in the country. It is one of the few states in the country where the Republicans are close to the Democrats in the number of registered voters and it is a state where the party is not severely split. Yet "unity" and "organization" brought victory only when the GOP provided acceptable candidates with acceptable positions on the important issues. On two occasions over the last six years—in the "right-to-work" disaster of 1958[3] and the Goldwater disaster of 1964—the party failed to do this, and Ohio is now solidly Democratic.

Bliss even failed to elect his dream candidate, Robert A. Taft, Jr., to the U. S. Senate in 1964. Moreover, Bliss had assumed that his delegation to the National Convention was united behind the favorite-son candidacy of Governor James Rhodes. But the illusory "unity" dissolved when Rhodes, its nominal repository, withdrew. Bliss should be an expert on the limitations of placing "unity" and "organization" first among priorities.

What is more, in 1964 the Republicans were better organized nationally than ever before. According to the Gallup polls, the Republican organizational effort exceeded the Democrats' by 40 percent; during the Eisenhower years, the Democratic effort

[3] Over the protest of Bliss, Ohio business interests managed to put on the ballot a referendum on the issue of a right-to-work law. A massive labor effort resulted in the defeat of Senator Bricker and most other Republicans who ran in Ohio in 1958.

always exceeded the Republicans'. Organization is indispensable, to be sure, but without appealing issues and candidates it is ineffectual. Unity, similarly, requires that the issues be confronted and resolved, compromised or amicably accepted; it cannot be achieved until the party provides programs and positions behind which to unify. The cant of "unity" and "organization" was the Trojan horse of William E. Miller's regime during his tenure as National Chairman, and in 1964 it disgorged the Birchers and segregationists who tore the party asunder.

Apparently little was learned from this experience. Although Bliss, as chairman of the National Committee faces special problems, particularly in fund-raising, which prevent him from becoming an ideological leader, there is no such excuse for Republican senators and congressmen. Yet it is in the Senate and the House—the party's only active official sources of ideological leadership—that the repression of the ideological facts of 1964 has been most complete. In some respects the Republicans are more conservative than ever. In the House the party is more securely under the control of the arch-conservatives than before the debacle, while in the Senate the right wing, though weaker than in the House, has been strengthened by the arrival of Strom Thurmond from the Democratic side of the aisle and by the electoral defeats of Kenneth B. Keating of New York and J. Glenn Beall of Maryland.

The decision of the South Carolina segregationist and militarist to join the "Goldwater Republican party" posed a major test for Senate Republicans. Thurmond demanded full credit for his seniority gained as a Democrat. The progressives adamantly opposed his demand; the right wing supported it. The fact that the progressives won the vote was encouraging. But in the end Thurmond got everything he wanted because of the willingness of the right-wingers to forgo their own seniority to advance him. Only the dramatic and self-sacrificing maneuvers of Senator Jacob K. Javits of New York prevented Thurmond from taking the vacancy on James Eastland's already Southern-oriented Judiciary Committee left by the defeat of Kenneth Keating. Forgoing another post he preferred, Javits pre-empted Thurmond, thus saving the cause of civil-rights and immigration legislation from a major setback which the party leadership apparently viewed with equanimity.

The remarkable aspect of the Thurmond affair was the inexplicable behavior of the two Republican senators from Iowa, a state where the party was devastated in 1964, losing five congressional seats. Policy Committee Chairman Bourke Hickenlooper, having secured Thurmond's presence on the Policy Committee on the grounds he was up for re-election in 1966, waived his own seniority on one committee to accomodate the South Carolinian, while his Iowa colleague, Jack Miller, waived his seniority on another. Neither had apparently learned anything at all, in either moral or political terms, from the electoral debacle.

Symbolic of the situation in the House was the standing ovation given South Carolina's Albert Watson by the Republican Conference when he switched to the party after serving as chief of the Youth Division of Citizens for Goldwater-Miller during the campaign. The election of Gerald Ford, Jr., as minority leader over Charles A. Halleck was hardly a progressive breakthrough. Angling for the Vice-Presidential nomination, Ford had accommodated Goldwater until the convention, when pressure in Michigan led him to give a seconding speech for George Romney. In the spring he went to Wisconsin to speak for Glenn Davis, an old McCarthyite, running against a progressive Republican in a congressional primary.

Still, Ford's election did reflect a recognition that the Goldwater catastrophe demanded some sort of change. He himself emphasized the need not only for Republican alternatives to Democratic programs but for initiatives in civil rights. Although he gave no indication of recognizing the vital need for regeneration of the party's appeal specifically in metropolitan areas, or of possessing the ambition or resourcefulness necessary for successfully pursuing his policy of constructive alternatives, he nonetheless did adopt a moderate rhetoric and emphatically rejected any revival of the Halleck coalition with the right-wing Southern Democrats. However, it soon became clear that Ford's mandate as minority leader did not extend much beyond the television display of his blond good looks. His tendency toward moderation was soon neutralized by the aggressive re-emergence of the right wing under the leadership of Melvin R. Laird of Wisconsin, his ambitious successor as chairman of the House Republican Conference.

First, Ford's candidate for the post of minority whip, Peter Frelinghuysen of New Jersey, was defeated by the popular conservative incumbent, Leslie Arends of Illinois. Then, to prevent Florence Dwyer of New Jersey, a progressive, from acceding to the position of ranking minority member of the Government Operations Committee, the right-wingers allowed one of their own, the late Clarence J. Brown of Ohio, to retain the post— in contravention of the new rule against a single congressman holding more than one leadership position. (Brown already was ranking member on the Rules Committee.)

The one-post rule was maintained, though, in the case of John Byrnes of Wisconsin, chairman of the GOP Policy Committee and ranking Republican on the Ways and Means Committee. Early in March, 1965, Byrnes was replaced as chairman by Goldwater-stalwart John J. Rhodes of Arizona.

Thus Ford has been surrounded by right-wingers in all of the party's leadership positions—more so, ironically, than Halleck was. In the process, Laird has emerged as the most powerful Republican in the House, and his ascendancy dramatizes the party's refusal to make ideological reforms.

Although his political philosophy is nearly identical with Goldwater's, Laird has escaped notoriety by exercising greater care in its expression. Unlike the Arizonan, who would sell TVA gratuitously for reporters, Laird never says more than is necessary to make a polemical point. Nonetheless, his voting was so obstructive during the Eisenhower Administration that his proposed appointment as Platform Committee chairman in 1960 was vetoed by Richard Nixon.

Laird went on to produce a book, *A House Divided.*[4] Like Goldwater's *Why Not Victory?*[5] it argues inanely for more courageous, militant, and moralistic foreign policies, with greater willingness to risk nuclear war, on the grounds that the Communists will always back down, and anyway, God is on our side. *A House Divided* is the product of the Karl Hess ("extremism in defense of liberty")–William J. Baroody school of political thought at the American Enterprise Association for Public Policy Research. Baroody is director of this non-profit institute, a right-wing omnibus, heavily supported by the late John Birch Society magnate J. Howard Pew.

In 1963 Laird was appointed chairman of a joint House-Senate committee on Republican principles. The committee provided the usual platitudes, but its real function was to advance Laird's ultimately successful campaign for the Platform Committee chairmanship in 1964. As platform chairman he again turned to the American Enterprise Association. Hess and Baroody contributed to the drafting and later became Goldwater's chief ideological advisers and speechwriters during the campaign.

On March 2, 1965, Laird delivered his first major address as chairman of the House Republican Conference. The speech contrasted sharply with Ford's statements as minority leader and may be considered the initial manifesto in Laird's campaign for the minority leadership, begun just weeks after Ford's election to the post. It also provided further evidence of the complete ideological banality of the Republican right.

In direct contradiction to Ford's often-repeated rejection of a coalition with the Southern Democrats, Laird stressed his belief that the principles of the Republican party in the House "are shared in full measure by some members of the majority party." He appealed to *"all* [his italics] who reject the Federal extremism of the Administration" to join in the fight against it.

Laird continued by citing a few constructive alternatives proposed by his friends, then gave a long apologia for the 1964

[4] Chicago: Henry Regnery Company; 1962.
[5] New York: Macfadden edition; 1963.

platform—attacking various misrepresentations of it. Granted, the platform was about as explicit as the Democrats' on civil rights, and in some respects was even superior; granted, it did not call for voluntarization of social security. But there is little that was good or constructive about it, and it remains difficult to take seriously a document which calls for liberation of the Ukraine.

The rest of Laird's speech was a drearily predictable, if occasionally sound, attack on the Administration. It reached special heights of absurdity, though, in its discussion of foreign and defense policies, an area in which Laird regards himself an expert. One quote will suffice as a measure of his expertise. He reveals with alarm: "We allow and even promote Socialistic forms of government throughout Latin and South America, totally ignoring the fact that Socialism is a vehicle for eventual Communist takeover." Throw in an apparently hopeful prediction of disaster in Southeast Asia, and you have the tenor of the current "loyal opposition" (Laird's phrase) in the House.

Laird's leadership continued on this level and he was prominently associated with the Republican congressional position on Vietnam well described by the *National Review Bulletin*[6] as reducing to "a) we wouldn't withdraw; b) we wouldn't fight; and c) above all, we shouldn't negotiate without first having fought and won." Although he is chairman of the House Republican Conference and an aspirant for the minority leadership, he has yet to offer any legislative or strategic proposal which much transcends the mandate of Goldwater's 1964 convention.

The progressive Republican congressmen, meanwhile, are in complete disarray. At the beginning of the session much was expected from the Wednesday Group, a very informal association of progressive and moderate Republican House members. But they have yet to get together even on a matter as basic as the acquisition of staff; they divided and neutralized themselves in the minority-leadership struggle between Halleck and Ford; and they seem to spend more of their time competing for individual

[6] August 31, 1965.

acclaim than advancing the progressive Republican cause. For petty personal reasons they have blackballed at least one liberal Republican from membership (Seymour Halpern of New York), while at the same time allowing themselves to be stymied on some issues by the presence of conservatives in their midst.

Such members of the Wednesday Group as Ogden Reid of New York, Bradford Morse and Silvio Conte of Massachusetts, Clark MacGregor of Minnesota, and Charles Mathias, Jr., of Maryland are among the most promising men in the Republican party, and perhaps in the future the group will be able to mobilize effectively. But at the moment most of them are distracted by thoughts of getting out of the House and moving on to higher office, while in the House Laird alone is more influential than all of them put together. Thus, even these men, able and progressive though they are, are unable to give the party the ideological leadership it needs.

The immediate political and ideological problems of the party are compounded by another deeper problem, already debilitating in 1960 and more portentous today than ever. This problem is the estrangement of the nation's intellectuals, collectively the intelligentsia, identified by their appreciation and understanding of ideas and scholarship. It is their views which—in continuous interaction with popular prejudices or "common sense" —form the national consensus. The intelligentsia either controls or deeply influences the nation's schools, colleges, and churches; its newspapers, magazines, and publishing houses; its radio and television stations; and a large proportion of the leadership of both labor and the business community. Normally the intelligentsia is enough divided between the two parties to obscure its influence on the outcome of elections. Today, however, this element, and particularly the elite of intellectuals, is overwhelmingly hostile or indifferent to the Republican party, and the party is overwhelmingly hostile or indifferent to them. This mutual antipathy is one of the most serious obstacles to a Republican revival. For it is intellectuals who must develop the new ideas and proposals on which a revival must ultimately depend.

Of course the malapportionment of the American intelligentsia did not happen overnight. Nor was it the result of some sly Democratic gerrymander on the nation's campuses. In recent years the Republicans as a party have been alienating intellectuals deliberately, as a matter of taste and strategy. Their approach combines aversion for the company of people smarter than themselves—the intelligentsia—and a kind of patronizing contempt for the intelligence of people poorer than themselves—the bulk of the electorate.

This attitude was incipiently present in the party long before its triumphant flowering in 1964. When Richard M. Nixon turned toward the cameras during the first television debate in 1960 and promised solemnly that a Nixon Administration would save the nation from the peril of dirty language in the White House, he caused shudders of embarrassment among Eastern intellectuals that would have been detectable on a good seismograph at Whittier; and he showed more disdain for the intelligence of his national audience than a scriptwriter for the "The Beverly Hillbillies," to whom the people turn for laughs, not, hopefully, for political leadership and wisdom. It is difficult to estimate the size of the clean-language vote, and no polling agency has considered it worth measuring. But one can safely say that only a small and diminishing sect feels strongly enough on the subject to vote for a Presidential candidate because of his position on it.

The incident itself is not important, of course, except as evidence of an attitude. Nixon's little homily showed a willingness to make himself look utterly ridiculous in the eyes of practically every intellectual in the country, in order to appeal to the millions of presumptive boobs, who, in the theory of H. L. Mencken, seek "boobissimus" for their leader. However, the truth is that most of the people are not that stupid, and most of them could sense that this man, obviously not a boob, was putting them on. The more important fact is that intellectuals—in the press, the churches, and the schools, and in business, union, and professional leadership—influence present and future elections in myriad ways, and it rarely pays to affront them openly. Lyndon Johnson might have discovered this in 1964 if the Republicans, in a really marvelous show of resourcefulness in protecting their stupidity margin, had not found a candidate, Barry Goldwater, even less compatible with intellectuals than the Democratic choice, who might otherwise have qualified easily as "boobissimus." Goldwater's nomination in fact represented a *reductio ad absurdum* of the trend of anti-intellectualism in the Republican party.

It is difficult to say when the trend began. The Democratic capture of the intellectual community is often placed in the thirties. But Seymour Martin Lipset of the University of California has suggested in *Encounter* that the Republican anti-intellectualism has its roots in the 1850's, at the party's very origins. He points out that the party in its early years cooperated with the Know-Nothing Party in a few states to elect local candidates. The Know-Nothings flourished in the 1840's and 1850's, and were given their name for their practice of responding "I know nothing" to all questions about their anti-Catholic and anti-immigrant doctrines. But the boobery of Know-Nothingism, Lipset to the contrary, was by no means limited to the Republicans. In fact, the Republican leadership explicitly repudiated the views of the Know-Nothings while the Democrats, in a bald appeal to this group, accused the first GOP Presidential candidate, General John C. Frémont, of being a Catholic in disguise, and a bastard to boot.

Indeed, the Republican party, if it did not exclude the boobs, did have an early attraction for their opposites, the intellectuals. The nation's most renowned minds quickly adopted the Republican label—men like Horace Greeley, founding editor of the New York *Tribune*; William Cullen Bryant, poet-politician; Peter Cooper, intellectual philanthropist; and Joseph Medill, early magnate on the Chicago *Tribune*. The founder of *The New York Times*, Henry J. Raymond, became Republican National Chairman under Lincoln.

After Lincoln, the benighted Presidencies of such nonentities as Grant, Hayes, Garfield, and Arthur severely strained the patience of Republican intellectuals. Many expressed their disillusionment with the party and some, such as Greeley, E. L. Godkin, editor of the *Nation*, and Henry Adams and Charles Francis Adams, Jr., led a rebellion against it. Significantly, however, American intellectuals did not leave the party, because the long-term alternative, the Democrats, was even less inspiring. In 1896 even the few intellectuals who did embrace the Democratic party left it to support the Republicans—not because William McKinley appealed to them but because they were repelled by Democrat William Jennings Bryan, a religious fundamentalist and radical agrarian. In much the same way, in 1964, Lyndon B. Johnson won over most of the few extant Republican intellectuals through Barry Goldwater's declaration for extremist demagoguery.

In our own century, intellectuals have been successfully wooed by Republicans under Theodore Roosevelt and Charles Evan Hughes, and lost again under Warren Harding and Calvin Coolidge. But the Democrats, with time out for Woodrow Wilson, still held the booby prize—condoning the Ku Klux Klan in 1924 the way the GOP convention condoned the Birch Society forty years later.

American intellectuals as a group did not find a home in either of the two major political parties this century until the Depression. This event, which was such a catastrophe for the country, proved to be a boon for the Democratic party. Franklin D. Roosevelt soon perceived that the times required new political and economic ideas; and he knew where to find them—in an intellectual community which, to an unprecedented extent, had despaired of American capitalism, was intrigued with Marxism, and was looking to the federal government for radical leadership. Although Roosevelt was in no way a doctrinaire Socialist, he succeeded in adapting many socialist programs to his New Deal purposes and attracting many leftist thinkers to his cause.

This Democratic appeal to intellectuals was aided by the Republican failure to respond persuasively. But by no means were all intellectuals captivated. One of the most prominent and articulate critics of the New Deal was Walter Lippmann, who supported Alfred M. Landon in 1936 and whose book *The Good Society,* written before World War II, still stands as a valuable critique of collectivist and socialist theory. Most college campuses, moreover, were relatively unswayed by the Roosevelt policies. Even Roosevelt's alma mater, Harvard, continued its Republican tradition, unbroken since the party's founding, and voted 3 to 1 for Hoover in a 1932 poll, 2 to 1 for Landon in 1936, and 3 to 2 for Willkie in 1940. During the college's tercentennial celebration in 1936, the Harvard *Crimson* wrote: "Let the presence of this man in the White House . . . serve as a useful antidote to the natural overemphasis on Harvard's successes."

However, the Republicans paid little attention to their diminishing number of intellectual supporters. The best that can be said is that from 1940 to 1960 the party equivocated. The refreshing ideological innovations of Wendell Willkie were unsteady to begin with and soon were inflated with the stale air of me-tooism; the constructive initiatives of the Eisenhower first term, so hopefully welcomed by a good portion of the American intelligentsia, coexisted uneasily with the manifest obscurantism of Senator McCarthy.

Many intellectuals supported Eisenhower for tactical reasons in 1952—to stop the Korean War and help stem McCarthyism in the GOP—and in 1956—to show support for the progressive initiatives of his first term; but their support for the party was provisional and in many cases could not endure Nixon's occasional demagoguery and indifference in 1960. The intellectuals turned decisively, but not overwhelmingly, to Kennedy. Although Nixon retained majorities on most college campuses and a majority of all college graduates, Kennedy was closing the gap everywhere, and among the elite took an overwhelming lead. The venerable Lippmann, after supporting most Republican Presidential nominees over the previous thirty years, turned conclusively to the Democrats, as did *The New York Times.* The Harvard student body rejected the Republicans for the first time, and its faculty went Democratic by a landslide. Kennedy was surrounded by eminent professors throughout the campaign and he made himself accessible to them. Nixon's brain trust was not nearly as large or impressive, and he did not pay much attention to it. It was clear by the end of the campaign that the Republicans were in trouble with the intellectuals.

In the 1964 campaign, Goldwater relied for policy advice almost entirely on a small group of associates of the American Enterprise Association for Public Policy Research, an organization heavily financed by extreme rightists. Both of Goldwater's leading intellectual advisers from the institute, Karl Hess and William Baroody, were known primarily as far-right publicists. Hess had been an editor of *American Mercury* during the anti-Semitic tenure of Russell Maguire[7] (although Hess later repudiated Maguire's racist views), and of *Washington World,* a very conservative publication, which he quit because it was too liberal for him. Baroody had been most closely associated with Congressman Laird (his son is Laird's administrative assistant), who served during the convention as chairman of the Committee on Resolutions and naturally turned to the right-wing institute for aid in drafting the platform. Although Goldwater did attract a few ultraconservative professors to his cause, like economist Milton Friedman of the University of Chicago, and cold-warrior Gerhart Niemeyer of Notre Dame, he neglected most of their proposals and turned instead to the more compatible Hess—a high-school graduate—and Baroody, neither of whom had ever published anything of academic value.

At the end, Barry Goldwater's campaign lacked even a scintilla of intellectual credibility. It was clear to anyone of the most rudimentary intelligence that, as President, Goldwater could not do any of the things he promised. He could not end crime in the streets, reduce the number or vehemence of Negro protest demonstrations, elevate the nation's moral tone, eliminate "off-color" novels and plays, banish the topless bathing suit, or

[7] *Facts* (October–November, 1959), a publication of the Anti-Defamation League.

alleviate the minor dissatisfactions and anxieties of affluent America.

On the defense issue, Major General Goldwater was preposterous. Secretary of Defense McNamara was hardly troubled to answer the charge that his vast expansion of American military power represented a program of unilateral disarmament, skillfully disguised by increases in defense spending. Nor was he impressed by Goldwater's arguments that Administration policies were leading to missile, bomber, and deterrence gaps, for he was up against what one Department of Defense official somewhat unfairly described as "the most dangerous gap in American politics—the one between Barry Goldwater's ears."

Goldwater's positions on crime and moral issues were equally specious. The right President, a President acutely aware—as Goldwater patently was not—of the need for a massive assault on the poverty, squalor, ugliness, and discrimination afflicting many American cities might have done something about crime and Negro protests. But Goldwater proposed no remedy beyond judicial stringency, schoolroom prayer, and tear gas. In the end, he became a dangerous joke among most intellectuals, and an object for apologetic sophistry even among the few right-wing intellectuals. He was attempting a direct appeal to the voters, circumventing all the more discriminating media of communications—the press and the intelligentsia—circumventing, as at times it seemed, even the gray matter of the people themselves. In his concept of "the whole man," so often cited in campaign speeches, Goldwater always seemed to leave out the brain.

It is true that the Democrats also pandered to visceral fears, the fear of nuclear war, or of a destitute old age. But there is a crucial difference. Goldwater's casual attitude toward nuclear weapons, his calls for total cold-war victory, and his speculations on social security had legitimately raised these fears; and the Democrats had programs supposed to alleviate them, such as Medicare and the test ban, both opposed by Goldwater. Thus the Democratic appeals—whatever else one thought of them— had a logical nexus with reality which Goldwater's lacked. The

Democrats proposed to do something about the sources of the fears which they exploited; Goldwater proposed to do nothing which would have any significant effect at all on the fears *he* exploited. Goldwater's demagoguery was devoid of the rationality of cause and effect.

Among Republican academic-intellectuals, Goldwater's appeal was so low that it was scarcely worthwhile for the Republican National Committee to send out mailings to its tested list of over 10,000 Republican professors. This list was compiled over the last several years by the RNC Arts and Sciences Division, headed during the 1964 campaign by Dr. Karl Lamb of Michigan State. Although mailings for Governor Scranton in January, 1964, had brought a phenomenal 25 percent return, only 4 percent replied affirmatively for Goldwater-Miller during the Presidential campaign. Only 300 professors—3 percent—indicated willingness to have their names used, compared with 1,100 in the inadequate effort for Nixon in 1960. Hostile responses came from the professors in such numbers, however, that the national appeal had to be explicitly divorced from all efforts of the division for local candidates. It was clear that any association with Goldwater was anathema even to the great majority of professors who were willing to work for Republicans on the local level in 1964.

The Republicans had thus resolved their problem of diminishing intellectual support by opting openly for the boobs —and with a vengeance. Any weakness among intellectuals was blamed on the intellectuals—they were hopelessly fuzzy-minded and socialitsic. The Republicans presented "boobissimus" and lost.

There is a real question now whether such a "boobissimus" will ever win in the future. It is possible that the people have come to expect better than "boobissimus" for their President. Perhaps most of them could see the anomaly of a major political party nominating a college-freshman dropout for the Presidency —at a time when qualifications for other jobs have increased to the point where some chief janitors are expected to have a college education. Nor it is implausible to suggest that people who are reassured by arrays of diplomas on the walls of their doctor's office might be unsettled by their absence in the office of the President. But—in deference to Lincoln—the primary issue is not the mere technicality of passage through college; it is the indifference shown by leading Republicans for the disciplines of logic and scholarship.

To say that intellectuals ultimately run the country seems preposterous to the average Republican, if not rather subversive and undemocratic. But in a very real sense, Republicans, over the last few elections, and particularly in 1964, have been re-belling against the dominance of the intellectuals. The rebellion has been articulated in many ways, as an opposition to the sin-ister power of an Eastern Establishment centered in New York, or of the liberal press, or of a circle of university "leftists," or of minorities and special interests. It expresses itself in the no-tion that, despite the electoral evidence to the contrary, the ma-jority of the people are really conservatives. In the view of the typical right-wing politician this does not mean merely that the people believe in less centralized government. It means that, deep in their hearts, they are narrow-minded, selfish, xenophobic, and racially prejudiced. If their prejudices were not confounded by vote-buying, journalistic misrepresentations, and me-tooism, it is argued, the people would turn overwhelmingly to a right-winger.

This view is often enunciated, somewhat evasively, in olym-pian polysyllables by *National Review,* and in the cruder idiom of *Human Events.* It underlies the approach of what passes these days for a "conservative movement" in the United States. Far from being idealistic, most right-wing politicians share with Dem-ocratic-machine liberals the belief that it is not important to appeal to the minds of the voters, only to their prejudices and appetites. Goldwater's campaign, a brute assault on the entire intellectual world, was based on the assumption that intellectuals are dispensable and that the people are heart-feeling right-wingers. They oppose foreign aid and immigration because they resent foreigners; they oppose civil rights because they fear Negroes; they oppose welfare programs because they begrudge public charity for the poor; they oppose the Supreme Court's prayer decisions because they are sanctimonious fundamentalists; and they oppose international negotiations because they see the cold war as a test of barroom virility. When the Republicans contrive a campaign designed to appeal to suspicion, xenophobia, fear, resentment, religiosity, and barroom virility, they need not be surprised if the intellectuals turn to the Democrats.

If Goldwater's defeat was not immediately caused by his affronts to the intellectuals, his affronts to them certainly made the defeat more durably crippling to his party.

In 1964, to a greater extent than ever before, college students just coming into political awareness, and college professors with lasting influence on their students and in their communities, were driven to the Democrats, many of them for years to come. Newspaper writers were more deeply antagonized than ever in the past, and editors and publishers from great Republican newspapers and magazines were massively alienated, along with their independent and Democratic colleagues. Novelists, artists, television writers, and moviemakers, also with incalculable long- and short-range influence on the views of the electorate, were driven into almost committed service for the Democrats. A series of recent books pillorying the right wing were appearing as movies during the election year. Among the most successful were *Fail Safe, Seven Days in May, The Manchurian Candidate, The Best Man, Dr. Strangelove, The Ugly American,* and *Point of Order;* the right-wingers could only respond with John Wayne preaching individualism at *The Alamo.* Even the word "conservative," once designating a valuable and constructive attitude in American political life, has become a pejorative to many because of the Goldwater caricature.

In a Presidential year, a party's mistakes can wreak deep and long-term damage. For most of the population, the images of the parties are most memorably projected during Presidential campaigns, and alignments are established for many years to come. The campaign of Thomas E. Dewey in 1948, almost twenty years after the Depression, was undercut by President Hoover's inadvertent association with that dire event. The intellectuals who surrounded President Kennedy and gave his leadership much of its vaunted eloquence and style were imbued with their Democratic liberalism during the days of Franklin D. Roosevelt and his cultivation of the intellectual community. So were many of the other journalists and scholars who refined and articulated the national consensus which so emphatically repulsed the overtures of Goldwaterism.

Of course the right-wingers reject the idea of such a national consensus led and articulated by intellectuals. Instead, they invent a national conspiracy. David Lawrence, the syndicated conservative columnist who edits *U. S. News and World Report*, and Frank Meyer, an ex-Communist now ideologizing for *National Review*, argue that the majority of the people hold relatively amorphous views which, when expressed, are apt to be conservative but which are distorted and confused by a national liberal establishment controlling the news media. William F. Buckley, Jr.'s first book, *God and Man at Yale*,[8] inveighed at length against the control of colleges by the intellectuals (of all people), expressing their views, preponderantly liberal, under the guise of academic freedom, despite the fact that most of the money for their salaries comes from more conservative parents and trustees. Donald E. ("Buz") Lukens, as National Chairman of the Young Republicans, was similarly distressed by the dominance of "liberals" in the press and proposed that his more literate right-wing followers infiltrate newspaper staffs.[9] Most right-wingers, in fact, find themselves unable to explain the widespread antipathy toward Goldwater among intellectuals with-

[8] Chicago: Henry Regnery Company; 1951.
[9] They might begin, incidentally, with the Young Americans for Freedom publication *New Guard*, which is right-wing enough, but only fitfully literate. One issue introduced the second installment of a three-page article on De Gaulle as follows: "This is the second and final half of a two-part series."

out imagining some far-reaching conspiracy encompassing most of the colleges and newspapers of the land.

Although Mr. Buckley would be quick to point out that conspiracies exist in the world—most notably something he would call, with some imprecision, the international Communist conspiracy—it is generally true that conspiracy theories of history reveal more about the desperation of their progenitors than about history itself. In any case, the burden of proof lies with the theorist of the conspiracy; and in this case it lies with the right-winger to show that colleges and newspapers discriminate against qualified right-wing applicants to a significant extent. So far the right-wingers have offered virtually no evidence in behalf of their theory, except an occasional column by Russell Kirk in *National Review* detailing obscurantist liberal atrocities at Michigan State.

However, the right-wingers have inadvertently contributed substantial evidence to support the more plausible theory that right-wingers do not prevail on the nation's campuses and on its newspapers, magazines, and book lists because they tend to be not only less numerous but also less knowledgeable and articulate than moderates and liberals. More tactfully, it may be said that intellectual training and sustained and systematic contact with political realities, though they do not preclude right-wing political views, do make them more difficult to maintain.

M. Stanton Evans was so hard-pressed in his attempt to name young right-wing intellectuals in his book *Revolt on the Campus*[1] that he resorted to listing a group of college newspaper editors and columnists and such other luminaries as "Dallas Roper, age 26, managing editor of the Monroe [Lousiana] *Morning World*, described by one prominent [though unnamed] journalist as the most important paper in the state, after the New Orleans, Shreveport, and Baton Rouge papers."

The Republican party, long tangentially associated with the positions of the far right, ardently embraced them and propounded them for a national campaign. Long indifferent to

[1] Chicago: Henry Regnery Company; 1961.

the nation's intellectuals, the party openly affronted them. The national consensus, long somewhat inhospitable to the Republicans, has now been decisively alienated for the first time since the Depression. The damage is great, but there are several reasons for believing that it need not be as lasting or politically incapacitating as the experience of the thirties, to which it is often compared. These reasons relate to the differing circumstances of the Hoover and Goldwater defeats, to the attitudes of the American intellectual today, and to the nature of the national consensus, so misunderstood by the right wing.

To begin with, unlike the Depression, which shook the lives of almost all Americans, the Goldwater movement—though it threatened international catastrophe—actually brought disaster only to Republican politicians. Republican politicians, hopefully, will remember Goldwater long. But the people may forget him more quickly than they forgot the Depression. At least they may not hold him against the Republican party as long, if only because people seem to remember politicians more for what they do than what they say. Thus if Lyndon Johnson should attempt now to liberate the Ukraine, as promised in the 1964 Republican platform, or if he should intervene in another Hungarian revolution with "appropriate nuclear weapons," as suggested by Goldwater in *The Conscience of a Conservative*,[2] no one would blame the Republicans for the consequences, in the then-improbable event that an election were held in 1968.

The Republicans thus were saved from the full destructive potential of Goldwater—by his defeat. The people could only guess, not experience, the catastrophe he portended, and they will not remember it as long.

Nor is the alienation of the intelligentsia likely to be as enduring as that of the thirties. Unless the Republicans choose to remain "the Stupid Party," as John Stuart Mill long ago called the Tories in England, they even may be able to win back most of the press—at least the publishers—and many of the intellectuals in time for the 1968 election.

[2] Shepherdsville, Ky.: Victor Publishing Company; 1960.

Unlike American intellectuals in the thirties, when the far-reaching crisis of capitalism led most of them to turn to radical ideologies, American intellectuals today are not preponderantly doctrinaire. Only a small minority are systematically Socialist; only a negligible handful are Communists. In fact, much to the frustration of the extreme left, a large proportion, perhaps a majority, of American intellectuals are moderates. Doctrinaire Socialist publications like *Monthly Review* and *The National Guardian* have circulations far below those of magazines like *The Reporter* or *The New Republic*. Few books are published anymore advocating unilateral disarmament or nationalization of industry. Dispassionate in tone, skeptical in temper, pragmatic in approach, even many of the most fiery radicals of the thirties now speak of an "end of ideology" and reject many of the pretentions of the most militant liberals. It is myth that most intellectuals have been rejecting the Republican party because it is conservative and they are dogmatic liberals or Socialists. The reason that most intellectuals have rejected the Republicans is that the party has not been paying any attention to them; and it has failed, for the most part, to present any coherent programs at all. It has been "the Stupid Party," and it has been pursuing the boobs. Winning back the intellectuals will not require particular appeals designed especially for professors, say, or church leaders, or editors, but rather a different *attitude*, one of honest and thorough scholarship in the preparation of issues, and of more constructive dissent and initiative in Congress. It will require a Presidential candidate in 1968 who can speak coherently about the nation's problems and offer workable solutions to them.

In their appeal to the nation's intellectuals, the Republicans are fortunate to have in Lyndon Johnson an opponent who has little respect for the life of the mind and little aptitude for communicating with the intelligentsia—an opponent, in fact, who is inclined to circumvent the intellectuals in an attempt to appeal directly to popular emotions, much as Goldwater tried in 1964. But the Republicans must return to their traditions in 1968 and propound rational, coherent, and specific programs, responsive to the obvious needs of the country. Then the party may be able to win back many intellectuals offended by Johnson's empty sloganeering, his personal vanity and refusal to listen to criticism, and his simplistic approach to foreign problems. (Democrats used to make fun of Eisenhower's limitation of all policy memoranda to two pages in length; shortly after taking office, Johnson reduced it to half a page.) Even so, it will not be easy for the Republicans to win back the intellectuals. The party has practically nothing to build on from 1964. But the time is auspicious if the party is willing 1) to repudiate all support by right-wing extremists or covert racists, and 2) to make a concerted effort, beginning now, to consult with scholars on the local, state, and national levels, and to develop workable programs, distinct from those of the Democrats and responsive to national problems.

If the Republicans can win back, or at least divide or neutralize intellectuals and the press—publishers, editors, and reporters —they can win back the national consensus also. It is nonsensical to believe, as Goldwater and *National Review* apparently do, that the consensus can be considered as existing apart from those who are capable of articulating it and making it intelligible; or to believe, as they explicitly do, that public expressions of minority interests by labor unions or ethnic organizations are somehow inauthentic and a perversion of our political system. It is Robert Welch and the John Birch Society, and occasionally *National Review* itself, who insist that the United States is a republic, not a democracy. Their point, at least as a semantic matter, as argued by the magazine, is well taken: the relevant distinction between the two forms of government considered with semantic precision (not common usage) relates to the nature of representation in the formation of a consensus. In a "pure" democracy as defined by the Greeks, sovereignty resides immediately and inalienably in the people, who express their will directly, as in a referendum or plebiscite. In a republic, the people confer their sovereignty on representatives, who under the terms of the transaction, govern according to their own interpretation of the true interests of their constituencies. It is clear that under these definitions the

United States is somewhat more republican than democratic, and that with the increasing complexity of political issues, it is, indeed, just as well to keep it that way.

One of the ways the republican nature of our political process is maintained is through the education of the American electorate by politicians, by schools and newspapers, and by special-interest lobbies and organizations, which argue how their own private interests relate to the general interest. This continual, essentially "republican" process does not allow the people to have their way on every issue according to their immediately undeliberated feelings; but it does prepare them to make relatively sophisticated appraisals of the qualifications and ideological approaches of political candidates over the long run, and it allows them to form a deliberated and educated consensus—as opposed to the right-wing view of a consensus comprising the uneducated prejudices of the majority.

It is ironic that the favorite candidate of the Birchers should have been victimized by the "republican" aspects of that American constitutional democracy. But that, in part, is what happened to Barry Goldwater. As he well knows, it was the intelligentsia, as represented by the press, the churches, the colleges, and other educated and influential segments of the population, along with organized "minorities" like Negroes and labor, which explained and propagated the implications of Goldwater's views and largely neutralized the effect of his most intellectually disreputable appeals.

Goldwater attacked each of these groups in succession during the campaign and ended in attacking even the clergy. It was remarkable, and somewhat disturbing, that he got as much as 40 percent of the vote.

In foreign policy the Republicans had a great opportunity in 1965 to attract intellectuals by sustained and intelligent criticism of the Johnson foreign policy. But the party leadership has been a convenient and unthinking accessory to Johnson's interventionism. By their jingoistic reflexes, the Republicans provided the President with a commodious shelter on the right to which he could repair after any foreign embarrassment or in any domestic political contingency. The protective value of this shelter has been tested repeatedly; it is the best political life and accident insurance the President could ask as he negotiates the treacherous tangles of international politics.

During the 1964 campaign Johnson nullified the political effect of Barry Goldwater's entire critique in foreign policy by a show of fireworks in the Bay of Tonkin. In May of 1965 the President escaped virtually unscathed from an operation in the Dominican Republic which eventuated in a series of blunders and prevarications, widely and authoritatively disclosed in the press but protected from the attack of leading Republicans by ritual anti-Communist alarms. On Vietnam Republican hospitality seems inexhaustibly elastic. By advocating in every crisis action more extreme than Johnson's, the Republicans have allowed Johnson always to appear more moderate and judicious than they. Meanwhile through 1965 the Republicans failed to offer a constructive general critique. On no issue has there been more need for a major party research project. The Republicans have scarcely participated in the foreign policy debate; they have merely assumed martial postures on the sidelines, serving as a foil for Lyndon Johnson. Intellectuals have been neither consulted nor allured. They have been ignored.

On domestic policy, the Republican road to sterility has been paved with the good but inadequate intentions of leaders Everett Dirksen and Gerald Ford. Ford is honestly committed to his policy of constructive alternatives. But the estrangement of the intellectuals and the hostility of the right wing have made it impossible to develop many good ones. For instance, the "constructive alternative" to the Democratic Appalachia program of 1965 was a reprise of the old Democratic Area Redevelopment program, opposed by the Republicans when it was introduced.[3] Neither of the two leaders has shown the vision to produce a legislative program which goes beyond the parliamentary exigencies of the session. Such a crucial, and appropriately Republican issue as

[3] *The New York Times,* March 3, 1965.

the revival of American federalism through alleviation of the states' tax problems was long left unattended by the leadership and then treated as a minor concern.[4]

Moreover, party leaders continue to voice the myth that Goldwater was defeated because of misrepresentation by the press, or because of his ad-lib remarks on social security or nuclear weapons. Certainly Goldwater's most extreme utterances made it a little easier to mobilize popular opposition to him; but the opposition of the intelligentsia would have been hardly less intense or monolithic—and hardly less effective—if Goldwater had been more deliberate in the expression of his right-wing views. Furthermore, the alienation of the intellectuals and the disintegration of the Republican consensus contingently assembled by Eisenhower began even before the end of his second term. After the party conclusively rejects the extreme right—which is the novel problem introduced with the Goldwater candidacy—it will have to deal with the problems which initiated the decline during the Eisenhower Administration. These are the problems which produced the defeat of Richard Nixon, which finally made possible the nomination of Goldwater, and which will persist even with the rejection of the radical right. Another of the key problems, often misunderstood and nearly as important as the hostility of intellectuals, is the party split.

[4] A major stimulus to new GOP thinking on the tax system was provided by a 1965 paper researched by the Ripon Society and promoted by the Republican Governor's Association. Another excellent concept adopted by the leadership in 1966 was the Human Investment Act's plan for tax incentives to businesses with retraining programs for technologically unemployed workers. The bill was developed chiefly by Rep. Tom Curtis of Missouri and Sen. Winston Prouty of Vermont.

Part Two

◇◇

THE MEANDERING MAINSTREAM

◇◇◇

CHAPTER 2

The Party Split

I N EARLY 1963 James MacGregor Burns, a historian and practicing Democrat, propounded in *The Deadlock of Democracy*[1]
his theory that our political system comprises four rather than
two parties, that the Democrats and Republicans alike are split
between a Congressional party and a Presidential party. Burns's
theory, to a progressive Republican, seemed false then and seemed
so in 1964 because only a few unimportant members of the Congressional party actually joined the internal struggle until it
was over.[2] Moreover, while there was no question that the split
within the Democratic party was historically fundamental, the
Republican division appeared at that point to be both newer,
and, hopefully, temporary. The split in the late fifties and early
sixties between the Democratic intellectual-liberal element and
the Democratic big-city machine "bosses" was usually susceptible
to opportunistic repair. The Northern-Southern split, however,
was so open and irreparable that the Democrats didn't even
bother to discuss it.

Yet by the spring of 1964 Professor Burns's thesis, whatever its
invalidity in detail, was beginning to seem plausible in its overall
theme of party divisions. There simply was no denying the in-

[1] Englewood Cliffs, N.J.: Prentice-Hall, Inc.; 1962.
[2] Cf. Chapter 6, "Revise and Dissent."

tensity of distrust between the progressives and the right wing of the Republican party.

Disunity in the GOP is a spirit both fugitive and persistent. Its origins extend back to the organizing coalition that made up Mr. Lincoln's party—the Free-Soilers, Northern Whigs, and Abolitionists. Unlike the Democrats, however, with their persistent but eroding North-South division, the divided Republicans can claim no tradition of sustained geographical, ideological, or personal conflict. One frequently cited theme of internal struggle has been the West versus the East, but that elusive division dissolves to inconsequence in diverse and ungeographical battles of big states against little states and "conservatives" against "progressives," and in the irrepressible vagaries of personality politics.

The nineteenth-century feuds are almost irrelevant to today's. In the fights between "stalwarts" and "mugwumps" one can discover the familiar profiles of the "old pro" and the "do-good citizen," but however fierce the battle then, civil-service reform is no longer an ideological issue in the Republican party. One finds "old pros" and "citizens" on each side of today's split.

Personalities are almost as useless as a historical guide. Most men lead short lives politically and leave few followers. Even direct family descendants take different positions from their political ancestors. William Howard Taft, who was a Theodore Roosevelt progressive in 1908 and an anti-Roosevelt regular in 1912 had a son, Robert A. Taft, who symbolized conservatism to a generation of partisans in the 1940's, and a grandson, Robert A. Taft, Jr., who describes himself as a "middle-ground" Republican and in 1964 had to beat down a "conservative" challenger for the GOP nomination for U. S. senator from Ohio.

Theodore Roosevelt and his Bull Moose bolters of 1912 "stood at Armageddon and battled for the Lord," and lost. While a handful of present-day Republicans profess to have carried away from that contest certain allegiances and grudges, its function as a traditional divider has long since been buried under the ironies and paradoxes of politics. One of Theodore Roosevelt's daughters, Mrs. Alice Longworth, a prominent supporter of conservative Robert Taft in 1948 (when she said of Dewey, defeated in 1944: "You can't make a soufflé rise twice") broke from the Republican party for the first time in 1964, voting for Johnson for President. An even more politically active descendant of Colonel Roosevelt, his granddaughter, Mrs. Andrew Williams of Seattle, did support the GOP ticket against Johnson, but earlier in the year was defeated for Washington State GOP National Committee-woman because she declined to help Goldwater before the National Convention and because the then-dominant right wing suspected (correctly) that her secret preference was Scranton. Another T.R. granddaughter, Edith Kermit Roosevelt, not only supported Goldwater before the convention but wrote ardent articles in radical-right publications extolling him and damning the mythical Eastern Establishment.[3]

Meanwhile, Teddy's ghost itself was conjured up by both sides of several questions in 1964; but by August it was consigned to the letters to the editor column of *The New York Times,* where former New York Congressman Hamilton Fish and a number of Roosevelt scholars debated where he would have stood on Goldwater.

There was an attempt to make geography an issue in 1964 with the "Eastern kingmakers" pictured by the Goldwater strategy as a long-standing Star Chamber that had dominated Republican politics since before living memory. But this East-West conflict was a campaign ploy with little historical basis, used at least partly to disguise an attempt of the Southern reactionaries to impose their own strategy on the national party. It is interesting to note however, that early in the century, the party did show a geographic division as well as an ideological and personal one. Except for T.R., the East tended to be "conservative" and the West—the "Sons of the Wild Jackasses"—"progressive." Nelson Rockefeller's maternal grandfather, Senator Winthrop Aldrich

[3] Edith Kermit Roosevelt: "Eastern Clique Grabs For GOP," *The Freedom Press* (November 25, 1964).

of Rhode Island, was considered by Westerners to be one of the most reactionary men in the Senate, as was Henry Cabot Lodge, Sr., grandfather of Henry Cabot Lodge Jr., the progressive Republican leader the right wing probably detested more than any other in 1964.

In the 1930's the geographical division made a mismarriage with the ideological split of that day and produced several mutant strains of the old splits which persist today in a schemeless tangle from coast to coast. The East retained its isolationist-conservatives from the twenties, but its dominant tendency in the thirties was internationalist in foreign policy and confusion in its domestic confrontation with liberal Democratic economic policies. That is generally its position today.

The Middle West was sternly opposed to the New Deal and unapologetically isolationist. With a few exceptions, the Republican party in this section is still economically conservative, but divided somewhat on foreign policy, including both isolationists converted to internationalism and isolationists converted to interventionism, with various shades in between.

In the 1930's the great plains and mountain states boasted a hybrid of East and Middle West. The Western progressives were New Dealers on economic questions and isolationist in foreign policy. The last of this species was Senator William Langer of North Dakota who died in 1959, and today the region is more conservative than the Middle West. Senator Goldwater's earliest Senate support came from Nebraska's Carl T. Curtis and Idaho's now deceased Henry Dworshak. The first of the few Republican governors to give backing to Goldwater's Presidential candidacy was Montana's Donald Nutter, who died in 1962.

The Far West, by tradition, has been faction-ridden and unpredictable. The one constant of Republican (and Democratic) politics on the West Coast is the predominance of personality over party in almost any given contest.

Historically, the Southern GOP has been a rotten borough, a pawn in the hands of Northern politicians who, unlike the Southerners, often actually held political office. In the late forties,

however, the old system began to crumble, first at the instigation
of Eisenhower supporters, who were economic conservatives,
foreign policy internationalists, and racial moderates. Whatever
its contribution to disunity in the 1960's, the Southern Republican
party will not fit into any tight scheme of historical analysis based
on geography.

There are exceptions to all these generalizations and indeed,
that is the point. One cannot chart a long history of internal
Republican feuding based on certain sustained themes (as many
of today's short order historians have tried to do) without dealing
in half-truths apt to be drawn and quartered as one reaches
further back into the tangle of the party's history.

This is not to say that the "progressives" of today, or the
"conservatives," can find no link with Republicans of the past or
that past events do not influence the party now. But it is to say
that there is no continuing thread that ties each group together.
While disunity provides counterpoint to Republicanism through
the years, overall unity has been the party's sustaining theme since
the Bull Moose break of 1912. This fact is difficult to grasp
now, after five years of heightened tension within the party.
During that time supporters of Senator Goldwater chose to invent a history of GOP internal conflict as a means of marshaling
further support, and so contributed to a view of present differences
within the party as major historical cleavages. In fact, their
analysis had the practical effect of creating new differences and
obscuring the novelty of their own factional extremism.

Nearly every revolution, large and small, requires a conspiratorial rationale for the dominance of the "ins." For the
Republican arch-conservatives of 1960–64, it was that the "liberals"
had captured the party through devious means in 1952 and
separated it from "real Republicanism."

Actually, despite the traumatic 1952 convention, the Eisenhower Administration attempted to reach a compromise between
the Taft conservatives—always less extreme than the Goldwaterites—and the progressives, who had engineered the general's
nomination. Not only did Eisenhower meet with Taft in Morning-

side Heights in September, 1952, to lay out a program acceptable to the conservative leader, but he made every effort to accommodate Taft after the election and before Taft's death in August, 1953.

Still the narrowly Republican Congress—the first since 1946, the second since 1930, and the latest to this day—resisted many of the more controversial items of legislation in the President's program, and in 1954 the GOP failed to maintain its control of either house.

Eisenhower continued to be torn between his long-range aim of fashioning a new Republican party, with the unpleasant necessity of directly rejecting the right wing, and his immediate need for cooperation from the GOP in Congress. In the end he chose to conciliate the right-wing leaders while setting a moderate example in his policies. However, Republican votes in Congress slipped further in 1956, even while Ike himself was winning re-election by a record plurality. In that campaign the GOP national ticket made a broad appeal to the metropolitan voter, with special organizational attention given labor and Negroes and with a comprehensively progressive platform. Eisenhower carried twenty-five of the nation's thirty-six largest cities. But of fifty-two congressional districts of greatest labor strength, the Eisenhower-Nixon ticket won twenty-seven, while Republican congressional candidates carried only eleven.

In *The Future of American Politics*,[4] written in 1951, a nonpartisan political analyst, Samuel Lubell, described the trends in American attitudes which could lead to a Republican victory. All the indices pointed to a candidate like Eisenhower. In 1956 Lubell wrote, in *The Revolt of the Moderates*,[5] that despite their propitious beginning, the Eisenhower Republicans had yet to renovate the full Republican party.

Indeed, rather than using his 1956 landslide as a mandate for internal reform, President Eisenhower made still further com-

[4] New York: Harper & Brothers; 1952.
[5] New York: Harper & Brothers; 1956.

promises with the right wing in Congress. Where in 1956 he had campaigned on a record of "Peace, Prosperity and Progress" coupled with a forthright appraisal of problems yet to be solved, in 1958, a recession year, he participated in GOP campaigns that played down economic difficulties and charged the Democrats with "socialism." The result was a disastrous defeat which put the GOP out of serious competition for control of Congress.

In the following two years the party at the national level did re-examine its posture on issues and organization. A national Committee on Programs and Progress was appointed by the National Committee, under stimulus from President Eisenhower, and received vigorous leadership from a progressive businessman from Illinois, Charles H. Percy. The "Percy Report," as it came to be called, presented a shiny, forward-looking image for the party and was the foundation for the 1960 platform.

Thus were conjugated the contradictions and compromises of the Eisenhower Administration. Bitter combat with Taft followed by propitiation of him; the submission of a wide-ranging program of social legislation, including establishment of the Department of Health, Education, and Welfare, followed by the refusal to openly attack Senator Joseph McCarthy; the conduct of a resolutely progressive national campaign in 1956, followed by the second-term alliance with the implacably conservative Secretary of the Treasury, George Humphrey, and finally by the establishment and support of the Percy committee. And during all the ideological vicissitudes, Eisenhower maintained a steady refusal to engage his own power in behalf of his own positions, even his own legislative program. Although the President did not suffer the likes of Senators Jenner, McCarthy, and Knowland gladly, he did suffer them quietly. Although he valued the support of progressive and moderate Republicans, he never showed them special favor, and he refused to defend effectively his Administration's court philosopher of modern Republicanism, Dr. Arthur Larson, when he was assaulted by rightists. Eisenhower led by example, never by threat or promise. And no matter how much rightists would flout his example, he would not openly reject them. This was the Eisenhower compromise. With Eisenhower out of office and the question of party direction for the future unresolved, the machinery established by the compromise was doomed to break down.

CHAPTER 3

◇◇◇

The Compromise Breaks Down

THE PRE-CONVENTION campaign and the 1960 convention broached the themes of the next four years. But most of the commenators and even most of the participants did not understand their portent.

In 1956 Vice-President Nixon beat back an inept "Dump-Nixon" move by Harold Stassen at the National Convention, and thereby became the logical candidate for President in 1960. But in 1958 he set the anti-"Socialist" theme of the disastrous midterm congressional campaign and after the election it was difficult to find many races where Nixon's speeches actually helped Republican candidates. In New York, however, where Nixon was only asked to appear after his absence became publicly embarrassing, the state GOP ticket bucked a national Democratic tide to win by a landslide, propelling Nelson Rockefeller into national prominence as a Presidential possibility. From then until the 1960 election the competition between Rockefeller and Nixon blinded most observers to what was really going on within the Republican party.

It was assumed by almost all observers except those who knew both Rockefeller and Nixon well that this was a reopening of the Taft-Eisenhower, "conservative"-"liberal" split of 1952, with Nixon now in Taft's position. This misconception was occasioned more by symbolic and political differences than by ideological ones. Rockefeller was a New York, big-city Republican, while Nixon was the small-town Horatio Alger who caught Alger Hiss and who had assailed the "socialist" Democrats in the recent 1958 campaign. Almost all of Rockefeller's backers were progressives. All of the right wing then prominent in the party backed Nixon.

However, Nixon received right-wing backing chiefly because there was no arch-conservative candidate in the race. A large part of his support, in fact, was from progressives—senators like Hugh Scott of Pennsylvania, Cabinet members like Attorney General William P. Rogers, and the chairman of the Republican National Committee, Senator Thruston B. Morton of Kentucky.

Rockefeller's quarrels with the Administration in 1959 and 1960, moreover, were not primarily liberal versus conservative at all. Only the question of a medical care for the aged was Rockefeller's position markedly to the "left" of the Administration's, and the New York governor was prepared to argue that social security financing of medical care, "with an option" for those persons with private insurance, was really the most "conservative" method.

Some of Rockefeller's proposals actually stood to the right of the Administration. His free-market ideas on agriculture won him a pathetic thirteenth-hour endorsement at convention-time from Secretary of Agriculture Ezra Taft Benson. Indeed, Rockefeller's farm program had been influenced by Benson, who disliked Nixon and privately had offered his advice to Rockefeller.[1]

---

[1] After 1960 Benson became chairman of the radical-right organization "We, the People!" and blessed his son's decision to become Midwest Co-ordinator of the John Birch Society.

It was defense and foreign policy which most concerned Rockefeller and which put him in substantial conflict with the Administration. Rockefeller called for a spending increase of 3.5 billion dollars for improved limited-war resources, more missiles, and a program of fallout shelters, and urged resumption of underground nuclear testing, a major break from Eisenhower policy. These planks in the Rockefeller platform could hardly be called "liberal," and he stressed them above all others.

Right-wing Republicans and Rockefeller's few liberal Democratic supporters were disconcerted by his candidacy. While liberals ignored the Rockefeller defense positions, right-wing Republicans were bemused by them. *National Review*'s editors could only comment, darkly but uncertainly, that Rockefeller's "hardness" on defense and foreign policy and "softness" on domestic issues were "the characteristic mixture found in the varied authoritarian, proto-fascist programs that have arisen out of the stultifications or turmoil of the twentieth century."[2]

Most Republicans, however, persisted in viewing the Nixon-Rockefeller feud simply as one between conservative and liberal. Political competition often sets up a spurious polarity in the eyes of observers and blinds them to areas of agreement. Rockefeller's competition with Nixon was the cynosure of Republican politics during his campaign for the nomination in 1959, and even through the 1960 convention.

On arriving in Chicago Rockefeller was welcomed by crowds of zealous supporters assuming with everyone else that his declaration of candidacy was imminent. His address to the Platform Committee was received coolly; it was considered a politically motivated retreat from his former position. What exactly, were Rockefeller's differences with Nixon? one member asked him. The governor's citation of defense and medicare alone irritated the members of the committee, who concluded either that the governor had been creating a tempest in a teapot over the previous months or that he was trying to conciliate them in hopes of support for his candidacy.

[2] *National Review Bulletin* (June 25, 1960), p. 1.

Barry Goldwater felt much more at home on the committee. It is constitutionally favorable to the right wing, since it gives small states equal representation with the most populous ones. Like Rockefeller, Goldwater did not involve the President by name in his criticism, but unlike the governor, he did not bother to soften his remarks by praising the Administration where he thought it had done well. "In foreign affairs," Goldwater told them, "we have moved with timidity and indecision; we have tolerated Castro's name-calling and confiscation of American property."

Goldwater droned on to domestic affairs, bitterly attacking all programs of federal aid for education and depressed areas, medical care for the aged, or support for the economy.

It is difficult to believe that those Platform Committee members who stood to cheer the senator were unaware that the Eisenhower Administration was backing programs of federal aid to education and to depressed areas, medical care for the aged, and support for the economy. But their ire still was directed at Governor Rockefeller, not the President and not the Vice-President, and so completely did they identify Rockefeller with the liberal viewpoint that the initial platform planks came unabashedly close to echoing Goldwater's speech.

The Arizona senator himself felt matters were so secure at the convention that he could afford to be magnanimous toward Rockefeller. He said on July 22: "The truth is that while Governor Rockefeller and I do disagree on many points, our areas of agreement far outweigh our areas of disagreement. And I would suggest," he said, speaking more accurately than he knew, "that despite Governor Rockefeller's recent apparent criticism of Mr. Nixon, these two men are committed to the same objectives and their areas of agreement are far more significant than the differences between them.[3]

Within a few hours Rockefeller had made a public repudiation of the platform, Nixon in response had telephoned him, and

[3] Barry M. Goldwater, *Newsweek* (August 1, 1960).

the two of them had met secretly in Rockefeller's New York apartment, with a telephone connection to the Rockefeller staff and to Platform Chairman Charles Percy in Chicago. Together they wrote the fourteen-point agreement soon to be called the "Compact of Fifth Avenue." Only on one or two points, chiefly medical care for the aged, could the two men not agree. The supposedly bitter ideological conflict between the two men was demonstrated to be illusory.

Goldwater now called Rockefeller a "spokesman for the ultra-liberals" and declared that Nixon had "sold out." But James C. Hagerty, Eisenhower's press secretary, informed reporters that the President did not agree with Goldwater's "sell-out" attack and that he thought things were "going all right."

Thus was the general ideological consensus among Eisenhower, Nixon, and Rockefeller revealed. The real difference between them was that Rockefeller, at least so it seemed then, was eager to make a logical extension of the Eisenhower mandates of 1962 and 1956. Nixon, up to the time of the compact and frequently after it, was more eager to continue the Eisenhower intraparty compromise and his drifting dalliance with the right wing. Both advocated strong civil-rights measures, for example, but Rockefeller returned again and again to this issue; Nixon wished to avoid it as much as possible. Style was the difference between them—style and strategy.

The Eisenhower-Nixon Compromise obscured the fact that the former President and Vice-President must in the last analysis be counted with Rockefeller in the party's progressive and moderate camp. The compromise, moreover, was in good measure responsible for what almost became of the 1960 convention and what did become of the convention and the party of 1964. In 1960 the President and Vice-President took little interest in the early development of the platform. Mr. Nixon did go to the trouble of vetoing the appointment of Representative Melvin Laird of Wisconsin as platform chairman because he was too right-wing, having voted against such pet Administration programs as foreign aid, reciprocal trade, and the National Defense Education Act.[4] But with the House leadership pushing for him, Laird was made vice chairman, and after the Fifth Avenue compact, he worked openly with other right-wingers to keep the fourteen points from being incorporated. In 1964 he was selected, and cleared without protest by Nixon, Rockefeller, and Eisenhower, to chair that year's Platform Committee, which once again, according to convention rules, was by composition favorable to the smaller states, most in the West and South, each one approximately equal in representation to the most populous states of the Northeast and Far West. In 1964, however, there was of course no outside intervention by a national candidate who represented more truly the party's national balance of power and interests.

In 1960 the compromise machinery paid no heed at all to the sudden emergence of Barry Goldwater as a champion of the right and a critic not only of the Democrats but of the Administration. Just as Rockefeller's opposition to Nixon's candidacy clouded the ideological congeniality of the two men, Goldwater's consistent support of Nixon before the convention obscured his broad policy breaks from the Administration. The emphasis, inevitable in an election year, was on defending the Republican candidate from the Democratic left.

Goldwater did work for the Nixon-Lodge ticket during the campaign. He made 126 speeches, mostly in the South and Southwest. Said I. Lee Potter, director of the Southern division ("Operation Dixie") of the Republican National Committee: "Demands for Sen. Goldwater to appear before Southern audiences are . . . in such volume that the Senator couldn't satisfy them if he spoke in three cities a day for the rest of the campaign." In Macon, Georgia, he stated that problems of desegregation should be handled by the states, a position fully contradicting the Republican platform.[5] In answer to a newsman's question as to what he would do if Nixon should lose, Goldwater said on October 8: "I'm for Dick Nixon. But on the premise the question presents,

[4] *Milwaukee Journal* (March 27, 1960).
[5] United Press International, October 8, 1960.

I will not hesitate to submit in 1964 for the Presidential nomination."[6]

Rockefeller was beset by charges that he had lost the state of New York by failure to campaign hard enough for the Nixon-Lodge ticket. The assertion was probably inevitable, but nonetheless unfair. Kennedy carried New York by 52.5 percent; his margin in neighboring Connecticut was 53.6 percent, in Massachusetts 60.2 percent. Indeed, a majority of Eastern states not only voted for Kennedy but gave him larger percentages than he got in New York. Moreover, the governor gave himself fully to the campaign. He scheduled four hundred major and minor speeches throughout the state on behalf of the Republican ticket; he maintained a sixteen-hour day; and with his help the New York State United Republican Finance Committee raised more money for the Nixon-Lodge ticket than for any previous Presidential campaign, overshooting its quota by 30 percent.

Had Rockefeller been a bit more cynical, he might have scheduled more speeches beyond the borders of New York—he made only eight out-of-state appearances during the campaign. These would have given him national publicity comparable to Goldwater's and removed some of the onus for the New York loss, which most politicians saw coming months beforehand. Instead, Rockefeller, with the encouragement of the national Nixon-Lodge campaign staff, tried to shore up Nixon's chances in the Empire State. But overwhelming majorities for Kennedy among the Negroes and Catholics in the cities wiped out Republican margins elsewhere in New York.

Facing such statistics in state after state, Republicans flapped and fluttered about in search for an explanation of the obvious. The right wing blamed Rockefeller, of course, and added, incongruously, that Nixon was also culpable for thinking he could win the Northeast in the first place. The still-hazy plans of the archconservatives required that the future emphasis be on the South. They also demanded new leadership. Senator Goldwater, during the January meeting of the Republican National Committee, in-

[6] Associated Press, October 25, 1960.

dicated he would be understanding if the moderate National Chairman Thruston B. Morton, decided to devote himself more fully to his Senate chores.

The official party line in late 1960 and early 1961 was vacuous and non-controversial, and hence irrelevant to treatment of the party's real problems. One began to wonder if the Republican National Committee would spend the next four years telling the world just how few votes per precinct in Illinois or Texas would have elected Mr. Nixon President. The party machinery of the Eisenhower Era was reeling, trying to find a safe place to stand.

Finally, the Research Division of the Republican National Committee under the direction of Dr. William Prendergast, released the agonizing news that the Nixon-Lodge team indeed had lost the election in the urban North. For this daring analysis, Prendergast became anathema to right-wingers, though he was strongly conservative. When the Goldwater new order arrived three and a half years later, he was among the first to have his resignation sympathetically accepted.

What the Research Division's statistics showed was that of forty-one cities with populations of over 300,000, the Nixon-Lodge ticket carried only fourteen. These same cities elected 123 congressmen, and only 40 of them were Republicans. In major states like Illinois, Michigan, Missouri, and Pennsylvania, the Republicans amassed large outstate pluralities which were inundated by the still larger Democratic pluralities in the major cities.

The plain implication of the election results was that the Eisenhower majority—founded on white, middle-class Republicans but indispensably including a substantial labor contribution and inroads even among the ethnic minorities of the biggest cities —was falling apart all over.

CHAPTER 4

◇◇

The Siren Drawl of "Dixie"

THE PROBLEM of the party after its 1960 defeat had two seemingly obvious dimensions. The first was that the party, and to a lesser degree the national candidate, had not developed and popularized programs that could attract support from an increasingly urbanized America. The second was partly a consequence of the first: the party was not at all well organized at the city and precinct levels of the major metropolitan areas. In Philadelphia, until the early fifties a strongly Republican city, the party had leadership that was widely suspected of collusion with the Democratic machine and on Election Day there were some 500 precincts out of 1,623 that were wholly unmanned by Republicans.[1]

But having mustered the courage to read the election returns to the gathered partisans, the national leadership of the Republican party in 1961 could not bring itself to suggest that an investigation of the Republican program might now be in order. In-

[1] *U.S. News and World Report* (April 23, 1960).

stead, it jumped right over that part of the problem and attacked with fast-fading zeal the dimension of "organization."

In June Senator Morton resigned his chairmanship of the National Committee. But before he left he appointed Ray Bliss, the GOP state chairman in Ohio, to head a committee on big-city politics. Representative William E. Miller (N.Y.), Morton's successor and previously chairman of the Congressional (Campaign) Committee, backed the Bliss Committee and it made its report at a National Committee meeting in Oklahoma City the following January, 1962. It revealed the full, sad disorder of the Republican organization around the country. The report called for new fundraising, research, and training programs; new divisions at national headquarters; invigoration of present activities, stunted by apathy; and continuous liaison with city-oriented lobbies and organizations. In short, it was a comprehensive blueprint for the reform of the Republican organization in the cities.

Having given the word, if not the will, to the National Committee, Mr. Bliss returned to Columbus and began a three-year staring contest with the encroaching Goldwater apparatus. Meanwhile, the Big-City Report became part of the pavement of good intentions for the right-wing advance. Not only was the residual machinery of the Eisenhower Era unable to grapple with the real issues that concern urban dwellers, it was unwilling to make more than rhetorical contact with them. Bliss's touted panacea of "Organization! Organization!" was never really applied to the big cities.

The verbal emphasis on organization, in fact, served two purposes for the Republican National Committee hierarchy. It diverted attention from its acquiescence in the subsequent Goldwater takeover, and it provided an escape from the ideological dilemma the takeover posed. When someone asked what issues the party was developing to meet the political realities of megalopolis, Chairman Miller would testily reply: "What the hell, we need muscle and money, not a new image." When one asked just what this "muscle" consisted of in the urban areas, the Republican National Chairman would demand: "We adopted a big-city report at a convention in Oklahoma City. Isn't that enough?"[2]

But somehow it was not enough. Under Miller the Republican National Committee not only failed to implement the Bliss report but even dismantled the few desultory operations which had been developed previously to deal with the party's urban problems. Over the months, Miller gravitated to an attitude of indifference toward the urban vote and then to sabotage of those attempts made by others to do the work he was unwilling to do.

Insiders tended to think that the congressman was just lazy. Staff workers at the national headquarters said that he appeared there approximately four times a month and that it was office policy not to disturb him over any matter before 11:00 a.m. He was seldom at his office on Capitol Hill where by 1963 his record of attending roll-call votes was 49 percent, the second lowest in the House. Some assumed, therefore, that the Republican National Chairman was always on the road, but if he was, his speaking schedule did not show it. Even Goldwater people grumbled that what the party needed was a paid, full-time chairman.

But sloth will not explain fully what happened to the national organization. In July of 1962 Mr. Miller told the authors, then editors of the unofficial Republican magazine *Advance*: "If the Republican party wants no dissension, they sure don't want me as their chairman. The only way to avoid dissension is to do nothing." To understand William Miller is to realize that even while seeming to do nothing he did cause dissension.

Under Miller the Republican attempt to secure labor support all but disappeared. The National Committee stuck its "Labor Division" into an obscure corner, staffed it with just one man, Robert Gormley, and ignored it. The Bliss Committee had called for "a continuing program of research, recording and dissemination of information of specific interest to the working man and woman," and for "bold statements of Republican positions." But

[2] New York *Post* (January 23, 1962).

the Republican positions were a mystery to the Labor Division. On the question of a national right-to-work law, for example, Mr. Gormley said: "This is a highly sensitive area." Right-to-work laws, implacably opposed by organized labor, had been the single most destructive issue used against the party in 1958. The 1960 Republican platform stood squarely against them. Every potential Republican nominee for President was opposing them, except one. But that one was Barry Goldwater, and Mr. Gormley, the Labor Division, was advised that he did not know the Republican position on this matter, or any other that was of interest to labor.

Few other moves of the official Republican leadership from 1960 to 1964 were so cynical and destructive as the option for the white South and the positive rejection of the Negro everywhere. For fifteen years, since 1948 and the National Chairmanship of then-Representative Hugh Scott of Pennsylvania, the Republicans sought to build a new party for the new South. Under Eisenhower and National Chairman Meade Alcorn of Connecticut "Operation Dixie" was given an exceptional organizational and financial base at party headquarters. The progressives in the party believed the South could be brought into the two-party system without Republican "me-tooing" of the Dixiecrats and without abandoning the party's traditional hospitality to Negroes in the North and South.

It was a long path from that decent and worthy beginning to the 1964 Republican National Convention floor where a Negro delegate from Maryland was taunted to leave the party by Alabama's neighboring delegation; where a New Jersey Negro broke down in tears and left the hall after being jeered as a "nigger" by Goldwater Southerners. Perhaps the most galling aspect of the corruption of the party's appeal was that so few progressives realized what was happening. Duplicity effected the change and hypocrisy shielded it from view.

Despite the results of the 1960 election, despite the census statistics showing the percentage of nonwhite population on the increase in every major city except Honolulu, and despite the program advocated in the Bliss report, neither the GOP Congressional (Campaign) Committee under Representative Bob Wilson of California nor the GOP Senatorial Campaign Committee under Senator Goldwater made any change in program to stimulate Negro confidence in and support for the Republican party.

Goldwater, in the Senate, not only failed to concern himself with the matter of urban voters (*"I* win in an industrial state," he said.) he also made it his business to discourage others. In a New York *Herald Tribune* interview on February 28, 1961, he said: "The Republican Party has not attracted Negro voters. It is time to admit we cannot get them and other minorities as a bloc . . . so let's quit trying specifically to get *these* groups." Although he was attacked for such statements by National Chairman Morton, Chairman Miller did not feel required to contradict the Goldwater strategy. Instead he moved to carry it out.

Miller's two staff men in the Minorities Division, both Negroes, were brought in early in 1961. One, Grant Reynolds, a lawyer from White Plains, New York, was a part-time employee. He believed the party must give full support to the civil-rights movement. He drew up a long list of projects for the Minorities Division—a program that would use contacts in every Negro fraternal organization and civil-rights group, maintain communication with the Negro press and regular press, work to encourage Negro Republicans to file as candidates for office at all levels, and to secure Negro votes for white Republicans. Reynolds became less and less popular with the National Committee leadership. The second staff man, Clay Claiborne of Atlantic City believed in a "bread-and-butter" appeal. His approach varied from talk about jobs for Negroes to free giveaways and other admitted gimmicks. Since the National Committee leaders at no time surrendered their antebellum conviction that Negroes were purchasable, they were more tolerant, if skeptical, of Claiborne.

However, the work undertaken by the Minorities Division decreased rather than increased over the years 1961–64, and for every project undertaken five or six were rejected. Neither Claiborne nor Reynolds made policy for the division. While they had two competing approaches to the problem of winning Negro votes for the Republicans, and the best approach was probably a combination of the two, neither man was given a chance at party headquarters. Never did the Minorities Division speak out on civil rights; there was no effort to publicize the party's legislative accomplishments of the past or to draw attention to the Republicans who were contributing to the progress of the civil rights bill of 1964. There was no prodding of the Democratic Administration, no exposure of its segregationist federal judge appointments in the South, no promotion of the outstanding civil-rights records of the Republican governors, all of whom (except for Governor Paul Fannin—of Goldwater's Arizona) had made exemplary progress in the field. One would never have known from the National Committee that the Republican party in 1962 was running a Negro for Attorney General of Massachusetts, Edward W. Brooke. However, after his victory, when the Republicans in Washington, D.C., Brooke's original home, held a testimonial dinner for him, Brooke did hear from Miller asking him not to mention the party's new alliance with segregationists in the South. Brooke was simply indignant and at the dinner proceeded to blast the "reprehensible, unholy and ominous" trend of the GOP—"the party I love"—in several Southern states.

At the height of the 1963 racial crisis, ten days after the civil-rights address of the President and the assassination of Medgar Evers, with the whole country absorbed in the issue, the Republican National Committee held a biennial meeting, in Denver, and failed to invite any of its Negro staff members. Operation Dixie's staff, however, was influentially present, and while the press intensively speculated about how the Republicans would respond to the racial crisis, the committee passed a series of resolutions on various issues, including one short one on civil rights that would have been perfectly acceptable to Governor George C. Wallace. It said merely that the President had failed "to deal effectively with the problems of civil rights and to foster an atmosphere of understanding and good will in which racial conflict can be resolved." It was not implausible after that for columnists Joseph Alsop, and Rowlands Evans and Robert Novak to conclude that the Republicans had written off the Negro vote for 1964.

The results were dramatic, though predictable. With no liaison between the Republican party and the big civil-rights organizations, their leaders assumed the GOP was hostile. Roy Wilkins of the NAACP, for example, told an *Advance* magazine[3] reporter in 1963 that only twelve Republicans in the House could be depended upon to support the public accommodations section of the omnibus civil-rights bill. Of course, 138 of 172 House Republicans later voted for the bill, and, moreover, when Wilkins made his statement some thirty Republican congressmen had already *introduced* the most extensive civil-rights legislation yet proposed in the House. So it was too with the party's own Negro supporters. Out of twenty-five Southern Republican Negro leaders interviewed by *Advance* in 1963, several of them featured in a *Newsweek* list of the hundred most influential Negroes in America, only one had ever *heard* of the GOP Minorities Division, and that one thought it was still headed by a man who had retired in 1960. The bitter irony was that every single one of these *Republican* leaders was receiving a weekly mailing from the Minorities Division of the *Democratic* National Committee under Louis Martin.

It was not for lack of funds that Negroes did not receive mailings from the Republican Minorities Division, because Chairman Miller hardly ever said "no money" to Operation Dixie. In an off-guard moment in Hershey, Pennsylvania, in 1963, he proudly stated that in the past few years $600,000 had been put into the well-staffed division. Its two-color, eight-page monthly newsletter based its appeal not on segregation, of course, but on defeating "the Kennedys" and promoting "states' rights." Its bad jokes, cutout stickers, and exclamation points alone

[3] An unofficial Republican magazine founded by the authors in 1961 and edited by them until its demise in 1964.

would have paid for the newsletter the party supposedly could not afford for the Minorities Division.

Certainly the case against Operation Dixie and the case against Southern Republicanism should not be overstated. The National Committee's Southern division cannot be held responsible for all the excesses of certain GOP segregationists. Nor should one make the mistake of confusing the outspoken segregationists with Republicans like those of Texas who merely pretend they never heard of Negroes, or with the few Southern Republican integrationists such as those in Atlanta who get up to 90 percent of the Negro vote.

But it is accurate to say that, because of its use of funds that might have been used elsewhere, Operation Dixie promoted the South at the expense of the Northern big cities, and Goldwater's Presidential hopes at the cost of the party's. As a lily-white operation it helped the worst elements in the Southern GOP at the expense of the better ones.

From 1960 to 1964 there was almost a 100 percent shift of leadership in the Southern Republican party. The most reactionary state was Mississippi, whose young chairman, Wirt A. Yerger, demanded after the Oxford crisis that President Kennedy be impeached and who invited Dixiecrat Governor Ross Barnett to speak at the Republican headquarters in Jackson.[4] Yerger was also the Southern regional chairman for the Republican party. The more "liberal" Republican parties, in Georgia and Tennessee, segregated themselves just as the states' Democratic parties were being integrated for the first time in a hundred years.

In 1962 private rumors floated North of segregationist campaigns being waged by certain Republicans in the South. People familiar with the national Republican machinery noted that it had been disproportionately geared to a right-wing campaign with an exaggerated Southern exposure. With U. S. Senate seats at stake in industrial states throughout the North, Barry Goldwater's Senatorial Campaign Committee was doting obsessively on races in South Carolina and Alabama. With more marginal

[4] "The Republicans Against History," *Advance* (Fall, 1963).

Democratic seats (55 percent or less plurality) in New York State alone than in the entire South, the Congressional (Campaign) Committee and the National Committee chose to invest in Dixie.

Despite the usual pattern of substantial outparty gains in midterm congressional elections, the GOP in 1962 added only four Southern seats while *losing* two in the North for a net gain of just two. In the Senate, Goldwater's Southern strategy won no Southern seats while effectively helping to lose four seats in the North.

This dismal electoral showing was cause for unrestrained jubilation at party headquarters. Senator Golwater was simply delighted the party's Senate candidate in South Carolina, William Workman, had made a barely respectable showing (43 percent) and that the nominee in Alabama, James Martin, had come within 7,000 votes of victory. These officials were not just whistling "Dixie." They knew full well that marginal gains in the South, whatever the price paid elsewhere, would improve the right wing's relative position in the party. It was not surprising, therefore, when a few weeks after the election the men responsible for the Southern strategy reacted with disapproval to a statement of criticism of the Southern campaign from Senator Jacob Javits of New York, and with snarling outrage when *Advance* issued a full-scale attack on the whole trend of party affairs. *Advance* compared the meager gains made in the South, even with the overwhelming commitment of the national party apparatus, to the impressive improvements made by individual candidates for state offices in the North. Working virtually without national help, they had won in Ohio, New York, Michigan, Pennsylvania, and Massachusetts—greatly improving on Nixon's Negro percentages—in considerable part because they took an interest in civil rights and party organization among Negroes. Statewide Republican candidates also won with over 40 percent of the Negro vote in Oklahoma and Kentucky.

What most disturbed *Advance,* however, was not the party's political stupidity, but its moral callousness. Negroes were being kept out of certain Southern campaigns by Operation Dixie and, at least in Alabama and South Carolina, the party was bidding against the Dixiecrats for the worst of the redneck, bigot vote.

Chairman Miller called these charges "ridiculous," pointing out that the Democrats had run a larger number of segregationist candidates than the GOP—as if the Republicans should emulate the historic Democratic schism—and implying that, unlike the Democrats, the *national* headquarters of the Republican party would sympathize with Dixie. Goldwater said segregation was not a "major issue" in any race he knew about. One gathers that as chairman of the Senate Campaign Committee, he did not "know about" the Senate campaigns in South Carolina and Alabama. Representative Wilson called the *Advance* attack "irresponsible and unfair," and falsely implied that it was aimed only at the five Republican House winners.

James Martin, the Alabama senatorial candidate, was so upset by the *Advance* charge that he came to Washington and held a press conference to "clarify" the "irresponsible" charges against him. He just didn't know how "*Advance* magazine gets its information . . . the race issue wasn't an issue in my campaign." No, sir, the real issue was the "un-Alabamian voting record" of the incumbent Senator Lister Hill. "Why that man voted exactly like Jacob Javits . . . I used Javits [i.e., campaigned against Hill as 'Alabama's Jacob Javits'] to keep Hill from using him."[5]

"Don't be misled," Miller piously advised the members of the National Committee, "our successes in the South . . . are the product of people dedicated to . . . freedom and sound government." Unhappily, the committee members had not heard senatorial candidate Martin when he cried out for "a return to the spirit of '61—*1961*—when our fathers formed a new nation to support their principles. God willing," said this "Republican" who protested that race was no issue in his campaign, "we will not again be forced to take up rifle and bayonet and preserve these principles . . . make no mistake, my friends, this will be a

[5] James Martin, press conference, (November 30, 1962).

fight. The bugle call is loud and clear. The South has risen! We have heard the call."[6]

The next year, in 1963, the Republican party of Kentucky took a gamble on a white backlash and ran Louis Nunn in an implicitly segregationist campaign against an integrationist Democrat. There was indeed a backlash, but it was partly nullified by a revolt (apparently against Nunn's demagoguery) by Republicans in Louisville's suburbs. Only the fact that much of the *Negro* vote in Louisville stayed with the GOP allowed Nunn to make it a close race. The Negroes responded to campaigning by Mayor Cowger, a Republican who had passed the first public accommodations law in any Southern city.

Nunn's loss in Kentucky, moreover, should be contrasted with the decisive victory for Senator Thruston Morton a year before and the overwhelming victory of Senator John Sherman Cooper in 1960. Both senators are integretionists, and Cooper had actually been a leader in the Senate civil-rights bloc.

In Mississippi in 1963 the Republican party dispensed with pretenses. It conducted such a wildly racist campaign that the National Committee leadership did not even bother to lie about it in the North. A photograph of the gubernatorial candidate, Rubel Phillips, with Senator Goldwater and a bust of Lincoln in the background, was widely used in campaign literature—with the Lincoln bust deleted. Mr. Phillips managed to lose 2 to 1, while the rest of the ticket went down by margins of 4 to 1 and more.

This grim outcome of a campaign that was neither moral nor victorious was joyfully hailed at national headquarters as a "moral victory." The full brass of the Republican National Committee was on hand to congratulate itself at a sort of moral-victory party held by the Southern GOP after the election. The crowd thrilled to "Dixie," announced as "the Southern National Anthem" and played instead of "The Star-Spangled Banner." Neither Chairman Miller nor anyone else murmured a protest when Mississippi's Wirt Yerger, in his moral-victory

[6] *Sumpter County* (Ala.) *Journal*, (November 1, 1962).

statement, upbraided the party's congressional leadership for "selling out" to the Democrats by supporting the omnibus civil-rights bill.

Notwithstanding the National Committee's sophistry, the Republican party in fact had been set back by the Southern strategy. In the South, the party had alienated the growing Negro vote without gaining a decisive portion of the diminishing number of segregationist whites. In the North, the Southern strategy had contributed to an equally thoroughgoing flop, with the Northern *urban* Republican voter for Congress rising only 2.5 percent from 1958's recession and right-to-work disaster. New England, once proudly Republican, actually cast fewer GOP votes (and a lower percentage) in 1962 than in 1958.

All the warning signs were out: the election results of 1962, the results of the special elections in 1963, the relative decline of Republican registration nationally, and all the polls. The Gallup poll showed the party officials to be out of step with rank-and-file Republicans. The Harris survey found that on nine issues raised by Senator Goldwater, a majority of Republican voters agreed with him on only three; and analyst Samuel Lubell summed up a series of national interviews: "Senator Goldwater's brand of conservatism may help the Republicans in the South but it weakens them in the nation as a whole."[7] Yet the party's National Committee continued its inherently pro-Goldwater Southern strategy, despite its manifest ineffectuality.

Thus the party machinery of the Eisenhower Era broke down and became the machinery of a faction. The Republican ship was sinking, but no one was ordered to bail. Bill Miller merely listened to the siren drawl of "Dixie" and led the passengers South to the bow. The bow rose higher and higher and seemed to point to the sun, which a bow will do as it follows the rest of the ship into the sea.

[7] Washington *Daily News*, (June 21, 1962).

CHAPTER 5

◇◇◇

Revise and Dissent

W HEN THE nominating was over and the acceptance speech was a few hours away, Robert R. Douglass, a Rockefeller aide in San Francisco asserted: "This was a defeat for the so-called Presidential wing and especially the governors, and this was a victory for the Congressional wing." He recited the list of congressional leaders who were for Goldwater and told the sad story of the twelve out of fifteen Republican governors who opposed Goldwater and who had flailed about ineffectually in their attempt to halt the Goldwater juggernaut.

But while it is true that the Goldwater nomination was a defeat for the Republican governors, it is only partly true that it constituted a victory for the congressmen. William Miller was a congressman, but his help to the right-wing cause redounded from his National Chairmanship of the party. Like Goldwater, he mattered little in congress. Senate Minority Leader Everett Dirksen of Illinois placed the Goldwater name in nomination in San Francisco, and House Minority Leader Charles Halleck of

Indiana seconded it. However, both of these men were late arrivals on the bandwagon; Dirksen, who sees virtue in inevitability, boarded well after the California primary, under heavy pressure from the pro-Goldwater Illinois delegation. Neither he nor Halleck was personally enthusiastic about the party nominee, who once had spoken sarcastically of them as "what we call the Leadership here."[1]

The Senate minority whip, Thomas L. Kuchel of California, was for Rockefeller and worked as openly for him as did any congressional leader for Goldwater. Senator Bourke Hickenlooper, chairman of the Senate Policy Committee, gave only marginal assistance to Goldwater, while the home-state organization of another leadership senator, Leverett Saltonstall of Massachusetts, worked alternately for Lodge and Scranton. The center of Goldwater activism in the Senate was reduced to Carl Curtis of Nebraska and John G. Tower of Texas.

In the House, the Republican caucus chairman, Gerald Ford of Michigan, remained neutral until the convention, when he gave a seconding speech for Romney. The Republican Policy Committee chairman, John Byrnes, ran himself as a Wisconsin "favorite son," perhaps to hold the state for Goldwater. The GOP Congressional (Campaign) Committee chairman, Bob Wilson, favored Goldwater, but managed to stay officially neutral while his staff plugged away for the Arizonan. Like Halleck, Minority Whip Leslie Arends of Illinois, and the ranking Republican on the House Rules Committee, Clarence Brown of Ohio, did little more for Goldwater than to endorse him after an appropriately long wait.

Almost the entire Republican Congressional Leadership from 1960–64 came from small towns in the central Middle West. These were the standpatters who succumbed to the Eisenhower Compromise with a yawn and now could not manage much more than that for anyone. Unimpressed by ideological fervor, whatever its source, they had left their passions in the fights of the thirties. To tell them that with Goldwater's nomina-

[1] Letter to *Advance,* published June, 1962.

tion they had just won a great victory would have required one to go wake them up.

A few younger, more ambitious congressmen like Representatives John Ashbrook of Ohio, Donald Bruce of Indiana, and John J. Rhodes of Arizona were the true Goldwater phalanx in the House. But there was also young and vigorous support for the Goldwater opposition from such men as Representatives Silvio Conte and Bradford Morse of Massachusetts, Stanley Tupper of Maine, and John Lindsay and Ogden Reid of New York. But Congress was only an important "second front" in the 1964 intraparty campaign. The main battle occurred in the state conventions and primaries.

However, to say that Goldwater's nomination was not a victory for the congressional Republicans is not to deny that they contributed importantly, if inadvertently, to it. Their contribution was ineffectuality. Their continual negativism, their failure to mobilize the party in the Congress behind a distinctive Republican program left a leadership vacuum that Goldwater moved aggressively to fill. As long as the party in Congress was inert, confused, and inarticulate, Goldwater's ideological manifestos and Miller's strategic decisions chiefly determined the direction of the party on the national level. The congressional inaction in the early years of the Goldwater ascendancy was almost as instrumental in his nomination as the uncoordination of the moderates in the final period. The slight revival in 1964, marked by statesmanship in the passage of the Civil Rights Act and by minor improvements in the leadership, was far too little and far too late to counteract the abdication of 1961 through 1963. This abdication, by giving the far right an opportunity to command the stage, was crucial to Goldwater's ultimate success.

In 1961 it looked as if Congress would be the arena for the Republican internal struggle. With Eisenhower out of office, Nixon defeated, and Rockefeller busy in Albany, the most important influence on the party, and, conversely, the party's greatest influence upon the nation, might well have come from Republicans in Congress. But this vantage position was used to observe or obstruct, not control, the history of the period. The progressive–right-wing split was resolved in stagnation—the politics of the vacuum center.

Progressives were eager to see the Congressional party follow the programs of the Eisenhower Administration and the 1960 platform. The rightists interpreted the election returns as a call for reaction. At every opportunity Senator Goldwater cited the fact that while Nixon went down to defeat, twenty-two new Republican congressmen were elected, and that "practically all" were "conservatives," which showed that "Our problem in the Republican party is that we haven't offered enough conservative candidates."

The facts, which never quite caught up with the fast-traveling senator, were these: First, several of the twenty-two were not "conservative" in the Goldwater sense, and the first chairman of the "class of 1960" was Robert T. Stafford of Vermont, a progressive; second, the GOP gains (twenty-eight Democratic seats were won, six GOP seats were lost, for a net gain of twenty-two) should have been measured against the loss of forty-eight in the catastrophic defeat of 1958. A district-by-district analysis would disclose that twenty-two of the twenty-eight "new" Republican seats were from districts safely Republican before 1958, and five of the remaining six had been Republican before 1956. In the swing-districts where Republicans made gains—as in Connecticut and Minnesota—the candidates who won were moderates, not right-wingers. In all, the election was hardly a mandate for Goldwater "conservatism."

But the progressive-rightist argument of 1960–61 was of secondary interest to the GOP congressional leadership. They enjoyed the new national spotlight, but they missed the guiding hand of a Republican President. To them the question was not so much whether to move one way or another but whether to move at all. They sympathized with parts of the Goldwater ideology, but only in their own fashion, which was obstruction rather than advocacy. "Our aim," said Senator Dirksen, will be "to modify [President] Kennedy's proposals."

The two leaders retained and embellished their weekly press conferences of the Eisenhower years, and what was once a dim light set unnoticed before the Eisenhower sun became, for a while, the Capitol beacon of the "Loyal Opposition." Rowland Evans, Jr., of the New York *Herald Tribune* early dubbed the new performance "The Ev and Charlie Show," and the name stuck. When *Advance* interviewed thirty prominent Republicans on Capitol Hill, from Bruce R. Alger on the right to Seymour Halpern on the left, only two thought the Ev and Charlie Show was helping the party, and those two were Ev and Charlie. Said Senator Dirksen: "You can tell how successful we've been by the amount of criticism we've had from the Democrats." Said Representative Halleck: "It must be pretty effective because the Democrats are always howling about it." Said a spokesman for the House Democratic Study Group: "But we *like* the Ev and Charlie Show!"

The more zealous right-wingers were restless under the Ev and Charlie reign, while the progressives, as individuals—always as individuals—were reluctantly rebellious. No sooner had the Eighty-seventh Congress organized in January, 1961, than twenty-two Republicans in the House bolted from the leadership to give the Administration just enough votes (217–212) to expand the Rules Committee. These twenty-two that the Dixiecrat–right-wing Republican coalition that had controlled the Rules Committee merely provided the Administration with a scapegoat for the failure of its legislative program. An expanded committee would permit the Democratic Administration ready access to a vote on the House floor, but it also would prevent the Democrats from imputing to the Republicans the blame for legislative inaction. Upon enlarging the committee to ten Democrats and five Republicans, President Kennedy still suffered Rules Committee defeats, and as Representative Thomas B. Curtis of Missouri, a leader of "the twenty-two" said eight months after the change: The main difference was that the Administration could no longer place the onus on the Republicans.

Representative Halleck had not seen it that way. Nor did he

understand the anxiety of marginal and metropolitan district congressmen when he asked them to oppose, without offering anything of their own, each new Kennedy bill to aid transportation or housing or raise the minimum wage. Halleck was a skillful floor leader, but as inept at long-range strategy as he was at public relations. By refusing to accommodate the progressives, he lost different combinations of them, often critical combinations on bill after bill.

Halleck was criticized by right-wingers as well as progressives (or "constructive conservatives" as some of them called themselves). He was indifferent to new suggestions, and was suspicious of their proponents. Instead of bringing issues before the whole 176-member Republican Conference four or five weeks before they came to a vote on the House floor, the leadership called meetings for the day before or even the very day of the vote. These meetings were not for free discussion, but to allow the leadership to exhort any waverers. Members willing to vote with the leadership often did so grudgingly, feeling the real weaknesses of the Democrats had been left unexploited. Halleck, especially, was inclined to oppose the Democrats on negative and tactical grounds.

By January of 1963 the grumbling against Halleck's leadership from all sides reached the point where a number of younger congressmen began to consider means of ousting him. Some felt that an assault on Halleck was ill-timed, that Minority Whip Leslie Arends was a more promising target. Still others wanted to inaugurate a complete new leadership from Halleck to Brown.

In the end the man they chose to challenge was Representative Charles B. Hoeven of Iowa, chairman of the Republican House Conference, and their choice for successor was Representative Gerald Ford. Hoeven, icily reserved and always willing to sacrifice vitality to brevity in his ordering of conference discussions, was considered an easy target. The leadership did not learn of the insurrection until the day before the annual caucus. Halleck was officially neutral. Others, including Hoeven, saw it as a "liberal" plot, although the insurgents included Republicans of every hue.

After his summary defeat, Hoeven angrily described himself as a "lamb for the slaughter"—an appetizer before the pièce de résistance, Charles Halleck—and some of the "Young Turks" who had overthrown him hinted that early 1965 would show him right. In the meantime, the Young Turks had, through Ford, all the power they needed to effect major reforms. The Republican House Conference elects the leadership, acts to affirm or reject the recommendations of the GOP Policy Committee, approves regular House committee assignments, and can confirm or reject the decisions of the minority leader.

Under Ford, the Young Turks moved to give more recognition to younger congressmen on the GOP Policy Committee, called more frequent conferences to discuss pending legislation, and attempted to put together task forces to study important national problems. But, by and large, inertia continued as the pattern of the party in Congress. Although Halleck usually moved if the Young Turks pushed, disappointingly, they pushed less and and less after their victory. The task forces on issues turned out for the most part to be shallow and unconvincing exercises in pedestrian rhetoric. The "reforms" of the Policy Committee merely provided new names for its roster. Ford himself offered little personal leadership in modernizing the party. Perhaps it was for such failures he was elected minority leader.

It is worth remembering that when Halleck first achieved his leadership position in 1959 by ousting the venerable Representative Joseph W. Martin of Massachusetts, it was with the help of Ford, Representative Melvin Laird, and other Young Turks who later turned on him. His call, like theirs, was for reform. It is hard to see that any of them were fully sincere, for the major problems of the Republicans in the House remained largely unattended from 1960 to 1964, and remain so today under Ford.

In the Senate inertia prevailed as well. Upon his re-election to the upper house in 1962, Everett Dirksen seemed to find new energy for his job as minority leader. More a shrewd judge than a creative innovator, Dirksen managed to walk the narrow line between the Senate GOP's almost evenly divided right-wingers and progressives and still, from time to time, to bring himself down decisively on the side of the angels. His measure of Administration proposals seemed to be: Is it really important to the nation? Is it likely to carry anyway? Can I change it enough to make it acceptable to a majority of Republicans?

On the Nuclear Test-Ban treaty, on the support of United Nations' bonds and, of course, on the Civil Rights Act of 1964, Dirksen chose to risk the backing of many powerful forces at home, such as the Chicago *Tribune*, to meet what he knew was the national interest, and the real interest of the Republican party. From 1961 to 1964 Dirksen managed to discard his image as the buffoon of the Ev and Charlie Show and to assume, every so often, the toga of statesmanship. There was very little opposition to Dirksen's leadership among Senate Republicans. "I never scold" was the way he described his method of persuasion, and if there was only minimum cooperation among the Senate Republicans under him, there was also a minimum of coercion and ample opportunity for the free expression of views.

However, the Senate Republicans, as a group, failed to provide the kind of constructive leadership the party needed from 1961 to 1964, just as it fails today. It waited for other, more vigorous forces in the party to lead.

The reasons for the inertia of the Republicans in Congress are as various as congressional constituencies. But two facts stand out. In the first place, the Congressional party—particularly in the House—decimated in 1958 and excluded almost entirely from many metropolitan areas, was not representative of the party across the land. Its vision of political realities was dimmed and its political energies misdirected by its concentration in less densely populated areas. Secondly, the organizational appendices of the Congressional party failed to function with either efficiency or vigor.

Except perhaps in Kansas and Vermont, there are today no "safe" Republican Senate seats. Given the increasing urbanization of America, every state contains a substantial city population. There are, however, some 40 "safe" Republican seats in the House (out of 435) usually won by pluralities of 55 percent or greater. They are largely rural, out-of-the-way districts, often malapportioned, and, like their counterpart safe Democratic districts, they tend to elect mild, mediocre, and "safe" congressmen. It is here where the Republican party is most secure that it is most torpid, and in politics still waters run shallow.

It is important to distinguish between, on the one hand, outstanding personalities who have taken a marginal or Democratic district and carried it by such pluralities that it becomes "safely Republican" as long as they are running, and, on the other hand, the men who represent districts in which the GOP registration so exceeds the Democratic that the competing records and personalities of the candidates become irrelevant. By and large, the party's House leadership comes from men representing districts of the second, uncompetitive sort. These men have little understanding of the prerequisites of successful Republicanism in marginal or Democratic districts.

Safe-district Republicans control the Republican Congressional (Campaign) Committee and orient it in effect toward winning *more* safe Republican districts, as if there were any more to be won, as if indeed this were the 1920's and 60 percent of the public was Republican, instead of the dismal 25 percent of today. The GOP Congressional Committee from 1960 to 1964 used the polls taken by congressmen in backwater Republican districts to show that the majority of Americans opposed this bill or that. The best parallel in political pulse-taking were the polls of 1936, which interviewed people with telephones and concluded that Landon would beat Roosevelt; indeed he might have—with the franchise restricted to those who could afford telephones in the middle of the Depression. And indeed Republicans today might win a national election restricted to districts which now elect

Republican congressmen (though even such a restriction would not have sufficed to elect Goldwater, the favorite of the Congressional Committee Staff.)

Until early 1963 Goldwater himself was the chairman of the Republican Senatorial Campaign Committee. There is no core of safe Republican seats in the Senate, and changing political realities have been whittling down the right wing until the progressives are almost as numerous. Since 1953–54 when the GOP last controlled the Senate, twenty-eight formerly Republican seats have gone Democratic. Only ten of the twenty-eight were moderates, while eighteen were men whom Goldwater would consider "conservatives." The right wing and the progressives each elected five new senators during that period, and the right also converted Strom Thurmond to "the Goldwater Republican party."

From 1955 to 1963 when Senator Goldwater chaired the GOP Senatorial Campaign Committee, his cumulative score was minus two. It was not much of an organization when he inherited it, nor was it much when he turned it over to Senator Morton in 1963.

His main staff assistant was and is Victor A. Johnston, a cynical old pro, as they say, who previously served on the staffs of Harold Stassen, Robert A. Taft, Thomas E. Dewey, and Richard Nixon. He was considered a fixture on the Campaign Committee, one of the Republican party's salaried pensioners. He took part in plotting Goldwater's nomination even when, after 1963, Goldwater was not his boss.

Goldwater, as chairman, kept few charts or records of Senate races, except as he said, "in our heads." No dossiers were maintained on incumbent Democrats, and the only things ever mailed out, a secretary said, "are occasional speeches of Senator Goldwater."

The Senatorial Campaign Committee was useful, however, as a vehicle for Senator Goldwater to "poop around" the country making invaluable contacts and, let it be said, helping raise a good deal of money for the party. Some $3,000 a month of that money, plus an average of $1,000 a month in expenses, went to one of Goldwater's personal ghostwriters, Stephen Shadegg of Phoenix, or rather, according to the spending reports that had to be filed with the Clerk of the House of Representatives, to S-K Research Laboratories of Phoenix, a manufacturer of nose sprays. Shadegg, who reportedly helped write Goldwater's *The Conscience of a Conservative* and his thrice-weekly newspaper column, owns S-K Research.[2]

As an organization for electing Republicans to the Senate, the Campaign Committee was ineffectual. Urging the National Committee to shy away from progressive, metropolitan-oriented appeals, Goldwater could hardly be expected to make them in his own department. In 1962 Goldwater and Victor Johnston predicted a gain of six or eight Republican seats, coming not from the urban North but from the South and West. The net loss was four seats. However, as Goldwater assured everyone before leaving the Senatorial Committee in 1963 to campaign more openly, supposedly for re-election to the Senate, 1964 could only see Republican gains. The year 1958 had been so bad that of the thirty-three senatorial contests the Republicans won only eight. Now at the end of this six-year term, the odds were 3 to 1 in favor of improved standing. Those were the odds, but the Senatorial Campaign Committee and the Goldwater candidacy managed to overcome them; the GOP suffered a net loss of two seats.

If the Republicans in the Senate or the House had desired, as a group, to have a more effective campaign committee, they could have had one. That they did not was a reflection of their overall confusion in confrontation with the Democratic threat and their own disunity. Important Republicans in both houses of Congress—Senators Scott (Pa.), Javits (N.Y.), and Kuchel (Cal.), Representatives Curtis (Mo.), Frehlinghuysen (N.J.), Schwengel (Iowa), and others—recognized the correlation between constructive, original Republican programs, party unity, and victory at the polls. But the leadership as a whole, and also the membership as a whole, ignored the need for honest research

[2] *Arizona Frontiers* (August, 1961).

as antecedent to a winning legislative program and an enlarged mandate at the polls.

Representative Thomas Curtis, a member of the Ways and Means Committee and the House-Senate Joint Economics Committee, struggled for months in 1961 before the leadership would permit him to organize a study of unemployment under the GOP House Policy Committee. Curtis's project used the talents of some forty Republican congressmen, right-wingers and progressives alike, and a score of Republican-oriented professors. "Operation Employment" was a conspicuous success, belatedly backed by the leadership, who suddenly discovered they had been for it all along. It provided the groundwork for the Manpower Retraining Act of 1962. This distinctive Republican program to reduce unemployment, authored by Representative Charles E. Goodell of New York, supplanted a sloppily prepared Administration bill.

For once, on one matter and for a few months, Republicans had a carefully developed and constructive alternative behind which all factions of the party could unite. One might have thought the example would inspire dozens of such projects, in both houses, to cover on a continuing basis the major issues confronting Congress. But the leadership, while no longer hostile to study projects like Operation Employment, was sullenly indifferent. "Well," said the late Clarence Brown of Ohio, "I guess it gives these young people something to do."

That apparently was Representative Halleck's attitude as well, for his response in 1962 to growing demands for research and new thought was to appoint Melvin Laird—a supposed "Young Turk"—to lead a House-Senate Joint Committee on Republican Principles, incorporating Republicans from each section of the country and each wing of the party. What resulted was a "Declaration of Republican Principles and Policy," something halfway between a platform and Senator Goldwater's proposed "Statement of Principles": a gassy blast of clichés that received press attention on a dull day and put Representative Laird in line for the chairmanship of the 1964 convention Platform Committee.

As Representative Brown might have thought, it gave the young people something to do.

But the Declaration of Principles and Policy, for all its vacuity, was celebrated more than the Operation Employment project. The leadership simply had no concept of the value of sound legislative research. In 1963 Chairman John W. Byrnes said that the Policy Committee would now "stop" publishing long reports, as if it had been normally so engaged, in order to give more time to working on special legislation and helping specific congressmen who requested help. Essentially that meant little research and very slight help of any kind to Republican congressmen. One staff man who managed to find time in his busy, subsidized schedule was Philip Brennan, who under the pseudonym, of Cato, authored a biweekly column for the right-wing *National Review.* Although he nominally represented all the House Republicans, he used the anonymous column to lambaste progressive congressmen, and even some right-wing ones, and to promote Goldwater.

In the Republican Policy Committee of the Senate no one would have thought of being so factional. First of all, the Policy Committee is uniquely subsidized by the federal government, thanks to the LaFollette-Monroney Reorganization Act of 1946. Unlike its Democratic counterpart, the GOP Policy Committee has, over the past few years, taken to heart the matter of economy in government and proudly turned back to the Treasury a goodly portion of its $175,000 subsidy.

This uncommonly generous, frugal, and nonutilitarian act deprived a nearly bankrupt party of funds for research and surely won it no votes. But it did serve to warm the self-esteem of the committee staff and its chieftain, Senator Bourke Hickenlooper of Iowa. In a way they had a point; certainly a party that feels no need for improvement of its ideas also needs very little money —even if it is free—to spend on research. It can sit back and watch the world, and the voters, go by. That was what the Senate Policy Committee did and does today.

It also performed the perfunctory tasks of record-keeping on

Senate legislation; it clipped and briefly quoted in a weekly *Memo* the timely, timeless remarks of Republican senators on the questions of the day; and it occasionally wrote speeches for Republican senators, who usually took advantage of this service only about once.

Much of the Policy Committee's day-to-day work was useful to Senate Republicans, and if not useful, inevitable. But it is against its well-subsidized potential that the committee's performance should be judged. With money literally to give back, and as the agent of a party withering from lack of new ideas, the Senate Policy Committee preferred menial service to the historic mission of creative research.

It is true that in both the House and Senate the policy committees were impeded in doing research by the divisions in their membership. However, it is only in research for specific, practical programs that such divisions can be overcome. But because neither committee would initiate true, well-researched scholarship, they betrayed their potential. The Republican party in Congress, understaffed as a minority on the regular committees and represented in its own apparatus by intellectual slouches and reactionaries, would only turn its aggressions back on itself. Goldwater moved into the breach.

CHAPTER 6

Miller
Surrenders
the Town

Aᴠᴛᴇʀ ᴛʜᴇ 1960 elections, Republican columnist and peni-
tent F.D.R. brain truster, Raymond Moley, wrote a book
on *The Republican Opportunity*.[1] In the midst of criticizing the
GOP for assorted failures and offering many constructive suggestions (including, unfortunately, the not so constructive but apparently *de rigeur* obeisance to "organization"), he added a rebuke to
the "pernicious Republican habit, so common among orators at
Lincoln Day dinners, of voicing criticism of their own party."

"Of their own party": the insidious attitude of sanctimony in
that phrase was one of the major traps hypocrisy set in the path
toward true Republican unity. In any case, Mr. Moley must have
been attending unusual Lincoln Day dinners from 1960 to 1964.

A little "voicing of criticism," well-aimed and properly docu-
mented, was just what the party lacked. The only harsh note at

[1] New York: Duel, Sloan, and Pearce; 1962.

those Lincoln Day dinners—harsh, bombastic, hypocritical quite often, and almost as inevitable as the lukewarm roast beef—was William Miller or some other leader calling for "unity." The jarring notes, the "voicing of criticism," did not occur at those dinners, in the open, but in private meetings with the press, in the cloakrooms of Congress, and in the precincts.

The essential question—whether the party should concentrate its appeal in the metropolitan North or in the South, and at what cost—was unmentionable in polite Republican company. Two other related causes of disunity, the controversies over the operation of the campaign committees and over the relative roles of the Republican governors and congressmen, were almost never discussed either—except, of course, everywhere outside party meetings.

Finally, one of the main causes of disunity in the Republican party was the viewpoint of Senator Goldwater himself, especially on such matters as the United Nations, foreign aid, free trade, the minimum wage, right-to-work laws, and civil rights. Still, so tight were "unity" regulations that criticism or defense of him had to be left to long-distance sarcasm or quip, reported in the press.

Perhaps Republican unity, at least by early 1964, was beyond recovery. But it is not unrealistic to suggest that the leaders of the party could have come together, surveyed their common ground, and decided upon what issues they could compromise their differences and on what others they should have a gentlemen's agreement to disagree. Like any unknown threat, disagreement would have been less fearsome when exposed to the light. Republicans needed to tolerate slight divergences from the party in either direction. At the same time, they needed to know what Republican orthodoxy really was. Republicanism was described as a "broad umbrella" under which many could stand, but no one was certain of the extent of the umbrella's periphery.

The urgent, historic issues relating to the demographic changes taking place in America and to the erosion of Republican ideology were never effectively raised. Even the question of the party's treatment of segregationists and radical rightists was avoided. Chairman Miller effectively repressed dissent over the segregationists, and as to the radical right, he just didn't "know where it is or who it is" and was "just not concerned."[2]

When a political party is in power, the national party head-quarters invariably serves the objectives of the President. When it is out of power, the national organization can back one party faction against another, as did the Democratic National Committee under Paul Butler during the Eisenhower years, or it can remain neutral, with an occasional assist to one group or another prob-ably being inevitable. It was the former that model progressives expected to see at Republican headquarters after 1960, with the direction of the party set in the pattern of the Eisenhower-Nixon Compromise.

But that was not William Miller's model. He came to his job with the blessings of Eisenhower and the quiet enthusiasm of Goldwater. His policy, officially, was one of neutrality, noninvolve-ment, and non-leadership. This attitude, under superficial analysis, was certainly bad for the party at a time when it needed vigorous leadership. But progressives could console themselves that at least there was not a policy of support for Goldwater. That con-solation, experience taught, was a delusion. Miller did not publicly go out to join the invader's camp; but he surrendered the town.

The rear-guard apology for the Southern strategy was in-valuable to the Goldwater cause. The first "Bill Miller for Veep" badges at the Republican convention of 1964 appeared on the breasts of delegates from Dixie. Miller himself let it be known in early 1963 that he would not run for re-election to Congress. His already safe Republican seat had been made even more so in the redistricting conducted by the GOP legislature in New York, yet in the 1962 election Miller's plurality had sunk to just over 5,000 votes. For some reason he also advised political leaders that he was going to resign as Republican National Chairman after the convention.

2 *The New York Times*, August 6, 1963.

Meanwhile the National Committee staff workers favorable to Goldwater, including Miller's chief assistant, William Warner, worked covertly for Goldwater, while those opposed to him—lacking the inclination for subterfuge—operated as the only true "neutrals" at party headquarters.

Policy often was checked with the Goldwater office itself. A group of reporters who had interviewed Miller in June of 1963 submitted the transcript to him for editing. Miller in turn submitted it to Senator Goldwater as he was afraid he had come out too strongly for civil rights in the interview. Sure enough, Goldwater did feel Miller had been too enthusiastically pro-rights, and the transcript position was appropriately diluted. None of the moderate party leaders was consulted.

About the same time a quarrel developed in the Young Republican Federation over the issue of which candidate had actually won the race for National College Chairman at its national convention. The argument was complex. A credentials dispute was at the heart of the conflict, and the outgoing legal counsel of the Young Republican National Federation ruled for the more moderate candidate, Ward H. White of Kansas. The incoming YRNF chairman, Donald E. "Buz" Lukens, elected head of all Young Republicans after the college group had already held its election, attempted to reverse the decision, and the matter was handed on to the senior party and Chairman Miller. Although White presented a long legal brief in his behalf and his opponent did nothing except move unchallenged into an office at the national headquarters, the chairman ruled against White. Miller's parting words, however, were more startling than his ruling. "Senator Goldwater," he declared one year before the nomination, "is going to the convention with enough votes to win, and if he doesn't his supporters are going to want to know why. We have to placate these people."

The vice chairman of the Republican National Committee, Mrs. Claire B. Williams of Florida, was the only staff authority to fight the Goldwater trend. Outside the staff the Rockefeller forces finally began to complain. Although they were only partly successful, the matter finally did come to the attention of the public through articles in the nonpartisan *Congressional Quarterly* and in *Advance*. When asked about the situation, Miller blandly announced that he had just issued a directive to all personnel that no participation in the pre-convention campaign would be tolerated.

A few days later the Evans-Novak column in the New York *Herald Tribune* reported that its check of National Committee personnel revealed that no Miller directive against intraparty intrigue had been received by anyone.

In an interview in the fall, another reporter asked Miller who might be Barry Goldwater's running mate if the Arizonan was the Presidential nominee. The National Chairman listed Governor William Scranton of Pennsylvania, Representative Gerald Ford of Michigan, and, candidly, himself.[3] Needless to say, Miller kept this interview off-the-record—he wanted to preserve "unity."

[3] Reported by Warren Weaver, Jr., *The New York Times,* September 6, 1964.

◇◇

CHAPTER 7

The Amenable
Moderates

THE BREAKDOWN of the Eisenhower compromise and the rout of its advocates in official party positions was a quiet, stealthy affair. It left the old leadership and, indeed, Republican progressives of all sorts unaware of their loss until it was beyond rescue.

No one who had participated in the formulation of political policy in the Eisenhower Era stayed on in Washington in a policy role after 1960. President Eisenhower himself became General Eisenhower, and retired to Gettysburg. Richard Nixon went into temporary seclusion and law practice in California. Former National Chairmen like Leonard W. Hall and Meade Alcorn were known to entertain private doubts about the course of affairs, but they too were wrapped up in private pursuits outside of Washington. Senator Morton, another former National Chairman, did complain publicly in February of 1962 that "We Republicans are being outmaneuvered at many levels, including the National, when it comes to handling issues. We are being placed in a position of complete negativism." But to do anything about the situation one year after resigning as National Chairman and one year before running for re-election to the Senate from Kentucky would have required a perverse sense of heroism Morton did not possess.

One senator eager to enter the fray was Hugh Scott of Pennsylvania, the jaunty and assertive National Chairman from 1948 to 1949. But Scott was even more tied down than Morton. Perhaps more than anyone else Scott grasped the realities of intraparty politics and was willing to risk his prestige to advance the progressive cause. He told William Miller he would denounce Operation Dixie all over the country if its staff chief, I. Lee Potter, spoke anywhere in Pennsylvania. He also was willing to go to the ends of the continent to raise money for moderate projects and candidates.

But Scott's talents were largely wasted nationally. In 1961 and 1962 he was occupied in an unsuccessful battle against the Old Guard city organization in his hometown of Philadelphia, and thereafter in a successful attempt to draft Scranton for governor. After 1962 Scott constantly goaded Scranton to enter Presidental politics. Since Scranton joined the race only in late 1964 and did not back anyone else before then, Scott as his chief supporter was stymied.

The Cabinet leaders upon whom Eisenhower had depended for programs and often political support dispersed to every corner of the nation. Like most of the compromise contingent, they assumed others were carrying the Republican party. Whatever might happen, the right people within the party would come out ahead when it counted. That, to these men, had been guaranteed by Eisenhower's nomination in 1952.

It is clear that the prominent Republicans of the Eisenhower years and the other moderate Republicans half believed one of the right wing's most persistent charges—that the Republican party over the last twenty-five years has been controlled by an Eastern-based group of "kingmakers," "liberal" Republicans who consistently thwarted the arch-conservatives' claim to power.

"The Establishment" is a phrase used loosely in England to describe the traditional ruling class, bound by old family, school ties, club, and political party. Some of America's right-wingers, such as William F. Buckley, Jr., in the late fifties began to use the word to describe what they considered a bipartisan association of political and economic leaders which discriminated against them. The similar theory of the left wing has been presented even more seriously by C. Wright Mills in *The Power Elite*.[1] Mills did not feel the right wing was left out of national decision-making at all, but that the Socialists and, of course, the unconscious majority of the people were.

As a description of a sociological phenomenon, the Establishment theory is imprecise to the point of irrelevancy. The bulk of leadership in politics and finance is indeed either moderately conservative or moderately liberal. This might be expected in a nation whose voters are divided the same way, where sociological conflicts are muted, where the economic system traditionally has operated to permit tension and dissent within a consensus for limited capitalism. Given the demographic statistics of modern America, and the historic development of our institutions of education and communications, it is not surprising that poltical leadership frequently polarizes at the coastal regions; that graduates of Ivy League schools and several other large universities across the country should be especially prominent in government; and that many of the largest magazines and radio-television networks should be headquartered in New York, the nation's largest city.

In any case, the debate with right-wing intellectuals on the subtleties of the "Establishment" concept was harmless enough. Unfortunately, however, the idea was not left in the more or less playful hands of men like Buckley. To a few zealous arch-conservatives the Establishment was not just a facile means of conceptualizing the American power scheme, but the *name* of a specific and self-conscious group of individuals who seek through often unethical means to control the politics of America.

Emanuel M. Josephson used such illogic to write a book called

[1] Oxford: Oxford University Press; 1956.

Rockefeller Internationalist: The Man Who Misrules the World.[2]
Its essential device is the implication of Rockefeller control of almost everyone and everything a Rockefeller touches. The web is
enormous. Rockefellers gave the land for the United Nations and
Nelson Rockefeller was one of the participants in the drafting
of the UN charter. Rockefellers have financial interests in many
countries, etc. etc., etc.; ergo, "Rockefeller" controls the United
Nations. By further innuendo, one is led to believe that this control is exercised out of some secret arrangement with the
Communists. Is it just a coincidence, Mr. Josephson wonders, that
the Council on Foreign Relations, of which several Rockefellers
are supporters and which has considerable influence on U.S.
policy as a nonpartisan study group, was for many years located
right across the street from the Soviet Consulate in New York?
Ironically, the Communist line overseas for years has featured the
same Rockefellers as agents in an immoral international capitalist
conspiracy, the Latin-American arm of which is described in the
anti-American book *The Shark and the Sardines,* by Juan José
Arevalo.[3]

Another of the conspiratorial tracts was *Must Barry Goldwater be Destroyed?* a widely distributed fifty-cent booklet written
by Frank Cullen Brophy, a friend of Goldwater and a member
of the National Council of the John Birch Society. Published in
Shepherdsville, Kentucky, by the Victor Publising Company in
early 1964, it opens with characteristic and rather impish glee
over the unease Barry Goldwater's candidacy is causing the
Establishment:

> After a half-century of progress toward submerging the
> United States in some vague semblance of world government, the
> American cadre of International Socialism has come face to face
> with a *bête noire* that dogs its heels by day and stabs its nocturnal
> hours with ghoulish nightmares. It is the definite prospect of a
> pro-American President of the United States and its name is
> Barry Goldwater.

[2] New York: Chedney Press; 1952.
[3] New York: Lyle Stuart, Inc.; 1961.

Next comes a pseudo-historical analysis of how the Establishment arose. The history of the Fall of Rome—the right loves the lesson of the Fall of Rome—is shown as a parallel to our own present national decay. "At last the Punic Wars were at an end, and the records disclose that Rome won them all; but the records likewise reveal that not so many years later [just five centuries, to be precise] Rome lost the Empire, from within." We learn that the Establishment, in collusion with the British, has been undermining America since it got us into World War I.

Most other analysts of the Establishment did not share Mr. Brophy's neo-isolationism or anglophobia, although through the election one did catch the Chicago *Tribune*, from time to time, implying in its front-page political cartoons that Western Europe is still receiving our foreign aid.

A more orthodox and more popular version of induced evidence on the Establishment was produced in early 1964 by the president of the Illinois Federation of Republican Women, Mrs. Phyllis Schlafly of Alton, a John Birch Society member. Her book, *A Choice Not an Echo*,[4] was sometimes sold, sometimes given away. The Goldwater volunteer from Panorama City, California, who passed out the books at the GOP National Convention in San Francisco said 750,000 copies had been distributed free in California alone.

While Mr. Brophy induces a conspiracy from foreign-policy events since World War I, Mrs. Schlafly is chiefly alarmed by the Establishment's alleged control of the Republican party since 1936. In that year "a little group of secret kingmakers laid long-range plans to control the Republican party"[5] to promote socialism at home and a soft-on-communism foreign policy. Mrs. Schlafly also warned against the verminous agents of "America Last" who, with European leaders, conspire in secret at nefarious Bilderberger meetings. (In reality, these are conferences on international political problems, sponsored by Prince Bernhard of the Netherlands, convoking such disparate leaders as French Socialist

4 Alton, Ill.: Pere Marquette Press; 1964.
5 Ibid.

Guy Mollet and American Republicans Gerald Ford and Clare
Booth Luce along with leading scholars.)[6]
   Richard H. Rovere, in 1962, wrote a hilarious spoof of the
Establishment theory in *The New Yorker*, later published as the
lead essay in a book. But the rightists were neither amused nor
outraged by the joke. John H. Rousselot, a radical-right congressman who became the Western director for the John Birch Society
after his re-election defeat in 1962, promptly placed the Rovere
article in the *Congressional Record* as further proof of what
he had been saying all along. Mr. Brophy is so gratified for
Rovere's scholarship that he quotes extensively from it, although he finds it a bit "surprising" that "one of Liberalism's most
articulate fellows" (Rovere) would so spill the beans on the
Establishment.
   It was easy to laugh at the creators of the Establishment myth
and then dismiss them as the crackpots they are. But it was unwise,
for several reasons. First, the myth gained great currency and
was a most valuable instrument for stirring up the Goldwater rank
and file to its characteristic abandon. People from Eastern states
and non-Goldwater Republicans everywhere from 1960 to 1964
were amazed when they were treated rudely by belligerents in
the Goldwater camp. What they did not know were the wicked
motivations and designs imputed to them by their antagonists.
Those arch-rightists whose hearts pounded with an indignant
and reckless passion necessarily believed the same hot blood
coursed through the veins of their opponents. The attitude and
actions, inspired by the conspiracy theory, eventually helped
separate millions of voters, including many Republicans, from the
Goldwater cause; but they also provided an unmatched zeal in
the Goldwater movement during the critical months before the
1964 Republican convention.
   Secondly, although few responsible observers believed in the
fairyland of the Establishment a few did accept the half-serious

[6] Mrs. Luce later became co-chairman of National Citizens For Goldwater-Miller, in which capacity she undoubtedly was kept under a suspicious
eye by Mrs. Schlafly.

Buckley use of the word to describe a *type* of person and a socio-political phenomenon. The glib use of the phrase was accepted, for example, by journalists who needed a colorful and terse handle for the opposition to Senator Goldwater. Stewart Alsop, a prestigious journalist and sometime Republican, wrote an article for the *Saturday Evening Post* in August, 1963, which blandly spoke of the Establishment as a real entity.

The greatest irony, however, and also the most tragic for the Republican party, was that the very people who best fitted the stock description of Establishmentarians, including many of the names cited by Mrs. Schlafly and others, were the most politically inept of all during the Goldwater boom. Many implicitly believed themselves that there was some sort of Establishment, but they were also sure that they were not part of it. Asked to help salvage a progressive's congressional primary race or to support a progressive GOP research organization, John Dokes of Establishment fame would inform his visitor that he was not active in politics anymore. He planned to help his own state ticket next fall, in a small way, but if the visitor wanted help from a real progressive Republican warhorse, he should see Mary Jones. Mary Jones would be flattered, eager to provide the name of someone who would be a more likely prospect than she, and she might—just might—give the visitor twenty-five dollars to get him out the door.

The chief demons to the true believers of the right were men like Henry Cabot Lodge and Thomas Dewey. After the 1960 defeat Lodge became disgusted with politics. He felt Nixon had organized a bad campaign and that he himself had been unfairly criticized for his role in it. Consequently, he refused to have anything to do with party affairs at any level during the next three and a half years and came out of his self-imposed exile only to take a secondary position in his son George's campaign for the Senate against Teddy Kennedy in 1962. He worked a while for Time-Life and then for the Atlantic Council. Finally, frustrated with inactivity, he applied to President Kennedy for an overseas foreign-policy assignment, and became U. S. Ambassador to South Vietnam.

But Lodge, the man who more than anyone else was responsible for initiating and masterminding the Eisenhower candidacy in 1952—at the sacrifice, it turned out, of his own seat in the Senate —could only view the developing situation from 1960 to 1964 with ignorance followed by surprise. The sentiment of alarm and outrage did not come until June, 1964, and the California primary.

Shortly after his return to the United States and before Goldwater's nomination, Lodge spoke to the National Press Club in Washington, and was asked a question both sympathetic and cruel: Surveying the Goldwater drive, did he not feel that much of his work to modernize the Republican party in 1952 was being undone?; and, also, how could the imminent right-wing takeover have been prevented?

You would have to have been a progressive Republican to understand the barbed implications of the question. Lodge paused for a long while. Well, he said, it was July 1 and the convention was still two weeks away, and the chances were really pretty good to salvage the party through Scranton. He reminded us that two weeks before the convention of 1952 Senator Taft had seemed a certain winner. There were many voices yet to be heard, he said, thinking of Eisenhower. But, "to answer the second part of your question, these things generally are prevented by enough people being willing to stick their necks out. That's the general rule. And you can judge as well as I can," he concluded with a faint smile, "whether enough people did."

And that other Establishment demon, Tom Dewey?

Thomas E. Dewey's name also brought a sure rise in the blood pressure of the Disestablishmentarians. At the 1940 convention Dewey sided with Senator Robert Taft in an unsuccessful attempt to keep that year's nomination from Wendell Willkie, but in 1944 and 1948 he carried off the nomination for himself and was one of the masterminds, with Lodge, behind the Eisenhower win in 1952. At the end of his third term as governor of

New York in 1954, he retired, officially and in fact, from politics. He was available for the annual fund-raising dinners of the New York Republican State Committee and spoke to the National Conventions of 1956 and 1960. But in 1964, knowing Goldwater would be nominated, he did not even attend. Only a few old acquaintances and those people doing business with his law firm could reach him on the telephone. Dewey had been an honest politician and a poor one financially; now he wanted to earn some money.

The same story could be told of almost all the players in the Establishment myth. Dewey's former adviser and Eisenhower's first Attorney General, Herbert Brownell, retired in 1956 and broke his oath of noninvolvment only in late 1964, when he came forward to manage the re-election campaign of Senator Kenneth B. Keating in New York. His successor as Attorney General, William P. Rogers, became so nonpolitical after 1960 that he was embarrassed to participate in an interview about the politics of the Administration he served under. Some, like late Labor Secretary James Mitchell and former Interior Secretary Fred Seaton, made abortive entries into state politics and after defeat at the polls returned to business.

Two former Defense Secretaries, Neil McElroy and Thomas Gates, Jr., were willing to act out an Establishment-type role if someone would ask them—but no one did. Gates did offer his services to Governor Scranton, and when the latter made up his mind to run for President a few weeks before the National Convention, Gates raised over $500,000 for him in ten days. Some likely Establishment types, such as former Secretary of State Christian A. Herter, were inducted into various positions with the Democratic Administration by two astute Presidents, and thereby kept out of the political arena. The mythmakers might insinuate that these men's jobs were just vehicles for continuing their alleged "control" of the Republican party, but a historian would be hard pressed to find examples of how this influence was exercised and upon whom.

One remembers seeing Mr. Herter at the 1964 Republican convention, after four years out of politics. He talked of the old,

old days when he was governor of Massachusetts, and while Scranton's battle for the delegates fizzled he took a guided tour of San Francisco's bridges. One remembers also during the platform fight that his cogent statement against giving the decision to use nuclear weapons to the NATO command could not be heard over the hubbub of the convention that Senator Morton, as chairman, would not gavel to order. When the Scranton floor manager, Senator Hugh Scott, asked thirty seconds' privilege for Herter to answer a demagogic attack on his speech by an Illinois congresswoman, Morton asked: "Are you kidding?"

Men like Herter, General Lucius D. Clay, John J. McCloy, Seaton, McElroy, and Gates have given the Republican party much more than they have received from it. They were experts and administrators; some of them had been in politics once, but they were not ambitious; they were willing to serve the larger goals of statecraft, even for a Democratic President. The Republican party benefited from them and should have honored them, which it did not.

If such men were the Establishment feared by the right wing, they surely constituted history's most incompetent conspiracy.

CHAPTER 8

◇◇

Progressive Initiatives that Failed

I N 1960 a prominent political scientist, Paul T. David, wrote in
The Politics of National Party Conventions: If some effective
instrument [of policy development] is to be formed when the
Republican party is next out of power, leadership from the party's
titular leader and national committee chairman, together with
the support and active participation of its incumbent governors in
competitive states, will undoubtedly be needed."[1]

In 1956 when the Democrats had been out of power for four
years, National Chairman Paul Butler put together a high-level
policy group called the Democratic Advisory Coucil, including
most of the top party leaders outside Congress (Majority Leader
Lyndon Johnson and Speaker Sam Rayburn refused to join). The
group did cause dissension within the Democratic party because
its very existence implied dissatisfaction with the congres-

[1] Menash, Wisconsin, 1958.

sional leadership. But the committee injected new vitality by developing the Democratic case against the Republicans through 1960 and by receiving constant front-page publicity. The Democratic platform of that year was derived from position papers of the Advisory Council, as were most of the issues of the successful 1960 campaign.

Senator Kenneth Keating was one of the first Republican leaders to apply to his own party after 1960 the lessons learned by the Democrats during the Eisenhower years. Soon after the election he proposed a permanent All-Republican Conference of top party leadership, from Congress and the National Committee, of course, but including also the more notable governors, former Administration officials, mayors, and the handful of celebrated Republican professors. By bringing to bear on policy all the voices of the non-congressional Republicans, there was reason to hope for a new burst of political creativity within the party. The familiar advisers of the Eisenhower era would stay familiar, while young political hopefuls would find a national forum. It was a worthy scheme: a grand Sanhedrin for the Grand Old Party.

Unfortunately, it was turned over to William Miller. It might well have been buried unceremoniously if General Eisenhower had not endorsed it. Eisenhower's endorsement, however, led Senator Keating to believe that his proposal would receive the respectful support it deserved, and for a while his confidence seemed justified.

Under a candy-striped tent at Eisenhower's Gettysburg farm in late June, 1962, one hundred Republican leaders finally did convene. In attendance also, over Eisenhower's opposition, was the press, making certain that no controversial issues would be discussed. Chairman Miller had assembled a long line of speakers, made giddy by the national press exposure, and they unwittingly served to filibuster the conference to death with the same anti-Kennedy wisecracks and turgid cliches one could find in any day's *Congressional Record*. It was another 100-dollar-a-platitude dinner and program, but without the 100 dollars. Perhaps, the money wasted on the affair by the National Committee was a small price to pay to dissipate the dreams of many that an All-Republican Conference would lead the party toward genuine unity and vitality.

The conference, nominally quarterly, did not meet again. Keating pressed for action for a while, but finally gave up. Other moderates, absorbed in their own activities, seemed indifferent, or even, in some cases, relieved. Some Rockefeller advisers had even feared it as a possible instrument of the old Eisenhower-compromise machinery to nominate Romney or Nixon.

But not everyone was so myopic. Indeed, the same disastrous first and last meeting of the All-Republican Conference saw the initiation of yet another instrumentality, this one by the group of men and women who had manned the Citizens for Eisenhower campaigns of 1952 and 1956 and the Volunteers for Nixon-Lodge in 1960.

The key man in initiating the citizens group was Walter Thayer, the president of the New York *Herald Tribune,* a veteran of Citizens for Eisenhower and Volunteers for Nixon, and a close friend of General Eisenhower. The former President himself was enthusiastic. "Through my first administration I tried to bring these people into the permanent party organization," he declared. "I worked like a dog to bring that about, but if I had it to do over again, I would have worked a lot harder."

Thayer committed his idea to writing in late October, 1961, in a letter to National Chairman Miller with copies to Eisenhower and Nixon. Both Eisenhower and Nixon immediately informed Miller that they supported the Thayer proposal and believed it should have his backing too. Over the winter, Thayer and Eisenhower met in Gettysburg and at the general's winter retreat in Palm Desert, California, sometimes alone, sometimes joined by others interested in the new citizens group.

By late spring of 1962 the plans for a National Republican Citizens Committee (later to become Republican Citizens Committee of the U.S.A. to avoid confusion with the regular Republican Committee) were presented to Chairman Miller with the blessings of General Eisenhower. George (Tim) Hermann, chairman of the Chicago's Republican Citizens League of Illinois, and Donald C. Frey, the staff director of the first city citizens association, the Los Angeles Republican Associates, were chosen to head the national group. It also was agreed that the "first" All-Republican Conference at Gettysburg in June would be the right place to announce the formation of the committee and sixteen Citizens Committee leaders were invited to be on hand.

Unfortunately, it was left to William Miller to announce the Citizens Committee. A few days before the Gettysburg conference he received a telephone call from Senator Goldwater, who had just learned of the citizens plans and was infuriated and fearful. No such autonomous group should be started in any case, but certainly not with the support of the National Committee, he argued. At the end of their talk Miller gave explicit assurance to Goldwater that there would be no announcement and no Citizens Committee. Goldwater took it as a commitment.

Although Miller was subsequently pressured by Eisenhower to confirm his pledge to cooperate with the committee, in fact he honored his commitment to Senator Goldwater rather than the one he made to the former President. In direct contravention of reassurances given to Eisenhower, Thayer, and other Citizens Committee leaders shortly before, he neglected to announce the formation of the group. The gathered press knew nothing of the Citizens Committee or the controversy. One reporter observed that "it's so hard to get a story out of these meetings." Only Earl Mazo of the New York *Herald Tribune*, who had been given the story ahead of time, wrote anything about the organization and he, of course, had not been briefed on the last-minute backroom struggle to get Miller's aid for the project over Goldwater's resistance.

But Goldwater's faithful operative on the GOP Senatorial Campaign Committee, Victor Johnston, who had been at Gettysburg and then seen the Mazo piece in the *Herald Tribune*, telephoned Senator Goldwater in Arizona (Goldwater, Romney, and Rockefeller had stayed away from Gettysburg in hopes of quieting Presidential talk) and told him of the Citizens program just hatched. After looking over the list of founders, most of them progressives, the Goldwater *cum* Victor Johnston conclusion was that "these were the same people who have caused most of our trouble." (Presumably he meant the nomination and election of the only Republican President in thirty years.) "It is unthinkable that they should be given another opportunity to lead us down the path to political destruction," he added, perhaps jealously protecting that role for himself and his own various citizens groups.

What Goldwater did not know was that the Republican Citizens Committee was not even slightly interested in stopping his putsch in the Republican party, chiefly because the committee members had no idea what was happening. In a "unity" move, a number of arch-conservatives were asked to join the executive committee, and later the national office encouraged the formation of a citizens group in Connecticut, under State Senator John Lupton, even after it became apparent that the group was a front developed by the Goldwater minority to harass the regular and vigorously progressive state organization.

In Los Angeles, San Francisco, Chicago, Sacramento, and Cleveland, the Citizens "Leagues," "Associations," and "Alliances," as they were variously called, followed the National Committee's example and took care to avoid ideological matters and Presidential politics and to stress organization.[2] Again and again the committeemen would declare, as did Walter Thayer at a national meeting of Citizens in Hershey, Pennsylvania, in June of 1963: "The Citizens Committee has no favorite candidates. We resolved unanimously last year . . . that our full support is available to *every Republican candidate nominated* [sic] for national office if that candidate requests it. That resolution stands and will stand."

When Thayer made the above statement most of the Citizens

---

[2] The exception to this approach, the Republican Alliance of Philadelphia, which lost in a fight against the notorious regular organization in that city, might have been disavowed by the national *Citizens*, except that David Maxwell was a leader in both groups.

members were still confident that a year later a moderate would
be nominated, through the efforts of others. But they did begin
to worry that after the primaries and the convention the moderate candidate would be saddled, like Eisenhower and Dewey
were, with a dreary Republican record in Congress.

So one year after the debacle of the All-Republican Conference in Gettysburg, the Citizens Committee met a few miles
away in Hershey to decide whether they should take up the
task of research once assigned to the conference. The debate
was secret and heated. Some members argued that Ev and Charlie
could only interpret a Citizens venture into issue research as
an assault on the congressional leadership's policies, and that the
Citizens should address itself solely to organization. But the
majority moved toward rebellion. If the congressional leadership
felt they had a corner on policy, they were wrong, and if they
felt research by the Citizens Committee implied criticism of
their own performance, they were right.

Once again General Eisenhower was enthusiastic, and in suc-
ceeding months the Citizens Committee organized a Critical
Issues Council to work through it under the chairmanship of
the general's brother, Dr. Milton Eisenhower.[3]

What was significant about the group was not its ideological
complexion. There were enough moderates so that on balance
their views would prevail, while there were enough rightists
to guarantee at least a reading among party conservatives. The

---

[3] Some of the most notable policy-makers of the Eisenhower Era were
assembled: Dr. Arthur Burns and Dr. Henry Wallich, professors at Columbia
and Yale, respectively; Health, Education, and Welfare Secretaries Oveta
Culp Hobby and Marion B. Folsom; General Lauris Norstad (Ret.);
UN Delegate Mary B. Lord; the late Labor Secretary James P. Mitchell;
Minnesota Congressman Walter Judd; former Defense Secretary Thomas
Gates, Jr.; and the head of the National Aeronautics and Space Administration, F. Keith Glennan. Most were identified with the progressive wing of
the party, but others were more conservative: Atomic Energy Commission
Chairman Lewis L. Strauss; Admiral Arleigh A. Burke (Ret.); Deane W.
Malott, president of Cornell University; Raymond J. Saulnier, member of
the Council of Economic Advisers; and Clare Boothe Luce, later co-chairman
of Citizens for Goldwater-Miller.

problem was that most of the members were "formers" of such unchallenged prestige that while they were happy to exchange opinions, few were willing to do the tedious research and hard thinking required to produce concrete proposals and ideas. Dr. Eisenhower's young assistant, James M. Clark, Jr., was patient and versatile, but he often found himself put down summarily by some of the status-conscious VIP's. Long negotiations were undertaken over the most picayune points and resolved in sterile compromises.

One of the council's finest papers, and the best prepared on the subject by any Republican in the 1960–64 period, was a thorough study of "Republicans and Civil Rights," researched and written by a group of young Republican scholars in Boston called the Ripon Society. The intra-council quarrel over the Ripon Society's admittedly strong positions left the study in most precarious straits for weeks. Through Bryce N. Harlow, General Eisenhower's former congressional liaison and speechwriter since 1960, Senator Dirksen and Representative Halleck lobbied against the paper and seemed to threaten at one point to denounce it publicly. When it did appear, it was without the degree of publicity fanfare the council gave other papers, and little public credit was accorded the Ripons for their work.

Nonetheless, against all the frailities of human nature—inconsistent resolve, fear of the wrath of Senator Goldwater and the congressional leaders, and distrust of new departures—the Critical Issues Council did produce a series of position papers that dealt, sometimes with incisiveness and sophistication, with the larger national concerns, like the Atlantic Alliance, Cuba, agriculture, foreign aid, and the international balance of payments. All were covered comprehensively by the news media. The Critical Issues papers were the best research performed by the party after it lost the Presidency. Yet both the council and its parent, Citizens Committee, in avoiding a factional commitment, committed themselves to increasing irrelevancy in Republican politics of 1964, which was dominated by a factional struggle.

With Goldwater's nomination, all the Citizens work was nullified. Even the members who had talked pro-Goldwater in the past seemed horrified after his performance in San Francisco, and Dr. Eisenhower was so upset by the prospect of the senator's nomination that he flatly refused to serve as Maryland's representative on the Platform Committee. The Critical Issues studies were scarcely noticed in the welter of Goldwater-position papers. Far from the anti-Goldwater movement the senator had feared, the politely moderate Citizens Committee spent over $200,000 that might have been used for factional purpose, and by its faithful aloofness neutralized important potential opposition to Goldwater.

When the senator was nominated, the Citizens Committee offered him their lists and whatever facilities he wanted, and thereupon reduced their staff to one secretary. During the campaign, most of the independent Citizens groups functioned in an organizational capacity; Dr. Milton Eisenhower returned full time to Johns Hopkins; Walter Thayer raised a war chest for Senator Keating in New York; and the honorary chairman of the Citizens Committee, General Eisenhower, revealed at the World's Fair in New York that he found the Presidential campaign "confusing." The future of the Citizens was left for a long and in 1966 still inconclusive post-election reappraisal.

Unable or unwilling to face the fact of Goldwaterism, the Republican Citizens plunged into organization and research. The moderate Republicans in Congress, on the other hand, dedicated themselves to improving the party's legislative program.

After the 1962 elections, Representative Tom Curtis and several House moderates tried to interest the leadership in giving official backing to a semiautonomous issue-research committee. The Curtis group reasoned that if the leadership was scared of new ideas or bored by them, perhaps they at least would give formal sanction to the efforts of those congressmen who felt differently. With such sanction, financial support would come more freely. Demonstrating their sincerity, the Curtis group independently raised and spent $5,000 in small contributions between November, 1962, and December, 1963, to put the operation together.

Minority Leader Halleck, House Policy Committee Chairman Byrnes, and his Special Projects chairman, Representative John Rhodes, were, as usual, quietly opposed. The position of Representative Ford as chairman of the House Conference was ambiguous, while the influential Melvin Laird pretended to support the idea while actually seeking to undercut it. Representative Bob Wilson of the GOP Congressional Campaign Committee, a personal friend of Curtis, gave the proposal his endorsement but grew vague when it was suggested that the study group be operated through his committee.

With House negotiations breaking down, the proposal's backers moved to bring in the Senate Republicans as partners. Senators Scott, Javits, and Prouty (Vt.) were extremely interested, and it was thought that the *ad hoc* Joint House–Senate Committee on Staffing could be incorporated with the joint study group under one Republican congressional office. Several of the potential financial angels for the research group expressed satisfaction with this proposal, and General Eisenhower's unofficial emissary in Washington, Bryce Harlow, was brought in to complete the arrangements. This, however, turned out to be a critical mistake. Mr. Harlow, a pleasantly shrewd politician, was a Southerner and an aide to Democratic Representative Carl Vinson of Georgia before joining President Eisenhower in the White House. After 1960, with a mandate from Gettysburg and an executive office with the Procter & Gamble Manufacturing Company in Washington, he managed to ingratiate many moderates in Congress, who considered him all the more valuable because of his reputed good relations with the right wing. Actually, his right-wing ties were very good indeed. Harlow's message-carrying, sympathetic advice, and patient negotiation for the moderates usually ended in their reluctant decision to do nothing or to capitulate to the right.

So it was with the House-Senate GOP study group. After a

written agreement on structure and procedure finally had been worked out in late 1963, Harlow cut out the Senate participants. Goldwater supporters were genuinely afraid that if men like Scott and Prouty and their staffs got together with certain House members and their staffs, even for the purpose of research, relationships might grow that would lead to collusive anti-Goldwater activity in national politics. The senators simply had to be isolated, and so they were. This decision infuriated some of the senators and potential financial backers, but Harlow made it stick. The study-group plan went back to the House for further negotiations in which, as one participant put it, "Harlow and Byrnes and Laird fiddle-diddled it to death."

The congressmen promoting the Curtis proposal, however, had not foreclosed other avenues of cooperation. Shortly before the Eighty-eighth Congress convened, Representative Curtis, Representative John Lindsay of Manhattan, and several other "constructive conservative" and progressive Republicans met in New York City to discuss how they could work together outside the formal party structure to develop a successful, positive legislative program. The group accepted an offer from Charles P. Taft, a former mayor of Cincinnati and a brother of the late Robert A. Taft, to help raise money to support a coordinating and research committee. The project came to fruition as an independent Republican Legislative Research Association, and its first effort after opening in Washington was on civil rights. Robert Kimball, a young Yale law student who worked for Representative Lindsay, was hired to spend full time on the legislative aspects of the civil-rights bills prepared by Republicans, while Frederick Sontag, a hugely energetic public-affairs consultant with several influential accounts among Capitol Hill Republicans, was assigned the task of coordinating political activities.

In the end, the little band of moderate activists in the House succeeded in getting forty GOP representatives, including nine members of the Judiciary Committee, to sponsor a comprehensive civil-rights bill (H.R. 3139), placed in the House hopper January 31, 1963. A month later President Kennedy submitted to Congress his first civil-rights message, calling for a bill weaker in several respects than the Republican offering.

Describing the work of the Legislative Research Association, Sontag cites the good publicity and the useful "credentials" the civil-rights effort gave the GOP. "But the Republican party paid a heavy price for its support of civil rights. When the party future was at stake in 1963 and '64 this fight in Congress tied up our most effective people, in the Senate as well as the House, and it bled us of money. What's more, the Democrats, because Goldwater did win the nomination, ultimately got most of the political credit for the bill."

When the civil-rights bill was passed in the House early in 1964, the financing for the Republican Legislative Research Association withered. Instead of shifting its efforts toward the forthcoming National Convention and the party platform, the participating congressmen let it collapse, despite its legislative success, and made no plans for reviving it in the future.

In Congress the Republican moderates were a minority, but even where they were a powerful majority—among the GOP governors—their cause stumbled and faltered. In 1952, when a majority of governors, twenty-five, were Republicans, Governor Dan Thornton of Colorado and Governor Dewey of New York made them into a unified pre-convention force for General Eisenhower and "modern Republicanism." With Eisenhower out of office in 1960, it made sense for the Republican governors, down to fifteen in number after the debacle of 1958, to develop a unified strategy for the annual Governors' Conference and to cooperate on projects of mutual benefit within the party.

The Republican governors had and have a special appeal to the electorate and a unique power. Unlike the members of Congress, they must personally accept the credit or blame for the way problems are handled by government; they are administrators and are expected to be initiators; there is no "seniority" for governors, and nowadays there are no "safe seats." Politically, governors are closest to the scources of real power in their states and are usually the best-known politicians within them. Ideologically, Republican governors in the post-Eisenhower years had a promising issue to develop, the revival of state government through new and combined emphasis on "states' rights and states' responsibility" (though not, of course, as a weapon against civil rights).

Progressive state government was an attractive inducement for Republican and Democratic voters alike. But its successful Republican practitioners among the governors failed to make common cause on the national level.[4] When they finally did try, their success was considerable, but without the indispensable element of "follow-through" it was, like the activity of the congressional progressives, short-lived.

In the summer of 1961 the governors of the fifty states gathered in Hawaii for their annual conference. Governor Rockefeller was widely regarded as the most glamorous state executive in attendance. The two political parties alternate control of the conference chairmanship, and as 1962 was the Republicans' turn the New York governor seemed the obvious choice for chairman. However, the Democrats, under the skillful influence of National Chairman John Bailey, decided that if possible they would like to see the prestigious post awarded to a Republican of less national promise. In this sentiment they were joined by, of all people, Victor Johnston of the Republican Senatorial Campaign Committee, who was in Hawaii as the unofficial representative of Senator Goldwater. If the Republicans had been united on a choice for chairman, the Democrats, despite their overwhelming number, would have been bound to acquiesce in it by a longstanding custom of courtesy. But Johnston lobbied from the outset for Governor Wesley Powell of New Hampshire—a man with

---

[4] Such Republican governors in 1960 included Romney, Rockefeller, Scranton, John Love of Colorado, Mark Hatfield of Oregon, Robert E. Smylie of Idaho, Elmer Andersen of Minnesota, and John Volpe of Massachusetts.

vaulting delusions of grandeur and little competence. With the Republicans split, the Democrats came out squarely for Powell and he was elected.

Almost all the Republicans later realized they had been conned out of an effective chairman by the Democrats in tacit collusion with the representative of a possible Presidential candidate who was not even a governor. They privately vowed to be better prepared the next year and even to essay a deft maneuver or two of their own.. Tentative plans were made for a meeting of the governors or their chief aides halfway through the year.

But July, 1962, brought another Governors' Conference, a few days after the All-Republican Conference at Gettysburg and only a few miles away, at Hershey, and the Republicans had not caucused since the previous year. Now Governors Rockefeller, Hatfield, and Andersen (of Minnesota) wanted to pass a civil-rights resolution and the Southern governors, playing a game of "U. S. Senate," filibustered it. Most of the other GOP chieftains gathered at the famous candy-bar resort were aching for the golf course. Once again Rockefeller was defeated, although (as became his trademark) he was able to claim a moral victory from the wide publicity given his losing battle and the exposure anew of the North-South split among the Democrats. As they departed, the Republican governors agreed that "next year" they just had to get organized.

The next year they tried. Repeatedly since 1961, *Advance* magazine had urged the Republican governors to organize. One editorial, in the summer, 1963, issue, caught the attention of Oregon's Governor Mark Hatfield, and he resolved that something should be done about the situation before the next national Governors' Conference. He wrote a lengthy memorandum to the senior Republican governor, Robert E. Smylie of Idaho, who in turn communicated to William Miller his and Hatfield's desire for action. Whether Miller was genuinely interested in the idea or merely responding to increased pressure, he contacted one other influential governor, John A. Love of Colorado, and then wired all sixteen Republican state executives to ask if they at least would like to assemble as a group before the upcoming Governors' conference in Miami Beach.

Hatfield's first objective was to gain the united support of Republican governors for a civil-rights resolution, and for the first time the Republican governors did use their small numbers to good advantage. With all the sixteen Republican governors except Scranton present, Rockefeller, Romney, and Hatfield outflanked the Democrats on almost every issue. Rockefeller accused the Democrats from the North of hypocrisy on civil rights and collusion with the Southerners. Under pressure from the White House to salvage some of their reputation of support for civil rights, Governor Endicott Peabody of Massachusetts prepared a "New England Declaration of Conscience" which individual governors could sign if they wished but which would not expose the Democratic split because it would not be voted upon. However, when Peabody asked permission to place his declaration in the conference files, Rockefeller called for a suspension of the rules to adopt it officially as a resolution. On a straight party vote, the Democrats, including Peabody, were put in the position of voting against their own civil-rights statement while the Republicans voted for it to a man. The conference maneuvers, engaging the attention of the press and public for almost a week, brought a considerable propaganda victory for the Republicans. This performance showed what the governors could accomplish by cooperation and planning and contrasted their position with that of the right wing on civil rights.

But the propaganda coup in Miami Beach was not so conclusive as the celebrating GOP governors seemed to think. Propaganda is not necessarily power. The unity of the governors was needed to help enact laws, instead of just resolutions; their planning was needed to influence the party's course, instead of just ameliorating its image; their enthusiasm was needed to help elect new progressive governors and congressmen, not just to evoke greater enthusiasm. More important than the publicity contest was what came of the plan for a Republican Governors' Association.

William Miller, as National Chairman, made his first appearance at a Governors' Conference in 1963. He brought with him to Miami Beach and the seaside Deauville Hotel Senator Thruston Morton, Goldwater's replacement on the Senatorial Campaign Committee; Representative Bob Wilson of the Congressional (Campaign) Committee; the leading GOP state chairman, Ray Bliss; and several staff members. In a breakfast meeting of Miller and his entourage with the governors, Mark Hatfield was made temporary chairman of the Republican caucus. Miller announced he expected to see the establishment of a GOP Governors' Association which would maintain liaison with the National Committee and, *through the National Committee,* with Congress. Miller left Miami Beach the following day, with the organizational structure of the GOP Governors' Association still inchoate.

It soon developed that a majority of the governors viewed their needs differently than did Miller. Specifically, they wanted *direct* access to the Republicans on Capitol Hill, and they also desired their association to deal with policy questions purportedly anathema to the National Committee. For this reason, several of the governors had asked Congressman Fred D. Schwengel, whose work for increased minority staffing in the House had familiarized him with congressional operations and who was known to favor closer relations between the party in Congress and the statehouses, to discuss with them how they could assist the party's campaign for staffing. When it announced its formation three days later as the permanent Republican Governors' Association, it adhered to Schwengel's concept of direct liaison with Congress rather than to Miller's proposal of liaison through the National Committee.

Governor Smylie was elected permanent chairman of the association and was enthusiastic over its prospects, calling it a "major breakthrough" toward making the governors a "third force" in Republican politics, after Congress and the National Committee. "It's long overdue," he said. Many of the Republicans, like Smylie, came from the West and were precluded by the distance from having regular contact with affairs in Washington. Some had Democratic lieutenant governors to whom they wished to leave their states as seldom as possible. Without a Washington staff, it would be very difficult for the governors, almost all moderates, to exert a collective influence on the party's national activities and position during the pre-convention Presidential campaign. Thus Smylie and the other governors left Miami in a sanguine glow of anticipation, assuming that somehow the actual money and manpower for the new association would appear. But far away in Boise, Governor Smylie had neither the time nor the fund-raising know-how to find it. Without making further plans, he called a meeting of the governors for September in Denver to take inventory on their pooled resources and plot an agenda of future activities.

Back in Washington gentle, homespun Congressman Fred Schwengel and a group of his colleagues labored to establish the formal liaison the governors approved in Miami and had asked Schwengel to establish. Michigan's popular Robert P. Griffin was chosen to represent the congressman at the Denver meeting of the governors. Somehow Chairman Miller heard of the plan and called Griffin, Schwengel, Gerald Ford, and Bob Wilson to lunch at the Capitol Hill Club, the glittering restaurant-retreat operated by the congressional GOP. There the Lockport congressman railed against the attempt to set up a congressional-statehouse liaison and warned that it could only result in party infighting. Schwengel said it was his recollection from Miami that the governors themselves had requested the liaison. Miller flatly contradicted him—no vote to that effect had been taken and no such expression had been voiced. Schwengel, who is not the infighting sort himself, was dumbfounded by Miller's statement. Back in his office was the copy of a document signed by the governors calling for direct congressional ties. But to ask time to get it would have been to accuse Miller of lying. Schwengel sat stunned, while his colleagues reluctantly acceded to the demands of the National Chairman.

No congressman was sent to Denver, except, of course, William Miller. When the governors assembled and confessed their penury, the National Chairman generously offered them all the money they needed, through his own good offices. He only asked that two innocent-looking clauses be inserted in the articles of association, and both were accepted. One stipulated that the treasurer of the National Committee would be the treasurer of the Governors' Association. The other stipulated that the National Chairman would serve as liaison with all other major Republican organizations. Since the National Committee was becoming more pro-Goldwater every day and the chairman himself could not find time to fulfill even his regular responsibilities, the two clauses effectively neutralized the Governors' Association as an independent force.

In the next nine months the association did nothing. No money was raised for it. The 1964 Governors' Conference in Cleveland found the GOP governors—the great bulwark of moderate Republicanism—so confused and demoralized that their tragi-comic performance of political ineptitude became hotter copy for the newspapers than their shrewd exertions of the year before. Governor Smylie, so hopeful in July, 1963, begged his colleagues in June, 1964, to let him resign, and as they were all even more depressed than he, they refused.

The governors, the moderates in Congress, the "Citizens," the former mandarins of the Eisenhower years—all these had taken initiatives toward reorienting the course of the Republican party and all had faltered. Their sad failures occurred concurrently, with each participant consoling himself with the thought that even if his own battle was lost there were others on different fronts still fighting. Those "others somewhere" constituted in a free-floating way the Republican "Establishment"!

◇◇◇

CHAPTER 9

Rockefeller

ONE SOURCE of power did continue to function undaunted throughout the post-Eisenhower years, and that was the largest and best-financed operation of all, the Presidential-campaign apparatus of Nelson A. Rockefeller.

Rockefeller repeatedly demonstrated the resilience of his ambition by rebounding from countless blows to his popularity and prestige. A reputation for bravery and tenacity grew up about him. One thought of him raising state taxes in early 1959 after his election as governor and going on television to explain why. One remembered him late that same year, determined jaw set forth, speaking under a large Nixon portrait while campaigning for President in California. One remembered him in Chicago in 1960, pulling a victory on the platform fight out of a loss of the Presidential nomination. Privately but profoundly depressed over his marriage, he thought briefly in summer, 1961, of leaving politics—but only briefly. He knew he had to follow his conscience ("I can't live a lie," he told a friend, not even for the sake of his life's ambition). He was divorced by Mary Todhunter Clark Rockefeller in 1962, but managed eventually to gain back the favor of the voters. He won re-election over a weak opponent by nearly the margin of his 1958 landslide. He raised taxes and called them fees, and amid the uproar plodded on in good humor. In May of 1963 he took a new bride—Margaretta ("Happy") Fitler Murphy, a brand-new divorcée—and while his popularity plummeted, went out on the fund-raising circuit and bore up with aristocratic patience under the examining eyes of his audience.

When he gamely announced he would seek the Presidential nomination and entered the primaries in 1964—Nelson Rockefeller "courageously slogging through the snows of New Hampshire" became a journalistic cliché that winter—he began to win some voters just on the basis of his "guts." When he was booed for his anti-extremist speech in San Francisco, the happy martyr of Pocantico Hills seemed in his finest hour; and when Richard M. Nixon, in introducing the nominated Goldwater at the end of the convention, invoked the names of those men who had opposed the winner, it was Rockefeller, even over Scranton, whose name won the greatest cheer—they admired his courage even if they detested him.

Rockefeller the slugger, who "loved not wisely but too well" —that's how the story may be remembered by Republican pros through the years. The taxes, the insults to Nixon in 1960 (which already seemed pale by 1964 standards), the divorce, they will say, could have been overcome if only he had not remarried. The other problems could arrest public attention for only a few weeks, but the remarriage was an ineffaceable stigma. His critics were given a subtle but corrosive weapon, while many longtime supporters felt betrayed and set adrift.

Governor Rockefeller was in New York that April evening when the headlines blared out the name and fact of Happy Murphy's Idaho divorce. The smug allusions in gossip columns and at East Coast cocktail parties now reverberated everywhere. Rockefeller was scheduled to deliver the main address to a Young Republican conference on minority groups in New York City. The national YR's, then in the hands of the more reasonable conservatives, had assembled members from all over the country for the party's first attempt in years to examine its appeal to

Negroes and nationality voters. It is likely no such meeting would have been called in the first place if the Young Republicans had not thought, like nearly everyone else, that the Eastern progressive, Nelson Rockefeller, would be the next Presidential nominee.

The right-wingers at the conference were amused at the "liberals'" new discomfiture. The moderates, and even those conservatives who had prepared themselves for the inevitability of Rockefeller in 1964, talked about it in dour tones and shook their heads. Then Rockefeller was entering the banquet hall and the radio reporters had microphones almost into his mouth. He kept smiling. "Are you going to marry Mrs. Murphy, Governor?" "No comment." "Do you know where Mrs. Murphy is right now, Governor?" "No comment." Still smiling, but his eyes becoming glassy. "No comment. No comment."

The crowd at the luncheon tables rose, a bit more slowly than usual, to applaud him onto the dais. They all ate rather quietly and then Jean McKee, the president of the New York Young Republican Federation, rose to introduce her governor. A picture of the attractive young lady greeting Rockefeller had appeared on the front page of one of the previous evening's tabloids under the Mrs. Murphy headline and several delegates to the conference were startled upon seeing her the next day and asked each other if that really was the mysterious "Happy" speaking. Miss McKee was as nervous as the crowd.

When Rockefeller had spoken and several questions had been asked one young delegate rose and solemnly began: "Governor, this is a rather personal question. But it concerns me very much and has been in the news lately . . ." Everyone in the room tensed and some of them audibly gasped. Rockefeller frowned. And then the boy asked, not about Happy, but if the Rockefeller family holdings in South America weren't really responsible for the governor's great interest in fighting communism there. The sighs of relief in the audience were louder than the previous gasps.

That was to be typical of many of Rockefeller's public appearances for a long time: respectful and formal hospitality from the audience underlaid with hypersensitivity to the problem never discussed—except universally in private.

The governor's advisers decided early that the subject of the remarriage would never be raised. Rockefeller himself was surprised and hurt by the intensity of the attack against him and was inclined toward making a television explanation. But that idea evoked invidious memories of Nixon's 1952 "Checkers speech" and was abandoned. A second version of the idea was discussed again and again: to have a background story, explaining all, leaked to a friendly female columnist. The Rockefellers had agreed with Dr. Robin Murphy to protect the Murphy children from publicity as much as possible, and when the governor and Happy were with them they dutifully forbade the presence of any reporters within camera-shot. But it would have been possible to have a question about the marriage and the children posed at a press conference and for the governor briefly to talk— not expatiate—about his feelings on the matter.

As it was, Rockefeller's standard response to questions was sufficiently vacuous to give the impression after a while that he felt the subject was no one else's business and therefore not worth discussing. A short, seemingly spontaneous expression of deep feeling might have provided the catharsis so many people really yearned for. But this proposal too was rejected, and it is hard for one to say with assurance that it was not properly so. Perhaps the staff at times carried their tactic of silence too far, pretending to themselves and to others that because people in meetings stopped asking embarrassing questions of the governor himself (usually it had been the coy, "Do you think your remarriage will hurt you politically?") that they had stopped thinking about it or talking about it in private. But in any case, the sympathetic observer could only insist that few men other than the governor and his wife were justified in judging his personal credo of love; it was not beyond politics, but it was beyond political critique. One could only feel sadness—sadness that any man in politics should have to suffer public censure for private behavior readily condoned by much of the public in their own experience; sadness for this very talented man's thwarted dreams; sadness for the old Rockefeller believers and for what might have been.

But then the sadness had to succumb to alarm. What would happen to progressive Republicanism and indeed to the whole party? Rockefeller had crippled himself as a Presidential candidate, but his incapacity—given his power, talent, and money— did not preclude his serving to stop Goldwater, reform the Republican party, and develop a winning program. After such service he could have had any position and role he desired in a Republican Administration, including the First Secretary of the Government, an innovation he had advocated in 1959. He could even quietly hope—realizing that after his remarriage overt self-seeking would not bring him the nomination—that selfless performance for a larger cause might prove his best weapon against prejudice, and that it might well kindle for him someday the kind of spontaneous combustion that propelled the early Goldwater, and Rockefeller himself in 1960. In any event, he would be assured of the gratitude and respect, grander than accorded many Presidents, that history reserves for its heroes who rescue an institution as important as one of the two leading political parties of the world's leading nation. If one could not in fairness judge Rockefeller politically on his remarriage, it was certainly fair to examine closely his record of advancing the progressive Republican cause.

By now it is held axiomatic that by staying in the race for President until after his loss to Goldwater in California's June primary, Governor Rockefeller manifested an almost sacrificial dedication to progressivism. His close aides argue that had Rockefeller pulled out of the race any time after his remarriage and before California, he would have been accused of "chickening twice" (the first time, 1959) and there would have been a massive shift to Goldwater in the party. By this retrospective view, Rockefeller was all that stood between Goldwater and the nomination.

But it can as persuasively be argued that he was all that really stood between Scranton or Nixon getting into the contest. "You couldn't *drag* other people into the race!" says George Hinman, New York's National Committeeman and Rockefeller's chief aide. But Hinman also admits that if someone else had come into the race, Rockefeller probably would not have gotten out, not before California. There also is no evidence that Rockefeller *tried* to get other candidates into the race. Certainly a promise of full support from him would have been rather persuasive to anyone even slightly willing to run. The truth is that Rockefeller—understandably—could not bear the thought of handing over to any reluctant dragon all that he had worked so hard for. Moreover, the fact is that the Rockefeller organization maintained more contact with Goldwater than with any of the other moderate Republicans, which is to say slightly more than none. It is true that for their part Scranton, Nixon, Eisenhower, Romney, *et al.* did nothing much to open lines of communication and cooperation. But Rockefeller was supposed to be the leader, Mr. Moderate, the man *in* the race.

What, it must be asked, did Governor Rockefeller do to stop Goldwater other than to pace him? Here the acknowledged strategy of the Rockefeller campaign is most revealing. The central premise was that nominations are most surely won through the primaries (e.g., Kennedy, 1960) rather than through the formal intraparty structure, and that given the indifference or hostility toward Rockefeller among the organization Republicans, the primaries were also the only possible route for him to take. Therefore, within the party, the governor's agents, chiefly Hinman and his assistant, Robert Douglass, merely attempted to make friends with as many people as possible, without involving the governor overtly or covertly in power-plays of any kind. They tried to attend most regional GOP gatherings and many on the state level. They made frequent "goodwill missions" to Washington ("just to check in") where they gossiped casually with senators and representatives they thought potentially useful.

Somehow, on such visits, moderate congressmen complained, George Hinman never got down to business.

Always polite, friendly, and noncommittal, the Rockefeller emissaries believed that someday, if the governor won the primaries, the organization would come around, and when that happened all the goodwill would pay off. This hope in turn reinforced the natural inclination to avoid interference in the workings of the party's various instrumentalities, for that might offend people who would be important to a smooth-functioning campaign after the 1964 convention. Thus, at least until 1964, there was only the slightest visible concern in New York that Chairman Miller was inveigling the National Committee into slavish attendance on the Southern strategy. Indeed, in December of 1963, when Rockefeller—falsely assumed by many to be bankrolling *Advance* magazine—was criticized for *Advance*'s attack on the segregationist Operation Dixie, the governor was very, very nearly persuaded to crank out a press release disavowing *Advance* and disassociating himself from its conclusions. He did not because the policy then was not to offend *anyone.*

It was said that Governor Rockefeller unwittingly befriended his enemies and tortured his friends. The governor's staff was willing to put in a good word to possible contributors or powerful politicians in states where moderate Republicans faced rightist primary opposition or a stiff general election. But hardly ever did the governor contribute money of his own, over or under the table.

Because of this attitude, the All-Republican Conference was given no encouragement and the Republican Citizens were unable even to get permission to start a local committee in New York City. The Young Republican contribution came to $2,500, and only for the 1963 *college* race. The Rockefeller organization simply saw no use in the YR's. But after the openly pro-Goldwater faction seized control, it mobilized untold numbers of passionately dedicated volunteers—the kind of workers Rockefeller could not get and who contributed decisively, along with the

John Birch Society, to his defeat in California. The story was the same for the Republican Women's Federation, seized by Goldwater zealots without a Rockefeller countermove. No boost was available, either, for those people engaged in long-term efforts to enlist minority-group voters in the Republican parties of the big cities, even though it turned out that a few thousand more of them in Los Angeles in June, 1964, might have changed history. "We didn't have a drive on in those areas," said Mr. Hinman much later, and he did not see why they should have.

The Rockefeller organization that spoke of its inability to "carry the whole world of Republicans on their shoulders" none-theless managed to put together, almost solely through the personal resources of the wealthiest man ever to run for Presi-dent, a paid campaign staff of some three hundred persons (a paltry seventy until the governor's formal announcement of candidacy) operating out of 30 Rockefeller Center, two converted brownstones on West 55th Street, an entire floor of an office building at 521 Fifth Avenue (later to become the Keating cam-paign headquarters), and a suite of rooms in the United Rubber Building on West 49th Street, not to mention the governor's Executive Chambers in Albany and the Republican State Central Committee offices in both Albany and New York. There were also, of course, offices and paid staffs in Washington, D.C., and in the primary states by early 1964. The price of the official campaign alone, according to reliable estimates, came to nearly eight million dollars.

Some of the finest talent in American politics was engaged in promoting the Rockefeller candidacy, and almost all were thoroughly dedicated to their task beyond personal emolument. But they often overlapped and efficiency was incredibly low. Centralization stifled spontaneity. Because money had always been available only for more staff to be utilized in New York and, after late 1963, for projects that would redound immedi-ately to the governor's campaign, the cause of progressive Re-publicanism in general suffered, and the grass-roots moderate never was given a ready vehicle for his concern.

Even the more important moderates could only be mystified by the subtle aloofness of Rockefeller's muscle-bound organization. In the autumn of 1963, before the assassination of President Kennedy, George Lodge, the son of Ambassador Lodge and the 1962 Massachusetts senatorial candidate against Edward Kennedy, offered his services to Rockefeller as New England coordinator. His qualifications for such a post were excellent, but he was waved off cavalierly by the high-riding New Yorkers, who were not ready yet to think about New England. After President Kennedy's death George Lodge became interested in the possibilities of his father being nominated, and the results in New Hampshire are well known.

Similarly, for eight months in the summer and fall of 1963, a vivacious Washington blond named Sally Saltonstall, a niece of Massachusetts Senator Leverett Saltonstall, and George Lodge's youth director in 1962, pounded on the doors of the Kafkaesque Rockefeller outfit, asking if it was not time for them to be thinking about a youth organization. The Goldwater Young Americans for Freedom, after all, had been functioning for four years. Finally she was told to prepare a memorandum on just what she would have a Youth for Rockefeller do. Wanting the best possible advice, she flew to Boston and consulted with Douglas Bailey, David Goldberg, and Paul Grindle, who had managed George Lodge's race in 1962. Bailey was already a research consultant to Rockefeller, but Goldberg and Grindle several months later were to commit themselves to the unannounced and unfinanced candidacy of Ambassador Henry Cabot Lodge and set out for New Hampshire to start the campaign.

With her report in tow, Sally Saltonstall presented herself at the Rockefeller office and once more was put off. In November she demanded to know one way or another whether there was going to be a Youth for Rockefeller and if she was going to work on it. The answer was further procrastination. In December Grindle and Goldberg decided to campaign for Lodge, and Sally, with her friend Caroline Williams, joined them. Essentially four people organized the successful New Hampshire Lodge campaign: Grindle, Goldberg, Sally Saltonstall, and Caroline Williams. The two girls, said Goldberg, "were absolutely critical" to the Lodge victory. "They built the aura of good will and fun. But moreover, they are 'pros' and tireless ones at that . . . These two kids physically made the thing work." To cap the irony, Miss Saltonstall's *father* and one of his friends—whose daughter was on Rockefeller's foreign policy research staff—became the two largest contributors to the budget-priced Lodge campaign.

The organizational follies of the Rockefeller staff betrayed the ailment attributed to New York Republican politicians since Dewey—parochial inattention to the rest of the country. Partly because of the Kennedy example, it was thought that it really did not matter how pro-Goldwater the state parties were or what the National Committee or any other formal organization did, because in the end only the results of the primaries would count. At the same time, Rockefeller, or his advisers, thoroughly underestimated the intensity of the feelings held by the new people to whom they were abandoning the party machinery. From late 1960 to July, 1963, Rockefeller tried to persuade the impassioned Goldwater ladies of the Women's Federation and other rightwing audiences across the country that, though they might not prefer him to the Arizona senator, he was a conservative whom they could accept after he had won the primaries. Said Robert Douglass: "We wanted to show that Governor Rockefeller had a brand of Republicanism saleable anywhere in the country. We tried to build up credits for him by staying close to the regular party and helping to raise money. . . . We were trying to show the party that what they believed in we believed in and that we had a fresh, ingenious application of what they believed in and that it worked." In nearly every speech Rockefeller would cite his record in New York State. "It made sense," said Douglass, "though some people forgot it fairly soon."

That they "forgot it fairly soon" was just the flaw in the whole approach. Rockefeller saw the party as something to be kept just friendly enough to accept the expected voice of the primaries, not as a series of organizations which were fundamentally hostile to him and therefore would have to be reformed. He did not want to build a new party, but just make the old one accept the fact of his popularity.

Toward this objective Rockefeller held several secret meetings in 1962 and 1963 with Barry Goldwater in the New Yorker's Washington home. Rather than fight the trend toward a segregationist party, he decided in 1963 to invite two of the Dixiecan ringleaders, John Grenier and James Martin, to discuss whether they all could work out a *modus vivendi*. (Grenier came; Martin did not.) With his incomparable resources, Rockefeller himself easily could have provided the money (or had the money provided) to make the Governors' Association independent of the National Committee. To have done so would have enhanced immeasurably the influence of the almost unanimously moderate governors. Rockefeller did not, of course, and George Hinman's statement that other moderate leaders were considered "potential rivals" explains why. Rather than helping to start a youth organization of progressive Republicans, or even meeting with young progressive leaders, as he was advised upon several occasions, Governor Rockefeller in 1962 hosted a quiet reception in New York for the leaders of the Young Americans for Freedom, in the naïve hope of neutralizing the ill-will which they bore against him almost as a *raison d'être*.

In early 1963 Rockefeller seemed headed for the nomination with anticipated primary victories the next year and the acquiescence in his victory of most of the party's right wing. He led the Gallup poll among Republican voters, with 41 percent to Goldwater's 11 percent. But when his remarriage destroyed his massive popularity and the glamour was gone, all the true feelings of his rightist friends were galvanized, and Rockefeller had no progressive Republican movement to fall back upon.

A month and a half after the Rockefeller remarriage, the Young Republicans held a tumultuous National Convention in San Francisco. Superficially, the battle for control of the group appeared one between the arch-conservatives and the even more arch-conservatives. In fact, while both leading candidates for

National Chairman shared a similar ideology, one was prepared to turn over the YR Federation to the Goldwater campaign and the other, who declined to announce his support of any Presidential possibility, viewed the federation as essentially non-ideological. He got no help from Rockefeller and ran his own campaign, while the campaign of his opponent, the winner, was masterminded by members of the National Draft-Goldwater Committee.

What Rockefeller did do, always, was make certain the New York State delegation to any assemblage was properly financed, and when his YR chairman, Jean McKee, returned from the West Coast with a memorandum on just how savage the convention had been, the governor was genuinely shocked. A few days later, on July 14, he issued a trenchant attack on the party's extremists.

"I am now convinced," the governor said, "that unless the vast majority of Republicans . . . are aroused from present inaction—whether this inaction stems from complacency, from fear or from fantastically short-sighted opportunism—the Republican party is in real danger of subversion by a radical, well-financed and highly disciplined minority.

"They are, in fact, embarked on a determined and ruthless effort to take over the party, its platform and its candidates on their own terms—terms that are wholly alien to the sound and honest conservatism that has firmly based the Republican party in the best of a century's traditions, wholly alien to the sound and honest Republican liberalism that has kept the party abreast of human needs in a changing world, wholly alien to the broad middle course that accommodates the mainstream of Republican principle."

"Mainstream" for Rockefeller excluded not only the radical right, but also the segregationism implicit in the Southern strategy. He did not mention Goldwater by name.

It was the kind of fighting statement for which Rockefeller is popularly known and its position bulked large in his campaign over the next year.

But several important moderates were skeptical of the Rockefeller assault, as was much of the press, and the cause of their skepticism was the governor's diminished standing in the polls. The right-wing takeover had been proceeding for a couple of years, they noted; why did he wait until after his remarriage to discover the fact? And even if Rockefeller had suddenly become alarmed by the takeover, he did not change his attitude toward the party structure and money did not become any more available for actually *doing something* about the rightists. The policy of indifference toward the Young Republicans was not changed— even a Youth for Rockefeller was not finally established until January, 1964. It was not until the final months that Rockefeller came to believe it was really the future of the Republican party, not his own, for which he was fighting.

In facing the inadequate Rockefeller in the winter of 1963–1964, most moderate Republicans had to admit their own feelings were ambivalent. Some dismissed Rockefeller as an unbridled egoist who refused to play ball unless he was always at bat. Such individuals sat glumly and irresponsibly on the sidelines of the contest that raged through the primary season. Others, however, decided that even with his liabilities Rockefeller was the one man actually in the game, he unquestionably was giving his all to it, and if he was helped, perhaps Goldwaterism would in the end be defeated.

Compared to the other progressives, moreover, Rockefeller was always a giant. The Scrantons, Nixons, and Eisenhowers of the Republican party were avoiding the contest as if it were a primary fight in someone else's county, between two candidates for sheriff, both equally fine fellows.

CHAPTER 10

The Primaries

"THERE's nothing wrong with Rockefeller," said Charles F. Moore, the blustery public relations chief of Rockefeller's primary campaigns, "that can't be cured by a win in New Hampshire."

In the final week of January, with rain falling in New York City and snow on the hills of the Granite State, most of Nelson Rockefeller's lieutenants were close to despair. The marriage "issue" had overshadowed all others that fall, and the Manchester *Union Leader*, a right-wing daily and the only large newspaper in the state, delicately pondered the moral issues in front-page editorials by publisher William Loeb, railing against "wife swapper" Rockefeller. Goldwater held a 7-to-1 lead in the polls, and one by one the state's leading Republican politicians announced their support for the senator.

Fortunately for Rockefeller, however, New Hampshire's GOP is so bitterly factional that it is impossible to get all its leaders on the same side of any fight, even a general election. When Senator Norris Cotton, Mrs. Delores Bridges (widow of the late Senator Styles Bridges), William Loeb, and the united leadership of the state legislature appeared as the Goldwater high command, the laws of political physics impelled their natural enemies to Rockefeller. With the New Yorker's personal charm and the promise of unlimited financing, former Governor Hugh Gregg, a conservative, and his sidekick, Bert Teague, were persuaded to head the campaign. Moreover, Rockefeller put together a large organizational staff, larger even than Goldwater's, and helped inspire it by indefatigable campaigning. "One, plus one, plus one, equals victory" is a hoary political maxim in sparsely populated New Hampshire and it was a formula Rockefeller understood.

The whole official Goldwater campaign opened sourly on a sunny January 3 in Phoenix, with the senator on crutches from a heel ailment and managing to inject into his nationally televised remarks a cursing out of a television mechanic. He subsequently flew to icy New Hampshire, without galoshes or a sufficiently heavy topcoat, confirming all the cultural suspicions of the local Yankees. When his foot was not in a cast that January, it was in his mouth. Asked in Concord if he did indeed favor abolishing social security, he said no, he just wanted to make it "voluntary."

Perhaps it was because he refused for some weeks to go on handshaking tours of town and city streets and spoke almost solely to assemblages of his own workers that he blundered so disastrously. His supporters cheered wildly when he said that U. S. Marines should be sent to the Guantánamo Naval Base in Cuba to turn on the water supply Fidel Castro cut off, but to many of the ordinary voters of New Hampshire the idea sounded irresponsible. Goldwater seldom saw such voters. Even at mass rallies, the local voters were kept at an impersonal distance not only by the raised platform and the troop of Goldwater cowgirls leading cheers in front of it but by the busloads of imported Goldwater supporters from as far away as Connecticut and Westchester County, New York. (The latter's presence was supposed to be a galling embarrassment to Rockefeller.) If Goldwater did not like to meet the people, it might have been because most of the "people" he met were from the Goldwater traveling mob.

Rockefeller's main problem, apart from Goldwater's popularity, still high in January's polls, was the plethora of noncandidates emerging in the headlines. When during the previous summer Rockefeller had decided definitely to enter the New Hampshire primary, the other moderates had indicated through various means that they would stay neutral. After the assassination of President Kennedy, with a Southerner now heading the nation and the Democratic party, it suddenly appeared that if the Republicans nominated a candidate from the urban North he might actually have a good chance to win the Presidency. Suddenly interest in a host of alternative candidates was stimulated in New Hampshire. Most important, as it turned out, was Ambassador Henry Cabot Lodge—"Henry Sabotage" to the Rockefeller people. In late January the pesky draft campaign by a Washington public relations man named Robert Mullen and his four Massachusetts cohorts, Robert Grindle, David Goldberg, Sally Saltonstall, and Caroline Williams, with the semi-secret cooperation of George Lodge, seemed threatening to the Rockefeller staff, but no more so than the Nixon effort.

In an attempt to stop the Lodge effort, Rockefeller tried for several days in the middle of February to get through the circuits to the ambassador in Saigon. When he finally did, the press inadvertently was made aware of it. Rockefeller was called to the telephone for a call from Saigon over a public-address system in the high-school auditorium where he was speaking. He asked Lodge to make a definite statement as to what his supporters should do. Lodge recited to Rockefeller the diplomatic code which he said prevented him from making any political statement. The upshot was to stimulate further interest in Lodge and abet the public credibility of the Draft-Lodge movement. Finally Charles Moore telephoned George Lodge and suggested that his political extermination was imminent unless the draft of his father was called off. But this empty threat had no more effect than the money half-seriously proffered a few weeks before.

By the end of February, with the primary just a week and a half away, the Rockefeller camp began to intercept those subtle impulses a public sends forth when it is changing its mind; Rockefeller was pulling ahead. Saturation television spots contrasting his views with Goldwater's had focused the voters' attention on issues rather than personalities. Rockefeller's fast-paced campaigning was drawing large crowds, larger than Gold-water's, even in towns so pro-Goldwater a few weeks earlier that the governor's staff had been unable to find local chairmen in them. A new buoyancy came to the Rockefeller camp and the national press quickly sensed it. Stories appeared all over the country about the enlarging hopes of Nelson Rockefeller. One place where they did not appear was in the Manchester *Union Leader.*

It is important to a politician that a shift in sentiment in his favor be covered by the news media, for that coverage not only reflects the changed trend but helps it to snowball. Rockefeller did not get such coverage from New Hampshire's largest and only statewide newspaper. Instead, the paper continued its personal invective against the governor.

Without money, time, volunteers, or support from party officials in the state, the Draft-Lodge campaign was as simple as it was brilliant, and it effectively exploited the right-wing concentration on Rockefeller. The Lodge group's New Hampshire chieftains, Grindle and Goldberg, pegged their hopes on a direct appeal to the voters, first through several mass mailings and, second, through television. The mail operation, a Grindle idea, was unique in the history of politics. Some 96,000 letters were mailed to Republican voters and each one contained a "Voter Pledge Card" to be signed and returned. In a business where a 3 percent return is considered normal, the Draft-Lodge committee received back over 9,000 cards (almost 10 percent). Out of these returns were culled the people who were to become the 1,800-man volunteer force for Lodge. Six thousand, in areas where Lodge was considered weakest, received another mailing asking the pledgers to hand out cards to their friends. The national Direct Mail Advertising Association was later to cite the Draft-Lodge letters as one of the most ingenious political mailing devices ever used.[1]

[1] *How to Win Your Election with Direct Mail,* Direct Mail Advertising Association, Inc., pamphlet, 1964.

Almost as inspired was the television commercial for Lodge, the two-minute film from the 1960 Vice-Presidential campaign, which was shown over the Manchester channel again and again in the last two weeks before the primary. At the original film's end, Dwight Eisenhower led up to an endorsement of Lodge for *Vice-President*. The Lodge for *President* backers in New Hampshire simply cut off the last portion of the film and put in a new voice, with a hand marking a ballot, explaining how to "write-in Henry Cabot Lodge" in the March 10 primary.

The two pronged Lodge campaign sent the Goldwater and Rockefeller machines reeling. A week before the election, the common consensus forecast a Goldwater defeat. Two nights before the primary, pollster Samuel Lubell described the massive second shift in sentiment occurring among the voters and indicating a victory for a non-candidate on the other side of the world.

The results had different effects on the Goldwater and Rockefeller candidacies. Defeat for Goldwater in New Hampshire disabused his supporters of faith in an irresistible rightist trend and sobered the pros. But it did not mean his immediate demise, for the Goldwater campaign was built on a grass-roots foundation that was politically shock-resistant. For Rockefeller, however, the defeat was the clear proof of his self-incapacitation. He no longer could pretend to be the popular choice, and he lacked an ideological or programmatic movement on which to fall back. No miracle could save him after New Hampshire, but maybe, just maybe, he thought, a series of miracles could.

Two Rockefeller failures were critical to the outcome of New Hampshire's primary. The first was the early and sustained mistake of overestimating the governor's personal appeal and underestimating the latent sentiment for other moderates. The Louis Harris poll showed in New Hampshire that four out of ten voters were bothered by Goldwater's positions on the issues, while an equal percentage was bothered by Rockefeller's re-marriage. But almost no appeals were made to voters *as moderates* to vote for Rockefeller on the grounds that a severe

Goldwater defeat in New Hampshire would open the door to the candidacies of other moderates.

The second critical failure was a misjudgment of the temperament of the New Hampshire voter. The Rockefeller high command was aware of the problem but they could not escape it. New York was always with them. Nowhere was this better exemplified than in the Rockefeller rally, euphemistically called a "New England Bean Supper," at the Manchester Armory on the Saturday before the primary. In attracting people, the affair was a great success. If, however, they had come to hear Rockefeller or to have the issues discussed, they were disappointed. What they got was, for once accurately described in the next day's *Union Leader,* a "nightclub show." Those appearing included Dave Garroway, a folk-singing group called "The Hunters," a championship bagpipe band, a stand-up comedian, two nightclub singers, an orchestra, and a tribe of "stars" to make walk-on testimonials. The latter included a professional football player, television and movie idols Troy Donahue and Connie Stevens, and others who passed by the microphone too fast to be noticed at all. People had come to be encouraged and confided in, but instead Rockefeller was just the warm-up for two hours of professional entertainment.

The walk-ons were inarticulate and one or two were actually incoherent, making it clear they were there for moral support only. (Presumably the audience did not know what their moral support cost.) The singers then sang a string of wholly inappropriate love songs to the political gathering including, to the vague unsettlement of the audience, "Make Someone Happy" ("just someone happy, *one* person happy, etc."). The comic imitated the same movie stars comedians imitated ten years ago and then told risqué jokes. It was as if a Goldwater saboteur had planned it all. The cost of knocking the spirit out of 3,000 supporters and curious voters came to $30,000, much more than the whole Lodge campaign.

On the evening of March 10 the communications industry took over from the politicians, and with computers and analysts, quickly announced a landslide for Lodge. The ambassadorial non-candidate got 35.3 percent of the 94,781 votes cast; Goldwater got 22.9 percent; Rockefeller, 20.5 percent; Nixon 16.6 percent; Mrs. Smith, 3.0 percent; and Harold Stassen, 1.4 percent.

One remembers the Goldwater people, almost beside themselves to get out of the state as fast as possible; the Rockefeller people grimly looking for a bright side ("a victory for moderation," Rockefeller said); and the happy Lodge volunteers, with Sally Saltonstall and Caroline Williams writing the results on a blackboard, their backs carrying for the benefit of the TV cameras behind them homemade signs reading "SEND MONEY."

There were nine weeks between the New Hampshire and Oregon primaries. The Goldwater people had time to explain away the New Hampshire defeat and a chance to win victories in the Indiana and Illinois races, without significant opposition. Badly advised, Rockefeller stayed out of the propitious Wisconsin primary of April 7, in deference to the pleas of the rightist state organization against a bitter fight in its own domain. Any voter can participate in the Wisconsin primary election, and Rockefeller's appeal to Democrats and Independents, as well as to the remaining La Follette Progressives in the GOP, might have won a significant upset, stalling the Goldwater bandwagon long before Oregon. What the party organization produced, of course, was a delegation officially pledged to Representative John W. Byrnes on the first ballot but, in fact, overwhelmingly for Goldwater.

In Illinois on April 14 Senator Goldwater, with token opposition from Senator Margaret Chase Smith, managed to win only 62 percent of the vote for President. But many Republicans who voted in the gubernatorial contest between Charles Percy and William Scott did not mark their ballots at all for President and therefore Goldwater won less than 50 percent of the total vote cast—an abysmal performance in a supposedly conservative Midwest state without significant opposition. In Nebraska, as the only name on the ballot, Goldwater got less than 50 percent of the votes cast, the others going as write-ins primarily for Nixon and Lodge, and in Indiana the senator got 67 percent against

Harold Stassen. In all these states with right-wing party organizations, the moderates were quiescent while the state parties
committed themselves and their delegates to Goldwater, despite
the clear evidence of his lack of popularity.

Prohibited by state law from entering the California primary
without a declared candidate, the Lodge forces decided they
would have to stake everything on an attempt to impress the
delegates with victories in Oregon and in the public-opinion polls.
But Oregon's primary, the graveyard of so many Presidential
hopes, was not cut to the New Hampshire pattern. Oregonians,
unlike the salty New Englanders, were simply delighted at the
prospect of all the Presidential excitement coming to their state.
With state law putting every potential candidate on the ballot, it
was a command performance, and Oregon was set to give the
visitors a good time. Then only Rockefeller showed. "Well, I
guess I'm the Lone Ranger," he said, and his literature echoed,
"He cared enough to come to Oregon." "He cared enough to
come."

Goldwater had taken a look at the polls showing Lodge a
runaway favorite and, nervously advised by aides that the more
he campaigned person-to-person the more votes he lost, decided
to plead "business in Washington." But back in New York,
Oregon's 1948 winner, Thomas E. Dewey, chuckled, and remarked
to George Hinman: "They like attention out there; I learned that."

There was more to Rockefeller's Oregon success, however,
than being there. His fast-paced ebullience was new to the West,
and in a small state it won friends. Also, all alone in the field, he
talked issues at greater length than before, in New Hampshire, or
later, in California. Moreover, unlike the efforts in New Hampshire
and California, the Rockefeller campaign in Oregon was well-
organized down to the precinct by Robert Price, John Lindsay's
longtime campaign manager.

Most important, he began to appear to the moderate citizens
of Oregon as the man to stop Goldwater. The professional and
executive class in and around Portland moved massively to
Rockefeller in the few hours before the election. Absentee ballots,

cast from four days to three weeks before the primary, gave Lodge 36 percent, Rockefeller 19 percent. On election day, sentiment among metropolitan voters had shifted enough to drop Lodge 9 percentage points and boost Rockefeller 14 over that absentee tally. The Harris poll caught the trend of the shift, but by neglecting to poll during the last two days of the campaign, missed its magnitude. The final vote was Rockefeller, 32.9 percent; Lodge, 27.7 percent; Goldwater, 17 percent; Nixon, 16.9 percent; Mrs. Smith, 2.9 percent; and Scranton, 2.0 percent.

It was Rockefeller's gladdest triumph since 1958. He would always be grateful to Oregon. But now he was eager for California, buoyed by the new enthusiasm and new workers suddenly appearing there. Nelson Rockefeller after Oregon was hero to the party's anti-Goldwaterites. On May 10 the Harris poll showed Rockefeller to have 45 percent, Goldwater 55 percent. On May 18, three days after Oregon, the figures gave Rockefeller 57 percent, Goldwater 43 percent.

Oregon was only the catalyst, however. Rockefeller and Goldwater both had been preparing for the June 2 primary for five months. Goldwater's major early supporter was former Senator William Knowland, a political Lazarus who was defeated for governor by a million votes in 1958 but who returned in 1963 to promote Goldwater, his former senatorial colleague. It was Knowland who headed the twenty-three-man California Advisory Committee for Goldwater, organized in September, 1963, to plot primary strategy. It was Knowland, among the Goldwater promoters, whose optimism revived most rapidly after the Kennedy assassination and who most persuasively argued with the senator to run despite the new problems posed by a Johnson candidacy.

The Goldwater strategy was to defend his early lead in the polls by firing away at President Johnson and pleading for party unity. He eschewed handshaking in favor of television and newspaper commercials designed to make him seem moderate, and mass rallies designed to inspire his workers to get out the right-wing vote. (Unlike most states, California does have a distinct

and self-conscious "right-wing vote.") Several Goldwater victories
in party organizations, most notably the Young Republicans and
the once-progressive citizens' body, the California Republican
Assembly, had provided the Arizonan with a trained army of
precinct workers, some 12,000 in Los Angeles alone, whose devotion would prove critical to the outcome of the primary. They
gave an early hint of their effectiveness by securing for the
Secretary of State, in only a few hours' time, more than the required number of signatures for Goldwater's nominating petitions.
Rockefeller's workers took a full month.

One of Rockefeller's earliest major backers was California
Senator Thomas H. Kuchel, re-elected in 1962 by 750,000 votes
in a state with a million-vote Democratic edge in registration.
Kuchel's first important contribution was to put Rockefeller in
touch with Spencer-Roberts Associates, a political campaign management firm which had conducted many successful races in
California, including the senator's. Most of Kuchel's own backers
quickly aligned themselves with Rockefeller, almost as much
from fear of the effects of a right-wing victory on the party's
future in California as from interest in defeating Goldwater as a
national candidate. With George Hinman helping to negotiate the
tangle of personal loyalties and feuds among the California
moderates, and with the help of Kuchel's staff, the Rockefeller
forces put together late that winter a *Who's Who* delegation of
leading Republicans that impressed even the Goldwater people.
Headed by Kuchel, the eighty-six Rockefeller delegates and
eighty-six alternates included powerful industrialists like Leonard
Firestone, Jr., and moviemaker Jack L. Warner; tried vote-getters
like former Governor Goodwin J. Knight, San Francisco's former
mayor George Christopher, and Congressman William S.
Mailliard; a group of the party's younger state legislators; and
a host of party officials, including National Committeeman Joseph
Martin, Jr., who had quit his post to work for Rockefeller. Republicans in the state's large Negro, Oriental, and Mexican communities, unrepresented on Goldwater's delegation, appeared on
Rockefeller's. At last the moderate Republicans had united be-

hind a candidate, if only in that one state, and, in concert, they seemed impregnable.

The Draft-Lodge enthusiasts were of great help to Rockefeller. They had expected to give him their support after a Lodge victory in Oregon in hope of his support for Lodge at the National Convention. But after the initial shock of their Oregon loss, the Lodge supporters made a dramatic trip to Los Angeles, where they formally endorsed Rockefeller anyway. Later, George Lodge flew to California to plead with Lodge-disposed voters in the state to cast their ballots for Rockefeller, and analyses showed that 2 out of 3 subsequently did so.

Another influential voice, the staunchly Republican Los Angeles *Times*, was raised in behalf of Rockefeller and moderation, as were practically all the other important California newspapers except Knowland's Oakland *Tribune*. The state legislators on the Rockefeller delegation, led by Assemblymen William Bagley of San Rafael and John Venaman of Modesto, organized as a "truth squad" to catch him in sleight-of-hand in changing the old positions.

Kuchel, through his assistant, Stephen Horn, took Goldwater to task for his record in the Senate. The Arizonan is fond of using the opposition's rhetoric in his counterattack and on March 14 labeled Kuchel, the minority whip in the Senate, "a Republican extremist," and on television the next day found him "out of the mainstream of the party." This gave Horn his opening and, pointing out that his boss was busy pushing the civil-rights bill through the Senate, he issued a lengthy study on April 19 comparing Goldwater's Senate support of the last Republican Administration with Kuchel's (52 percent as opposed to 75 percent in 1958–60, by tabulation of the *Congressional Quarterly*), and showing that on "25 major issues specifically favored by the Republican National Platform of 1960 . . . Barry Goldwater has opposed all 25 and favored none." Kuchel had supported all 25 and was joined nearly every instance by the rest of the party's Senate leadership and on 23 of 25 occasions by a majority of Senate Republicans. The Horn memorandum received wide attention in the California press and was repeatedly used by Rockefeller and speakers for him.[2]

The combined assault of the Rockefeller campaign had put Goldwater well behind the New Yorker by all indices two weeks before primary day. Back East the moderates, considered a mighty "Establishment" by the Goldwaterites, were seized and immobilized by excited spectatorial anticipation of what might happen as soon as Rockefeller had finished off the senator. Rockefeller's own supporters were using terms like "irresistible thrust" in considering the new chances of the governor after victory in California. It was supposed that a private offer to finance his own campaign and provide his own organization might be decisive with party professionals, pessimistic in any case about the party's chances in 1964.

Meanwhile, the seismographically sensitive skin of Richard Nixon, a professed fatalist, began to detect the vibrations of a Seventh Crisis, brought by the whisper of a coming draft. Nominally neutral in California, he had watched his old supporters there split between the two camps, the majority of official supporters going to Rockefeller. Those voters naming Nixon as their first choice gave a majority to the governor in the polls, but split evenly in the final vote. Three days before the California primary, he privately predicted a Rockefeller victory and told friends he was ready to heed a call to service.

An alternative to Rockefeller and Goldwater that excited wider interest was Governor William Scranton. But Scranton honestly did not want to run, though his staff made extensive plans on the assumption of a Rockefeller victory in the primary.

Two activists among the immobilized moderates were Elmer L. Andersen of Minnesota, one of the party's most knowledgeable and progressive governors until his 91-vote re-election defeat in 1962, and Walter Thayer of the New York *Herald Tribune.*

[2] Ironically, it also served as the basis for Senator Hubert H. Humphrey's speech to the Democratic Convention with its celebrated refrain, "But not Senator Goldwater!"

Although both had favored Scranton, they felt a Rockefeller victory in California was necessary to keep the nomination open, and they were dubious of the forecasts of an easy Rockefeller triumph. They thought the most effective means to help the Governor would be to have Dwight Eisenhower declare publicly for a "progressive candidate." There was no chance of an explicit endorsement of Rockefeller by the general since he had sworn repeatedly not to back a candidate before the nomination and, moreover, had only slightly higher regard for Rockefeller than for Goldwater.

In private, General Eisenhower admitted that Goldwater was a lot more right-wing than he thought any nominee should be. However, a year earlier, before it even occurred to him that Goldwater could be nominated, the general had been effectively neutralized by his sometime adviser and speechwriter, Bryce Harlow, and by his former Secretary of the Treasury, George Humphrey (who was already raising funds for Goldwater). Applying soothing injections of "party unity," they convinced him he should take no stand on the Presidential race of 1964. And when that position because embarrassing in light of Goldwater's increasing success, they suggested to him that the situation could not be changed at so late a date. The effect was to paralyze the influence of the most popular Republican in 30 years during his party's most critical period.

Eisenhower, of course, was not just a helpless victim. He accepted the treatment in large part because it adapted so well to his own disposition to ease further and further out of public life. He felt that, like former Presidents Truman and Hoover, he deserved a rest in retirement. He sagely concluded that to hire even one political assistant was to increase the pressure on himself. Instead, he spent his government staff allotment on personal servants. He turned over the bulk of work on his memoirs to his talented and devoted son, John, and the politcal problems to Bryce Harlow in Washington. General Eisenhower remembered former President Harry Truman's abortive and somewhat embarrassing attempt in 1956 to have the Democratic convention nominate

New York's Governor Averell Harriman for President. Often citing this experience, putative friends of Eisenhower urged him to stay out of intraparty struggles.

Fortunately for the moderates not all of General Eisenhower's companions advocated inaction. Breaking into his seasonal routine of golf at Palm Desert, California, in the winter and Gettysburg in the summer was the increasingly alarmed counsel of a stream of visitors, including his brother, Dr. Milton Eisenhower, who warned that Goldwater might win the convention despite a bad showing in the primaries before California. Three days after the Oregon primary, Governor Andersen, accompanied by the late Nathan Crabtree of Minneapolis, public relations vice-president of General Mills, met with Eisenhower in Gettysburg. For some time the general paced the room declaiming on the need for a more progressive Republican party and declared finally that he was going to say the same things in his speech to the National Convention in July.

Then Andersen quietly pointed out that July would be too late. A party that had just nominated Goldwater for President would hardly entertain an appeal for progressivism from Eisenhower. The last chance to influence events was nigh. Of course, Andersen told the general, an exertion of influence need not take the form of an open endorsement of anybody. Rather, he suggested, it merely could *describe* the type of candidate and program Eisenhower favored and let the voters do the interpreting.

Andersen's idea appealed to Eisenhower. It seemed a way out of his dilemma. But he wanted to get some further advice on the matter before committing himself and decided, with Andersen and Crabtree still present, to telephone Walter Thayer. General Eisenhower respected Thayer's political judgment, and, of course, he could not have sought guidance from anyone more agreeable to Andersen's opinion.

It was a sign of Eisenhower's relative political innocence that at this point his main worry was whether anyone really was interested in a personal statement as to what he thought about the nomination, and upon reaching Thayer, that was his first question. Thayer allowed that the people certainly would be interested. Eisenhower then assented. During the next week the telephone lines between the *Herald Tribune* and Eisenhower's large office on the campus of Gettysburg College carried long discussions of the forthcoming statement. Eisenhower traveled to New York and Thayer came to Gettysburg, taking with him Raymond Price, the *Herald Tribune's* young editorial-page editor. The final draft was cast in the political rhetoric of progressive Republicanism with its implicit criticism of the right wing, including words like "responsible," "forward-looking," "positive," etc. It had special praise for the 1960 platform, which Rockefeller had helped write, which Goldwater had denounced, and by which the Horn memorandum was showing Goldwater to be outside the Republican mainstream. It proudly proclaimed the very accomplishments of the Eisenhower Administration that at the time had been anathema to Arizona's junior senator—extension of social security benefits, raises in the minimum wage, hospital construction, medical care for the aged, aid to depressed areas. It also used several arrows directly from the campaign sheath of Nelson Rockefeller, a call for "loyal support of the United Nations," a warning that "in today's nuclear-age there is no . . . room for impulsiveness," and the admonition that, "As the party of Lincoln we Republicans have a particular obligation to be vigorous in the furtherance of civil rights."

Thayer released the exclusive Eisenhower article to *The New York Times* as well as to the Associated Press and to United Press International. The news of Eisenhower's apparent intervention brought elation to the Rockefeller ranks in California and gloom to the camp of Senator Goldwater. The senator, speaking that Monday at Redding, California, jokingly appeared on the stage with an arrow tucked under his arm, giving the illusion, in profile, that he had just been shot in the back. When he was asked why he thought Eisenhower had done it, Goldwater adopted the conspiratorial tone of Phyllis Schlafly and darkly imputed the statement to a "mysterious clique in the East that nobody seems to know about but everyone agrees is in existence."

There followed one of the most consequential weeks in American political history. Rarely have the events of any period so short prejudiced so much the future of the Republican party as the events of the week from May 26 to June 2, 1964.

Through the week Nelson Rockefeller plied an argument that seemed sure of success. It was that Goldwater was not a conservative, but a reactionary who opposed social security and the United Nations and favored reckless adventures in foreign policy; that as a result, Goldwater was opposed by Eisenhower, Nixon, Romney, Scranton, and Rockefeller, who was, therefore, the proxy of the other leading moderates in California; that "extremists" of the right backed Goldwater and were a threat to the party and the nation.

Goldwater began the week on the defensive, as he had been since the campaign began in January and would be until it was over in November. He urged "unity" of the party and said his critics were destroying it. He said he was being outrageously misrepresented by Rockefeller and by the press: that Eisenhower and the other moderates were not against him, that there was, however, an Eastern Establishment machinating against him, and that the extremism charge against his followers was just a smear.

Although Goldwater first seemed to admit he had been the object of Eisenhower's oblique attack, he recovered his political sense and denied it soon after. Eisenhower had left him the latitude, scant though it was, to obscure the statement's meaning. What Goldwater and his advisers shrewdly understood was that many voters had not read the Eisenhower article and that many who had might not be sophisticated enough to know, for example, that Rockefeller was running on the 1960 platform and Goldwater was running against it.

The middle of the week saw a steep rise in the number of bomb threats, acts of vandalism, obscene telephone calls, and other harassments of the Rockefeller camp. Part of the growing agitation among Goldwaterites could be traced to a mailing the Rockefeller forces had sent to nearly two million voters over the previous week. Included in it was a reprint of a *Look* magazine

article presenting Goldwater's more controversial quotations and
self-contradictions, together with a pamphlet suggesting that
Lodge, Nixon, Romney, Scranton, and Stassen shared a philosophy
opposed to Goldwater's. The title of the pamphlet was *Whom
Do You Want in the Room with the H-Bomb Button?* Rockefeller
agents in the field reported from meetings of volunteers that even
among the governor's backers there was grumbling about the
alleged intemperance of the pamphlet. Behind the scenes Goldwater sent telegrams to the non-candidates suggesting that the
Rockefeller pamphlet was exploiting their names and asking if
they were or were not neutral in the race.

But on Wednesday night Rockefeller's campaign seemed
to be on a rising crest. The latest private polls from the Northern
half of the state showed a lead over Goldwater of 60 percent
to 25 percent, while Spencer-Roberts' volunteers and paid workers, telephoning over seven hundred thousand Republicans the
week before, found that the division was nearly even in Los
Angeles County, with a full 50 percent "undecided."

On May 28, before heading his campaign North again, Rockefeller convened a critical meeting of his strategists at a station
KTLA television studio on Sunset Boulevard. Its purpose was to
screen a film he had had prepared, called "The Extremists."
The joint Rockefeller-Kuchel staff script had avoided sensational-
ism in editorial content, but the testimonials and documentary
footage were sensational enough and held the viewers in rapt
fascination. Here on film were the leaders of the radical right and
their views on politics and political technique; here, to tell his
own story, was the man from the Los Angeles suburb, whose
meeting on civil rights was raided by a band of admitted John
Birch Society members; here was the schoolteacher in Oakland
whose Republican Assembly organization was literally seized
one evening by the mass invasion of a local Birch chapter; here
was the Lutheran minister and active UN supporter whose house
was bombed while he was nearby, participating in a panel discussion on the subject "Is the Radical Right a Threat to Democracy?"; here were the hate sheets that had started a mass scare

with a story of Red Chinese troops under UN command, poised on the Mexican border and about to invade the United States.

The older, more established Rockefeller backers from California tended to believe the film should not be shown; the younger strategists and Charles Moore argued strongly for it. The rightists will just cry smear, someone suggested. "But it's all true!" said Athalee Clark, Rockefeller women's director, and reminded the Californians of some of their personal experiences. Both Rockefeller and Kuchel were favorably impressed by the film and wanted to show it, but they also were impressed by a plea against "ruining" the party for the future, and when the meeting broke no firm decision on whether to show the film had been made. As with most decisions, the advocates of inaction had a special advantage—inertia—and the movie was never released.

On Friday Governor Rockefeller was in San Francisco to speak to the famous Commonwealth Club, and at the day's end he left for New York and a weekend with his wife. The final trip North, rather than staying in the pivotal, populous South, was probably a mistake for Rockefeller. Leaving the state during the second and third days before the primary was unfortunate, too, but unavoidable—Mrs. Rockefeller was expected to give birth over the weekend.

Goldwater meanwhile was stumping the South, and his fortune was turning. Seven hundred campaign workers, many of them ladies distributing Mrs. Schlafly's book, came out for a breakfast meeting in Inglewood and heard their crusading leader promise to take vengeance against the Establishment: "A handful of people in the Republican party will not change the principles of that party to those of the Democrats if I have anything to do with it!"

But Goldwater's effective high-level opposition was shrinking down to even less than a handful. The supposed Establishmentarians were falling over each other bringing help for the faltering commander whose army each hoped to enlist after its defeat. Romney, Scranton, and Nixon all sent telegrams avowing neutrality. As Senator Goldwater wryly observed, he really did not need the telegram from Mr. Nixon, because he already had received one telegram, a telephone call, and a letter also pledging neutrality

On Friday afternoon Senator Goldwater purchased one million dollars' worth of weekend advertising in newspapers, radio, and television, most of it in Southern California. Rockefeller was spending a lot that weekend, too, but less, and his ads had been prepared long before Goldwater's. Indeed, from reading a newspaper or listening to competing television blurbs, it was difficult to tell who was running against whom. A host of prominent moderates stared out from an ad for Rockefeller, but these same moderates were quoted in Goldwater ads—the quotations lifted from old thank-you's-for-speaking-at-our-fund-raising-dinner and the like—appearing to lavish praise on the Arizonan.

"I think Social Security should be voluntary," said Barry Goldwater, quoted in a Rockefeller ad. "I have always supported Social Security and the record proves it," Senator Goldwater declared in one of his own ads. (The "proof" was that he voted for all of three out of twenty-two social security bills in the Senate during the fifties, and the "record" also shows he was joined in those votes by every other U.S. senator.) Another Rockefeller ad innocently asked in its headline: "Where Does Ike Stand in the June 2 Primary?"

Senator Kuchel discovered on Sunday just how much money Goldwater was putting into the cleverly deceitful advertising operation and urged that Spencer-Roberts secure time to answer on Monday. But Bill Roberts said that it was too late to buy air time.

That was also the weekend for which "The Extremists" had been scheduled for repetition. A survey by Louis Harris later revealed that the number of Republicans concerned about the threat of extremists declined over two days that weekend from 48 percent to 33 percent.

Also on Sunday, General Dwight D. Eisenhower arrived in New York City for the annual meeting of the International People-to-People program. He was in a good mood, did not expect questions on politics, and was irritated when a reporter asked if his statement of a week before "read Senator Barry Goldwater out of the party."

"I never attempted to read anyone out of the party," the general tartly replied. "You people [the press] read Goldwater out of the party, I didn't."

The question, of course, had been loaded. The Eisenhower statement by no reasonable interpretation read anyone out of the party. It merely specified the kind of candidate the general hoped would be the Presidential nominee and did so in a way that precluded Goldwater. In this one inept remark, Eisenhower destroyed completely the value to the moderate candidates of his May statement. The Goldwater camp immediately broadcast the news.

Monday morning saw the great pendulum of victory swinging perceptibly toward Goldwater. He was losing the stigma of his extremist friends while Rockefeller was losing the implicit support of his moderate friends. The issues had become more cloudy, and Goldwater's cries of misinterpretation and misrepresentation had become more credible. The other moderates had unwittingly punctured Rockefeller's claim to their proxies. The polls had shown all along that when the voters were asked to pick between the two candidates on the basis of personality alone Goldwater was the runaway favorite. Moreover, the birth of Rockefeller's son on Saturday had directed attention back to Rockefeller's greatest personal weakness, his remarriage. The tasteful Goldwater camp celebrated the new addition to the Rockefeller family with a series of weekend ads sponsored by "Dedicated California Women for Goldwater" showing that "Senator Goldwater is a True Family Man."

There is no question that by Monday the race had lost much of its ideological content and was narrowing as far as many voters were concerned to a two-man popularity, or unpopularity, contest. Goldwater's advertising barrage had blunted the extremism charge by representing the senator as a staunch supporter of the UN and social security; Eisenhower and the other moderates had pitched in with their "neutrality"; and news media wrap-up stories asserted that if Goldwater lost he would be down to four hundred delegates' votes, while Rockefeller would be up to that figure. The governor had said during the middle of the past week that if he won in California he would win the nomination. Now this same prediction in the newspapers, though no longer coming from him, was losing him votes. The question was less now whether one was pro- or anti-Goldwater, but which man one personally disliked least.

Goldwater meanwhile began his day back in Washington over breakfast at the Capitol with Dr. Milton Eisenhower. Dr. Eisenhower is not a devious man, and when Barry Goldwater asked him to breakfast to talk about the Critical Issues Council of the Republican Citizens Committee he could think of no reason to refuse, although it was the day before the California primary and he wondered how Goldwater, who never had shown much interest in the Critical Issues Council before, could spare the time. Personally, Dr. Eisenhower abhorred the idea of a Goldwater Presidency even more than a Goldwater nomination, but he also believed in courtesy to senators. He had very little to say for reporters after the breakfast, but Goldwater, calculating the column inches in the Los Angeles *Times*, was expansive. General Eisenhower's brother, he said, expressed some criticism of the way he and Rockefeller had been attacking each other rather than President Johnson. But that delighted him, he said, because "that is something I've been saying all along. Republicans should be united and reserve criticisms for Democrats."

When Senator Goldwater arrived back in Los Angeles that early evening he had one priority message for the wild throng at the airport: "Let's make sure we get our troops out!" That summed up his campaign.

Rockfeller, finishing his tour, arrived at the airport soon after Goldwater and a good half of the senator's crowd had waited to ambush him. "Get out, Rocky! Get out, Rocky!" they screamed when his airplane at last came to a stop. The Rockefeller band played and the Rockefeller crowd shouted "We Want Rocky" to drown out the taunting "We Want Barry." When the governor did step out onto the ramp, in the blinding spotlights, he must have thought the roaring cacophony was all friendly, and more than half of it was. But then he heard the "We Want a Leader, Not a Lover!" chant. "I'm glad to see so many Goldwater followers here. It's the first time I've had chance to talk to you," he said at last.

That was Rockefeller, still trying to make his points on the last night, and that summed up *his* campaign.

◇◇

CHAPTER 11

The Goldwater Stoppers

T HE CALIFORNIA primary clinched the Republican nomination for Barry Goldwater. *Human Events,* the right wing's weekly tabloid, exulted afterwards that "Arrayed against the Senator were the powerful Eastern Establishment (including Ike, no matter what he says now), the press, the Communists, U Thant, Ralph Bunche, Jimmy Hoffa and the polls."[1] A less deluded analysis would show that arrayed against Goldwater was merely the feckless neutrality of the Republican moderates and a candidate whose crippling personal weaknesses were never fully overcome.

The turnout was exceptionally large, with 2,170,000 Republicans voting. Only 68,000 ballots separated the two candidates. Rockefeller carried nearly every county in Northern California and Goldwater carried all of Southern California except Santa Barbara, the city whose newspaper three years before first exposed the John Birch Society. Senator Goldwater said his victory showed him to be the true representative of the "Republican

[1] *Human Events* (June 13, 1964).

mainstream," to which Governor Rockefeller could only retort, "We got a meandering mainstream."

The other moderate leaders were stunned by the California results. Facing re-election in highly Democratic Rhode Island, Governor John H. Chafee endorsed Governor Scranton for President on June 4. The same day in Harrisburg, however, Scranton told newsmen that there were no "extremely basic differences" between his philosophy and that of the Arizona senator, and that he would even consider a draft to run as Goldwater's Vice-Presidential nominee. Because of his deferential temperament, Scranton did not consider himself anything more than the leader of Pennsylvania, and, by necessity, of that state's Republican party. He maintained minimal interest and virtually no involvement in the national struggle which preceded California.

Like Eisenhower, Scranton is a man of many moral and few ideological absolutes. Perhaps that is what attracted the retired Gettysburg general to the young Duke of Scranton. "Duty" was the critical word Eisenhower employed to help convince Scranton to run for governor in 1962, and it was the mandate to which he himself, as a military man, felt most inclined to respond. Where his chance for personal comfort lay with inaction (which, he could flatter himself, Harlow and Humphrey considered to *be* his "duty"), it was "duty" unalloyed which motivated Eisenhower's original statement on California. It was "duty," mixed perhaps with frustration, that prompted him three days after the California primary to telephone Scranton to suggest a meeting on "the Presidential thing," and it was on the question of "duty" that he planned to focus the discussion.

Eisenhower, Scranton, Romney, Nixon, Rockefeller, and several eminent GOP governors all wanted to stop Goldwater, and good fortune had arranged the annual Governors' Conference in Cleveland for the week after the California primary. They all were there, each proceeding with a different plan which he failed to present to the others at all or at the right time, each still trying to protect his own reputation, each so volatile in his appraisal of the situation that people began to wonder if GOP moderates were by nature manic-depressives. Nearly every one of them seemed to present himself as the prospective giant-killer, then to push forward someone else, and finally to withdraw in favor of apathy, with the stand rearranged into varying sequences by each of the great leaders. It was a comic-opera, where all of the cast were prima donnas, and each singing only arias, each from a different score, and all at the same time.

On Saturday Scranton and Eisenhower met in Gettysburg, and the former President asked the governor to announce his availability for a draft by a majority of the convention (his "duty") and to schedule more public appearances. Before leaving Eisenhower, Scranton agreed to take a more "available" stance. Indeed, he was to appear on CBS's "Face the Nation" television program the next day, Sunday, and would announce his new decision then. The general was pleased and said he would be watching. The evening newspapers carried stories speculating on a Scranton announcement of candidacy. In Cleveland, meanwhile, George Romney, whose own staff had left all the Goldwater files back in Lansing, was moving Saturday night toward a strong denunciation of the front-running Arizonan, and also a possible candidacy.

The subsequent Romney broadside at Goldwater, made despite disparaging comments from other moderates ("George, you're six months late," said Mark Hatfield), was one of the roughest of the campaign so far. Goldwater, he said, held views wholly opposed to traditional Republicanism and his nomination could lead to "the suidical destruction of the Republican party as an effective instrument in meeting the nation's needs."

"I'm not so naïve that I don't know what the odds are," he said, slapping back at Hatfield and the others. "I realize it's late . . . But plenty of uphill battles have been won . . . I will do everything in my power to keep [Goldwater] from becoming the party's presidential nominee."

Scranton, who had not consulted with the other governors after the Eisenhower discussion, was preparing to "Face the Nation." The strongest of the four statements he was considering called a Goldwater nomination "a blueprint for disaster," and made known his own availability. In his ninth-floor hotel suite a few minutes before air time, he and his wife posed for photographers while a crowd of aides and reporters scurried about. A hotel assistant turned on a promotional record of Bob Hope welcoming the governors to Cleveland and, in the din, the telephone rang in the bedroom. A Scranton aide took the call, conferred with the others a moment, and then whispered to the governor that General Eisenhower was on the wire. The aides much later moaned that they had thought the general's call to Scranton was "to beef him up." But what Scranton heard on the telephone was General Eisenhower saying he did not want to be part of any "Stop-Goldwater cabal" and urging Scranton not to join one either.

Scranton that Sunday afternoon informed the world that there was no split in the party at all, only a misunderstanding here or there. The sadly deflated governor stressed his points of agreement with Goldwater and dismissed the others, including even civil rights, as minor. He had no intention whatever of running against the senator. He also now thought inappropriate Richard Nixon's suggestion that he run for Vice-President. With left-handed generosity, he countered, let Nixon run for it. Progressive Republicans across the country were dismayed by the performance, and Claire Booth Luce disgustedly called Goldwater to announce her support.

In Detroit for a speech, however, Scranton's new Vice-Presidential suggestion, Richard Nixon made the ominous observation that Goldwater was, despite all, still not nominated and new opposition could emerge at any time. If a deadlock did develop, and "if the party is unable to settle on another man," he would willingly accept whatever role the party might ask him to take. "And if the party should decide on me as its candidate, Mr. Johnson would know he'd been in a fight."

On Monday evening General Eisenhower came to Cleveland and the conference. He seemed subdued, as if wary of contamination from the infectious atmosphere of despair. In a meeting with the Republicans before an address to the full conference, he pathetically urged "unity." When the governors explained just what "unity" behind Goldwater would mean to the party's chances in their states, he cut them off—he just had to leave to get to that speech.

At the banquet itself Senator Goldwater suddenly appeared. He ate, grandly shook hands all around, posed especially with General Eisenhower, and left for Washington.

At midnight Richard Nixon appeared and was briefed by Governor Rhodes. Waiting for him was an invitation from Romney for conversation the next morning.

At 7:00 A.M., Tuesday, Romney and Nixon talked for a while in Nixon's suite. When the Republican governors, sober and beaten, joined Nixon for breakfast, they found him, to their astonishment, the apparent new champion of the anti-Goldwater movement. He wanted them to put a "third force" into play against Goldwater (he considered Rockefeller number two) and, according to participants, he seemed to mean George Romney one moment and Richard Nixon the next.

During breakfast Bill Scranton whispered to Romney that the Michigan governor had his certain support if he did choose to run. Grabbing Nixon on the way out of the breakfast and on his way to a press conference, Romney hurried him into a nearby men's room to confide his growing interest in the race. Nixon, according to Romney, encouraged him, and they arranged to meet after Nixon's press conference.

Now, at the conference, Nixon attacked Goldwater on the very issues for which—in a unity ploy—he had defended him two days before in Detroit—the United Nations, diplomatic relations with the USSR, social security, right-to-work legislation, TVA. "Looking to the future of the party," he declared, "it would be a tragedy if Senator Goldwater's views, as previously stated, were not challenged and repudiated." (This was the man who shortly after called Scranton a "weak man"—because he changed his mind so often!) Then Nixon met with Romney.

According to Sherman Unger, a Nixon aide who was present,

Romney informed Nixon he was ready to run if a majority of the other governors and Nixon would draft him. Nixon, says Unger, tried to point out the difficulties in putting together a campaign overnight, but Romney was busy scribbling notes for a press statement and finally looked up to ask if he could say Nixon had urged him to run. Nixon, according to Unger, somewhat reluctantly said yes—because he thought a number of candidates in the race would be healthy for the party. But according to Romney, Nixon did ask him to run and he informed Nixon he was "not willing to become a candidate in the usual sense," but did intend to wage a fight over the platform.

In any case, after this final Nixon-Romney meeting, Romney did tell the press that Nixon had asked him to run.

Richard Nixon's motives have fascinated political professionals and amateurs alike ever since he entered public life and he probably has been psychoanalyzed at a distance more often than any modern celebrity except, perhaps, Marilyn Monroe. Just what was his "game" from 1960 to 1964 can be speculated upon by everyone, because no one other than Richard Nixon, and maybe not he, knows for sure.

The closeness of Nixon's defeat by John F. Kennedy in 1960 was the next-best thing to victory. It left him the support of most of the Republican rank and file (whatever Rockefeller and Goldwater might say), and the conviction of almost everyone that he was counted out of a fair share of Cook County's popular vote and hence Illinois' electoral vote (even though with them he still would have lost). Even though there was no gainsaying the personal rejection of Richard Nixon by the voters of California in the gubernatorial race of 1962, California's disillusionment was not America's. Millions who had not experienced the state campaign still idolized Richard Nixon and millions of others still highly respected him. From California 1962 to California 1964 Nixon rode the roller coaster of national popularity, always rising highest when the others dipped down. In early 1964, six months after Rockefeller's remarriage and two months after the Kennedy assassination, Nixon was favored for the

Presidential nomination in a Harris poll by 43 percent of the Republicans, with only 23 percent for Goldwater, 22 percent for Rockefeller, and 12 percent undecided.

Was Nixon trying to operate the roller coaster as well as ride it? Many critical observers pointed to evidence during 1963 and 1964 that the official Nixon posture of aloofness and neutrality was being stretched to the point of deception. Their evidence suggested that though Nixon might realize that he could not court the party, that it must court him, he nonetheless did actively seek to stimulate its ardor indirectly and directly. Indirectly, he flirted first with the Goldwaterites by coy aloofness from any endorsement of the civil-rights bill until very, very late, while freely rebuking the Negro demonstrations in favor of it. On foreign policy he began parroting verbatim the Goldwater rhetoric of "Total Victory over Communism." Also, periodically, Nixon denounced alleged "Stop-Goldwater" movements.

Later, after California, when Goldwater was the undisputed front-runner, with supporters who were invulnerable to the wiles of imitation, Nixon turned suddenly to parrot the moderate argument against Goldwater, verbatim, right down the "mainstream."

Besides wriggling in and out of other people's ideologies, Nixon went well beyond his pose of strict aloofness in Nebraska and Oregon by communicating directly with his managers there. According to an Evans-Novak account at the time, his neutrality posture also did not prevent him from attending a strategy conclave of all his main supporters, presided over by former Secretary of the Interior Fred Seaton, on May 30 in New York's Waldorf Towers. Anticipating a Rockefeller win in California's primary, Nixon scheduled an eleven-state speaking tour to follow it. The kickoff was to be a testimonial dinner on Long Island for Congressman Steven B. Derounian and the guest list featured a half-dozen top Republican leaders who had not committed themselves to either Goldwater or Rockefeller. The facts do show that *at the very least* Nixon cooperated with his supporters and arranged his plans so that he would be within earshot if the call to duty came.

But whatever Nixon's "game," he failed at it. If he was seeking the Presidency, he misjudged the nature of sentiment for Goldwater and the realities of delegate-gathering (he did not have to go after delegates in 1960). His strategy at Cleveland—arriving at midnight when the hopes of the progressives had just turned back into pumpkins—finally exposed his hand. Most of the governors as well as the press quickly decided that the attempt to push others into the race without promising to support them was neither the helpful stance of an elder statesman nor a call to arms; it was a coy straddle, Nixon angling for Nixon again. Goldwater shared that judgment, too. "He's sounding more like Harold Stassen every day," the senator snapped, and for men like himself and Richard Nixon that is a cruel comparison indeed.

If, however, Nixon really was trying to remain "neutral," he failed also, and it was an even more spectacular failure than Eisenhower's. His pursuit of Goldwater during the California primary to remind him of his impartiality infuriated Rockefeller, while the Cleveland attack on Goldwater and the Romney flirtation (if that was all it was) outraged the senator. The remark about Scranton's "weakness" could not have won many friends. How was Nixon serving his principle of remaining above the battle and free to campaign for any nominee?

So Nixon misunderstood his political position in 1963–64 and was unable to do either his party or himself any good. By failing to provide practical, pertinent guidance to a party that needed it far more than a deceptive aura of "unity," Nixon neither led nor deserved to lead. His greatest asset after his gubernatorial loss was the respect in which he was held by the party pros, and consequently his greatest potential contribution to the party was to guide the pros as they tried to steer the party from disaster. By going beyond marginal maneuvering, or even genuine neutrality, to positively renounce any claim to the nomination and to lead an early effort for Scranton or Romney, he would have served the best interests of his party. By acting from conspicuous personal disinterest, he would have made himself a genuine compromise possibility—losing his political life, he might have gained it.

But enlightened self-interest was not Nixon's meat in the days the GOP struggled desperately over its fate. If nothing else, the Cleveland Governors' Conference revealed that among the moderates even operators like Nixon would suffer with the rest. As for the governors themselves, on Wednesday they dispersed, dispirited and disgruntled, angry with each other and themselves. Said Senator Hugh Scott: "All the heroes have run. Only us cowards stand."[2]

Much later in a private, but well-circulated paper delivered to the most important moderates, the Ripon Society detailed the "wholesale slaughter" Goldwater's nomination would mean to the party. Their predictions of the number of Senate, House, and state legislative seats that the party would lose came almost precisely true on November 3. Only as regards governorships (they predicted the loss of five then held, while only one was actually lost) were the Ripons overly pessimistic. But their pessimism led not to resignation but to a call for a last-ditch stand.

The society concluded that "Aside from ideological reasons, and aside from the desire to nominate a candidate who is adequately prepared for the Presidency, it is vitally important for the future of the Republican party that the nomination of Goldwater be contested with all of the strength his opposition can muster. We believe that it is possible to stop-Goldwater, but we believe that even if it were not possible to stop him, his nomination should be contested." A fight would show the voters that at least a struggle was going on and that Republicanism was not synonymous with Goldwaterism. The moderate officeholders who battled at the convention would have a better chance of convincing constituents later on that they were what they said they were. Many moderates, thinking of saving face after Cleveland and remembering Rockefeller in 1960, talked about devoting themselves to a platform fight as the way to exhibit their distinctive position before the nation. But the Ripons branded the idea as a self-deceptive

[2] Murray Kempton: "The Bleating of Sheep," *New Republic* (June 20, 1964).

rationale for defeat. Only a Presidential contest would grasp national attention, they said, and only it would activate the people who must remain active to reform the party after the inevitable November debacle.

Fortunately for the Ripon Society's strategy, Governor William Scranton was having similar thoughts. He was feeling foolish and indignant as well. Goldwater's Senate vote on Wednesday against cloture in the civil-rights debate brought a new realization of the senator's basic commitment on this, perhaps the most important domestic issue of the decade. Scranton on Thursday evening, June 11, surrounded by friends and advisers, decided to become a candidate.

By midnight, after Scranton's "I'll do it," Senator Scott and Pennsylvania Republican Chairman Craig Truax had telephoned all their potential supporters around the nation, and also Goldwater. The next day, by special invitation, the governor opened his campaign with an address, in many ways his best, before the Maryland Republican State Convention in Baltimore.

Speaking straight to the party and its interests, Scranton said: "We will convene [in San Francisco] in four weeks' time to select the man who best squares with the enduring principles of the Republican party, not to embrace a cause which has no roots in American history.

"We will convene there to select a man who can lead the whole ticket to victory up and down this nation, not to embrace a cause which has written off most of America." The progressive Maryland Republicans rose to their feet, exuberant and relieved, as the Pennsylvanian declared: "We will leave San Francisco a united party, but united behind our traditional principles, not behind some weird parody of our beliefs."

It was to be, as Scranton said, a "good fight," the first which the party progressives had thrown themselves into in years. It did not matter so much that they knew they were going to lose: At last they could unleash themselves in an unequivocal commitment to their cause. And with the supporters and organzations of Rockefeller and Lodge in the lead, most of the progressive

Republicans did indeed enthusiastically pitch in for the last-ditch stand.

Most of the Goldwater people guessed that the Scranton race was only a show and they were incensed. It did not seem fair, now that the party was theirs. The true believers of the Establishment myth were not only angry but a bit frightened; who could know what sensational sorcery the "Eastern Liberals" had prepared?

It was their resentment in June that flamed out so hatefully at the convention in July. Probably never have such an obviously doomed candidate and his supporters been so fiercely over-killed by opponents in their own party. It was like a murderer who cannot stop at just killing his victim but must mutilate him as well. The reason was that after its fight, at last, the progressive Republican corpse wore a mocking smile.

Part Three

◆◇◆◇◆◇◆◇◆◇◆◇◆◇◆◇◆◇◆◇◆◇◆◇◆◇◆◇◆◇◆◇◆◇◆◇◆◇◆

THE PYRRHIC VICTORY PARTY

CHAPTER 12

◇◇

A Star Is Born

MOST ANALYSTS of the Goldwater movement have made the mistake of viewing it through the prism of the Republican party. As the original Goldwater supporters belatedly maneuvered themselves into the party, the movement assumed a variety of synthetic and deceptive shapes which misled many observers, among them many conventional Republicans, into believeing that Goldwater's candidacy, though somewhat more conservative than most, was essentially not unusual. During the period of Goldwater's masquerade as a typical Republican in the tradition of Eisenhower and Taft, he acquired large numbers of conventional Republican followers who indeed lent his campaign an aspect of party authenticity. Even before the masquerade began, he attracted some traditional Republicans to his cause through his appealing personality, which they felt would make him a good candidate, and through his conservatism, which they were sure he would modify over time just enough to fit the more traditional Republican pattern. But the movement, at its core, was always just provisionally Republican. It was originated, animated, sustained and, in many areas, controlled by the nonpartisan far right, and its strategies and purposes were always dictated more by the interests of the far right than by those of

the Republican party. The party, as historian Richard Hofstadter
has put it, became a right-wing front.[1]

Until Goldwater swept onto the scene, most of the far-
rightists rejected both parties indiscriminately. In fact, some of
them found more truly sympathetic supporters among Southern
Democrats like Strom Thurmond and James Eastland than within
a Republican party which had rejected their inspirational leader,
Senator Joseph McCarthy, and was led by Dwight D. Eisenhower
and Richard Nixon, both considered to be contaminated by
liberalism, if not implicated in the international Communist conspiracy. Goldwater himself shared many such attitudes in
modulated form, and to the end his movement was ambivalent
toward the GOP.

Goldwater began his political career as an aggressive fighter
for economy on the Phoenix City Council, but not as an instrument
of the radical right. Elected to the Senate on Eisenhower's coattails
in 1952 over Majority Leader Ernest McFarland, he took his place
as a strongly conservative Republican. But he received more
publicity for his aeronautical derring-do than for anything else—
certainly more than for his political ideas, which seemed incon-
sequential since he had shown no aptitude for translating them
into legislative accomplishment. It is doubtful that the Republican
senators who voted him chairman of their Campaign Committee in
1954 were aware that they were giving a national pulpit to a
right-wing evangelist.

Yet this, it soon became clear, was what they were doing.

Victor Johnston, the committee's staff director, has said:
"I've been on this Committee for 18 years, and we've never had
a chairman like Barry. He's by far the most active chairman we've
ever had. If anybody would ask him to come and give a speech,
he'd go."[2] Goldwater traveled over a million miles and made over
a thousand speeches during his three two-year terms as chairman.

[1] *The Paranoid Style in American Politics* (Alfred A. Knopf; New York:
1965).
[2] James M. Perry: "Barry Goldwater," *The National Observer* (1964),
p. 73.

His faculty for raising money for Republican candidates, an estimated two million dollars, and his fairness in its dispensation, attested to even by progressive Republican Senator Clifford Case, led most senators to overlook his indefatigable use of the office for personal advancement, not only among Republicans but also among the most lurid nonpartisan right-wing extremists.[3]

Goldwater had become a hero to the whole American right in 1958 when he overcame massive labor opposition to defeat McFarland again for the Senate. It is possible that by moderating his positions and rejecting extremism he then could have become a respectable, if somewhat intransigent, conservative Republican senator in the tradition of Robert A. Taft. But Goldwater's rejection of this course was in fact almost total, though he managed to persuade many Republicans of his party loyalty. Instead, Goldwater chose to become the agent of party realignment through the incorporation of the extreme right into the Republican party. His policy, like that of many gullible or ambitious right-wingers, was one of "no enemies on the right." Goldwater used the Republican party for prestige and respectability. But he relied on the far right for political muscle.

One of the most fatefully important episodes in Goldwater's rise to national power was the publication, in 1960, of his first book, *The Conscience of a Conservative*, which sold 85,000 copies within weeks after it came out. This book, offensive to most traditional Republican politicians who read it but greeted exultantly by the extreme right, was the product of cooperation between Goldwater and members of both the rational and the lunatic right.

The lunatic right was represented by Leo Reardon and his

[3] In 1959, for instance, Goldwater addressed "We the People!" despite the fact it is riddled with segregationists, anti-Semites, and other assorted kooks. The March, 1960, issue of the organization's newsletter, *Free Enterprise*, instructed its subscribers to read *The Cross and the Flag*, then published by Gerald L. K. Smith, described by a group of congressmen before the House Un-American Activities Committee as "America's most raucous purveyor of anti-Semitism." Goldwater's indiscriminate peregrinations also took him to the Manion Forum, run by John Birch Society National Council member Clarence E. Manion.

Victor Publishing Company, which published the book. Reardon, currently vice-president of the Birchite Manion Forum, was the personal political agent of Father Charles Coughlin just before World War II, when, according to Arnold Forster and Benjamin R. Epstein of the Anti-Defamation League,[4] Coughlin was running an anti-Semitic and pro-Nazi operation. Manion, a National Council member of the John Birch Society,[5] advised Goldwater in the writing of the book.

The somewhat more reasonable right wing was represented on the project by L. Brent Bozell, who provided the rhetoric. An editor of *National Review* and one of its most elegant stylists, Bozell gave the book the messianic tone which made it such a rousing success on the far right. His inimitable style appeared four years later in Goldwater's ringingly eloquent, though essentially misguided speech against ratification of the Nuclear Test-Ban Treaty.

Bozell has a bent for catalytic verbiage. It was he who penned the McCarthy attack on the Watkins Committee as "the handmaiden of the Communists." This phrase, more than any other, resulted in the censure of the Wisconsin senator. But it is doubtful that Bozell will ever again write anything so fraught with political consequence as *The Conscience of a Conservative*. It was in this book that Goldwater almost irretrievably committed himself to the extreme right. Not only was the book written in the tone and idiom of the extremists—eschewing only their obsession with internal communism—but it was also published and distributed by one of the most extreme-rightist publishers. One of Victor's few other efforts was Frank Cullen Brophy's *Must Goldwater Be Destroyed?*, the paranoid and phantasmagorical study of the Eastern Establishment.[6]

Goldwater's book gave an incalculable boost to his national reputation and notoriety as a leading spokesman for arch-conservatism. It also gave an incalculable financial boost, esti-

[4] *Danger on the Right* (New York: Random House, Inc.; 1964).
[5] Ibid.
[6] Cf. Chapter 7, "The Amenable Moderates."

mated by other publishers at over $500,000, to Leo Reardon and the Victor Publishing Company, which had complete rights to the book and sold it to MacFadden for paperback publication. However, Goldwater did not emerge fully into the public consciousness until the 1960 Republican National Convention in Chicago. He emerged there, ironically enough, not as an intransigent sectarian but as an attractive spokesman for party unity with a valuably enthusiastic following, which he delivered without reservation, so it seemed, to a grateful party.

Goldwater's speech, withdrawing his candidacy and urging support for the ticket, came as a particular relief to the delegates, both because he had reacted angrily to the rejection of most of his platform proposals, and because his rampant floor demonstration had made the delegates apprehensive as they prepared to nominate Nixon. It seemed a reproach, reviving the sense of guilt some of them still felt for rejecting Bob Taft in 1952. So the anticipation was electric as Goldwater walked dramatically to the podium; and the gratitude redounded overwhelmingly when, speaking solemnly, he called on his "conservative" followers to "grow up" and give full support to the national ticket.

In the minds of many delegates this performance contrasted memorably with Rockefeller's no less sincere but almost comically overdone protestations of support. His Nixon hat and sash and Nixon buttons, his Nixon speeches and Nixon campaigning, all could not dispel the atmosphere of bitterly frustrated ambition, the feeling of distaste for the candidate, that clung to the governor at the convention. Rockefeller's commitment to the Republican party has always been deep and unstinting, but to millions of Republicans, Barry Goldwater emerged from the 1960 convention as the very exemplar of party loyalty while Rockefeller remained ironically suspect.

It was Goldwater's speech of withdrawal that was responsible—a political masterpiece in its dramatic timing and in its sincere, somber delivery, apparently addressed to his supporters, but poignantly reaching every delegate, as well as a huge television audience. The deftly paced sequence of Governor Fannin's nomination speech, the wild insurgence of the demonstration, and the quiet authority of the speech of withdrawal all suggested the hand of a master of political theater. It was a moment unexcelled in Goldwater's entire career as a national leader. After acquiring the almost inalienable support of the far right through his book and his speeches, he had moved to become a respectable Republican, warmly acclaimed by Republican delegates.

Yet, as at almost every crucial juncture in his career, it was the extreme right which was largely responsible for his showing. Goldwater's actual delegate support was too small to make him a threat to the equilibrium of the convention without the belief that he led a large and consequential movement in the party, which might have been alienated by the progressive approach of the platform. The best-selling reception of Goldwater's book contributed to this belief. But just as important were the series of meetings and rallies that culminated so riotously on the convention floor—and these were orchestrated, to a large degree, by the far-out right.

His speech to the convention was revealing. Who were these supporters of his, these "conservatives" he was talking to and about? They were not loyal Republican "conservatives." They were "conservatives" who had cost the party "election after election," according to Goldwater, their champion, because they "get mad and stay home." "We must remember" he said in his speech, implicitly threatening the delegates as he reproached his supporters, "Republicans have been losing elections not because of more Democratic votes but because conservatives often fail to vote." He ended with his now famous exhortation, more momentous than most delegates knew at the time, "Let's grow up, conservatives. If we want to take this party back, and I think we can some day, let's get to work."

Goldwater knew his supporters better than anyone else, and they had a lot of growing up to do indeed. There were four principal groups. All of them, with the possible exception of the

Youth for Goldwater for Vice-President, were deeply implicated in the extreme right.

Kent Courtney, the New Orleans extremist, working closely with Harry Everingham of the far-out "We the People!" conducted a large Goldwater petition campaign, staged the largest Goldwater rally, and provided many of the Goldwater placards used at the convention. The rally, held the day before the convention at the Morrison Hotel in Chicago, turned into an extremist-right-wing conclave. Courtney (called "quite a guy" by Goldwater in an interview with *U. S. News and World Report*) and his wife Phoebe are notorious Birchers who are associated with the White Citizens' Council. They produce one of the most virulent of all the far-right newsletters, *The Independent American*. Neither husband nor wife had ever supported a Republican before Goldwater. In fact, the year before they had instigated another meeting in Chicago to start a third party.[7]

Birchers Robert Welch and Tom Anderson, both at the earlier meeting, returned in 1960 to address Courtney's pre-convention rally for Goldwater, also addressed by Aubrey Barker, GOP delegate from Arizona and co-chairman of another of the Goldwater organizations, the Goldwater Coordinating Committee. The other co-chairman of this latter committee was Gregory D. Shorey, Jr., chairman of the South Carolina delegation to the convention. According to *The New York Times*, Shorey claimed to be "in constant touch with Goldwater."

Youth for Goldwater for Vice-President provided much of the personnel for the demonstrations on the convention floor. They were mostly too young to have acquired extremist records, but after a post-convention meeting with Goldwater they went on to establish Young Americans for Freedom, a nonpartisan rightist youth organization whose membership includes right-wingers of all shades of opinion, from relatively moderate to extremist. YAF's nonpartisanship, before Goldwater's nomination, was scrupulous. Refusing to heed their hero's convention plea,

[7] William F. Buckley, Jr., was a featured speaker.

the board of directors declined to endorse Nixon in 1960 (too liberal).

The effort with Goldwater's closest personal involvement was Americans for Goldwater headed by Birchers Manion and Brophy. Goldwater's daughter Peggy was guest of honor at the opening of the headquarters and "non-candidate" Goldwater held his press conference there the next day.

Such was the Goldwater movement in 1960 as it first appeared at a National Convention—chiefly manned and organized by extreme rightists. Yet Goldwater was allowed to pass as a reputable conservative Republican. In fact, he was never really exposed. Goldwater's claim that he was misrepresented by the press, is in this respect partly, if ironically, true. Although the press reported some of his far-right associations, it continued to regard him first as a Republican candidate to be taken at face value not as the leader of a complex of far-right organizations attempting to infiltrate, capture, and transform the party, and loyal to it only to the extent they succeeded.

All Republicans are inclined to resist the idea that Goldwater is a real extremist himself. He is an appealing man and he seems honest. He is not a bigot, or a paranoid believer in an internal Communist conspiracy. However, since the beginning of his career as a national figure, Goldwater has exploited and encouraged right-wing extremism. Also, consciously or unconsciously, he has associated himself with rightists in the John Birch Society and out of it, who—at least in political terms—are anything but the "fine" men he calls them ("the finest in my community," he said once).[8] These far-right associations have not been a casual aspect of his political success. Until he became the Republican nominee, his emergence on the national level was primarily the achievement of the far right, some of it of the most extreme right; traditional Republicans, unaware of the full implications of Goldwaterism, were almost always uninfluential followers.

It is important to dispose of the notion that John Birch Society members are "fine people," who should be considered apart from

[8] *Time* (June 23, 1961).

their leader, Robert Welch. An *Advance* magazine reporter, Alice Kepler, attended a recruiting meeting of the Birch Society in Washington, D.C., where the society might be expected to be relatively moderate. Yet even here members freely expressed anti-Semitic sentiments, despite the angry insistence of the "Major Coordinator" that anti-Semitism was "the downfall of all previous conservative movements" (unnamed). Welch's books and magazines were available, but those in attendance went even beyond Welch in their racist attitudes. They were not "fine" people; they were bitter, hateful people.

Goldwater, however, refused to repudiate the John Birch Society. Why? asked Mary McGrory in February, 1962. Because, Goldwater explained, *"my effort has always been to bring all elements of the right into the Republican party"* (author's italics.)[9] That was the meaning of his speech at the Republican convention in 1960, when he appealed to all "conservatives" to join the Republican party. At the time he gave the speech, the only "conservatives," as he calls them, who were not already in the Republican party, were radical rightists who reject both parties, segregationist Democrats, plus a few mavericks like Senator Frank J. Lausche of Ohio, long a favorite of Goldwater's. In 1961 when he was chairman of the Senatorial Campaign Committee and responsible for managing the national party's contribution to a campaign against Lausche, Goldwater told the authors, "No Republican can beat him. Besides he's a good man to have around." Goldwater has never been a very firm party man when right-wing Democrats are involved. He has often expressed his view that a realignment of the parties is needed, along "liberal" and "conservative" lines, with progressive Republicans moving into the Democratic party.

After the 1960 election, on November 10 he made a statement to *The New York Times* that Nixon lost because he was a "me-tooer." Then he said: "Those who believe in the traditional philosophy of government, which is clearly identified with the Conservative cause, might very well decide the nation could

[9] Washington *Star*, February 15, 1962.

benefit from a realignment of the parties and a more frank disclosure of the philosophy of each group."[1]

Thus Goldwater stood after the 1960 election—the hero of a fanatic following with many of its most important members outside or on the fringes of the Republican party and determined to transform it, and at the same time the favorite of a large minority within the party who considered him the exemplary Mr. Republican and were oblivious of the implications of his far-right connections. There he stood—dismissed as a serious Presidential possibility by most political analysts because of his eccentric views, and yet the only Republican with a serious movement committed to him for President. His problem as he well understood and as he proclaimed in his speech at the convention was that so much of his movement was then committed not to the Republican party but to views anathema to the majority of Republicans.

The Goldwater following—particularly the racist Southerners and the Birchers—were outsiders who would not be welcomed or invited in by the Republican leadership. They would have to come in on false pretenses, often with the complicity of the National Committee under Miller, or they would have to be, quite literally, party crashers.

[1] *The New York Times*, November 11, 1960.

◇◇◇

CHAPTER 13

The Party Crashers

GOLDWATER'S attack on Nixon as a "me-tooer" just days after the 1960 election signaled the beginning of his campaign for 1964, whether the senator knew it or not. His people had been ready for a long time. For many of them it was a crusade, heavenly ordained, and one does not hold up a crusade for tactical political maneuvering or to await the results of public-opinion polls. The right-wing purpose, as it unfolded through the years, was nothing short of saving the Republican party and the country from mortal peril—primarily from socialism and communism, but also from threats even more urgent because only a few initiates were even aware of their existence. There was no time to lose. It would take more than a twelfth-hour Goldwater's Ride to arouse the people against the nefarious "Bilderberger Conspiracy,"[1] for instance, as later revealed by Phyllis Schlafly; or to mobilize the public against the "Gnostic Peril," even as alarmingly described by L. Brent Bozell; or to save the country, as an anonymous New York pamphleteer put it, from "The Communist-Rockefeller plot to

[1] Cf. Chapter 7, "The Amenable Moderates."

poison your water." The right-wingers were impatient to start at once, without dreary preparations. For victory, they—like the Communists of the thirties—felt they could depend on the American people, provided they were warned of the danger, and in the words made famous by Mrs. Schlafly, given "a choice not an echo."

The candidate, despite his catalytic remarks, was less intrepid and messianic than his supporters, and he was not yet inclined to mistake the voice of Phyllis Schlafly for the voice of the American people or the voice of God. As a politician (and he had always balked at seeing himself as a messiah) he was not sure either that he could win the nomination or that his nomination in 1964 would advance the cause of "conservatism." Moreover, Goldwater must have been influenced by the conventional notion that it is unbecoming for a politician to show premature interest in the Presidency. Accordingly, in the early stages, the senator left the various "Goldwater for President" organizations to cope alone with their multifarious enemies, the most important of which was their own factionalism and confusion—as well as the complete incomprehension by many right-wingers of elemental political realities.

In 1961 Goldwater's real need, which he never fully understood, was to down-play his extremist opinions and supporters and mobilize and consolidate his potential support among reasonable conservatives within the party. To do this, he would have to establish a realistic campaign organization to conduct his national political affairs, and he would have to take a consistently careful and responsible position on the issues. But when such a group, the National Draft Goldwater Committee, did finally emerge, it was without any indication of sympathy from Goldwater; and, moreover, he declined to accommodate its purposes by moderating his views. He continued "just pooping around," speculating in public about TVA, social security, Negroes, and the bomb, attending to his gargantuan speaking schedule for the Senatorial Campaign Committee, writing his arch-conservative column, and in general intensifying his support where he was already strongest—on the

far right, much of it outside the party—and increasing his unac-
ceptability among the moderates, who were already in it.

He revealed his rationale to Mary McGrory when asked why
he refused to repudiate the Birch Society: "What good would it
do me to condemn the Birchers? Do you think the New York
delegation would weigh what kind of a conservative I am? They
would just want a liberal anyway."[2] Perhaps because he associated primarily with sympathetic party officials, he seemed to
believe that it was only in the East that moderates were crucial
to Republican strength; perhaps because at first he did not expect
to get the nomination, he completely ignored, or else completely
misunderstood, the requirements of a national campaign against
the Democrats; perhaps because he was deeply and sincerely
committed to his concept of conservatism, he was unwilling to
compromise or modulate his views; and perhaps because he mis-
took the fervor of the far right for numerical strength, he believed
they could win him not only the nomination if he got them into
the party but also the election. In any case, in the crucial years
of 1961 and 1962, he neither divorced himself from the extremists
who had conducted his unauthorized campaign in 1960 nor indicated that he would take a different approach in 1964. His only
intraparty efforts, and they were thus of enormous importance,
were for the Campaign Committee. Otherwise he seemed to be
taking the long-term approach, focusing on public education and
on youth.

The importance of Goldwater's emphasis on young people
should not be underestimated. His appreciation of their value
in providing spirit, manpower, and favorable publicity for a political movement has always been among his important advantages
over the moderates, and the takeover of the Young Republicans
by his supporters foreshadowed and contributed to his takeover
of the national party. Nor was his showing among youth a spontaneous expression of wide popularity. His youth effort was conscious and persistent and, according to all the public-opinion
polls, went against overwhelming majority resistance to his views.

[2] Washington *Star*, February 15, 1962.

The youth for Goldwater made themselves heard and felt partly because their antics made good copy; but more important was that they were well organized and amply financed.

Ample financing was not exorbitant by right-wing standards. Youth activities are relatively cheap. Because most young people are not organized politically at all, a relatively small sum can send "a wave of the future" flooding the newspapers and magazines of the land.[3] According to the figures available on the contributions of right-wing foundations, corporations, and individuals to "conservative" youth organizations, their annual budget probably does not exceed five-hundred thousand dollars, the bulk going to Young Americans for Freedom and the Intercollegiate Society of Individualists. This total should be compared to the twenty million dollars lavished annually on all far-right organizations, and also to the estimated total of three hundred thousand dollars devoted to all explicitly progressive Republican groups—for young and old—including the Republican Citizens Committee.

Young Americans for Freedom was developed from the Youth for Goldwater organization so prominent at the 1960 Republican convention. Meeting with the youth leaders for several hours in Chicago on the day Nixon was nominated, Goldwater suggested the formation of a national "conservative" youth organization. In accordance with his desire to reach beyond the GOP, he did not suggest that the group ally itself with the Republican party. Thus, when YAF emerged soon after on "Great Elm," William F. Buckley's family estate in Sharon, Connecticut, the group took an expressly bipartisan position. Not only did its board of directors refuse to endorse Nixon against Kennedy, but YAF adopted Senators Strom Thurmond and Thomas Dodd, both Democrats at the time, as two of their favorite active politicians.

After a year or so when it appeared regularly in newspapers

[3] The supposed conservative "revolt on the campus" was succeeded in the press by a putative far-left anti-Vietnam "revolt" in late 1965. Neither represented much more than the mobilization of already committed minorities among American youth.

and magazines across the country as evidence of a right-wing revival, the group began to decline. Despite all its money and political support, YAF, like much of the Goldwater movement, was
essentially a newspaper tiger. It gave a public impression of
growth and vitality, but it foundered on public resistance and
apathy toward its ideology. At the beginning YAF officials resorted to the device of egregiously inflating their membership
figures. They started counting at 10,000—the number of "members" of the other conservative groups, which had given YAF their
also loosely tabulated lists—and continued counting to 23,000 in
the summer of 1961. But despite the similarly trumped up Goldwater boom with all its attendant publicity, YAF never much exceeded that figure and, in fact, soon began to lose active members.
Even its first chapter, at Yale, which the then-National Chairman,
Bob Schuchman, had lent the unique gift of his sense of humor,
fell into desuetude along with Schuchman's sense of humor when
Goldwater began to get serious.

Apart from self-exposure, YAF's prime function was infiltration of the Young Republicans, and it was perhaps in this role
that "the rising tide" made its biggest splash. The right-wing insurgence in the YR's, as in the rest of the party, was more a
product of organization and financing than of pervasive strength.
The right wing recognized the importance of the Young Republicans and encouraged and subsidized their faction in YR elections.
Progressive and moderate Republicans ignored *their* YR support.
The result was predictable. In three years the party's official national youth organization, once a redoubt of moderation, succumbed not merely to party-line Goldwaterites but to an extremist
element heavily infiltrated by Birchers.

As in the national party, California was the pivotal state—
moving from moderation to right-wing extremism just in time to
give the Goldwater forces a providential margin of victory. At
the 1961 National YR convention, California had provided much
of the margin for a moderate triumph. In 1963, the state's votes
were decisive in the triumph of the far right.

The takeover began with a victory in Los Angeles County,

won on non-ideological issues by men who nonetheless secretly represented the extreme right. Robert Gaston, the leading figure in this operation, and ultimately a key figure in the Goldwater takeover of the national YR's, has been one of the most colorfully outspoken right-wingers. His devastating tendency to shoot from the hip at one point even won him a stern rebuke from Barry Goldwater. Gaston had made remarks about Dwight Eisenhower which did not take into consideration the great improvements Goldwater had seen in the general in the three years since he left the Presidency.

Ironically enough, Gaston, like so many of the Goldwaterites, had not only been a Democrat himself but had supported Eisenhower in 1952, and only recently had come into the Republican politics. His political mentor was John Rousselot, the persuasive Birch Society evangel. But the nature of Gaston's political leadership is not conveyed by his speeches or affiliations. His primary quality is tactical resourcefulness. Normally, victory in the Los Angeles YR Convention, though important, would not have been immediately convertible into control of California YR politics, much less into a dominant role at the Young Republicans National Convention. But Gaston and his followers used their new positions to produce literally hundreds of new, ostensibly right-wing YR clubs in Los Angeles and across the state. Many of them existed only on paper or were created simply by giving a second name to a YAF or Birch Society chapter. The third largest YR chapter listed in the college federation, for instance, was a militantly rightist 500-man club at La Sierra College which evidently had mushroomed up overnight in celebration of the Gaston victory. This group, purportedly as big as the club at Berkeley, turned out not to exist.

Many smaller right-wing clubs also dissolved on investigation and there was no way to be sure which of the new creations was real as the 1962 state convention approached. Moreover, the right-wingers made a practice of invading and disrupting moderate local chapters to such a degree that many moderates resigned in disgust. With the far right transporting delegates by private plane and outspending the moderates by an estimated two to one despite contributions from Nixon and several other moderate Republican leaders in California politics, the Gaston forces took almost every office except that of chairman. The moderates retained technical control of the college division in a wild meeting at which the right-wingers, some of whom brought guns, were finally subdued with the help of the police. But Gaston and his supporters, now in control of the board of directors, simply refused to recognize the victory.

Soon after the State Convention Gaston declared himself a candidate for National Chairman. The YR National Convention was scheduled the next year in San Francisco and the right wing prepared for it exhaustively. Because of Gaston's volatility, the Draft Goldwater Committee supported Donald E. ("Buz") Lukens of the District of Columbia for chairman, and Lukens won a close second-ballot victory over Charles McDevitt of Idaho, who was within two votes of winning on the first. But it was Gaston and his followers who dominated the publicity from the convention and who ultimately decided its outcome. Sitting in the front rows munching on peanuts and sucking on oranges injected with vodka, the Californians maintained a steady racket, and with far-rightists from other states made it impossible for outgoing National Chairman Len Nadasdy to manage the convention. At one point they even rushed the podium in protest of an adverse ruling. With a steady flow of points of order and appeals to the chair, all business was stifled for a twenty-four-hour period early in the convention while right-wing leaders, including congressmen, applied pressure on shaky opposition delegations which otherwise would have given McDevitt the victory. One reporter characterized the convention as a "snake pit." In fact, the extremists so overwhelmingly dominated the scene that few reporters noticed how close they came to losing the vote.

This successful operation at the YR convention in San Francisco was paralleled in the national Republican party, and reached its climax just a year later in the same city. The relation between the two conventions was not merely symbolic or coincidental.

Capture by Goldwater of this largest of all American dues-paying political organizations importantly contributed to his capture of the party itself the next year, particularly in California, where the YR's provided a large proportion of the fanatically dedicated workers who gave Goldwater the victory in that decisive primary. The YR's should not be depreciated. Lukens told the press after the 1964 election they numbered over 500,000 nationally, including 100,000 teen-age Republicans (TARS), and were represented on 1,100 college campuses.[4]

The YR performance for Goldwater was an impressive indication of the group's potentialities. The most important national party organization that he fully controlled by 1963, they gave him the futuristic aspect of a candidate of the party's youth and provided him innumerable volunteers across the country. But perhaps the most important contribution of the YR's was social. They had introduced to each other and to practical politics much of the leadership for the National Draft Goldwater Committee. Members of this committee intervened continually in YR politics, and many of them were veterans of the "syndicate" group which had controlled the YR's most of the time for fifteen years. More than any other group it was the Draft Committee that turned Goldwater's gaggle of competing extremists into an effective political concert.

The committee was begun largely on the initiative of F. Clinton White, a public relations man from Rye, New York, and William Rusher, the Victorian publisher of *National Review*. White had been a key member of the YR "syndicate" with Rusher during the early fifties. Once a member of the Dewey organization and Assistant Commissioner of Motor Vehicles in his administration, he had conclusively alienated New York progressive Republicans by supporting Walter Mahoney against Rockefeller for the gubernatorial nomination in 1958—thus becoming, like so many of the Northern Goldwater leaders, an outsider to the Republican establishment in his own state. In 1960 White was further estranged. As organizational director of Citizens for Nixon-Lodge,

4 William K. Wyant, Jr., St. Louis *Post-Dispatch*, December 7, 1964.

he was tactlessly ignored by the candidates, and moreover came to feel they were conducting a weak, unprincipled "me-too" campaign. With Rusher injecting high-test political philosophy, the formerly bland Motor Vehicle official was growing an ideological tiger in his tank.

Rusher had not been militant in the YR's, but during the early fifties he began the process of smoldering disaffection with the course of American policy that later flamed out in his fervid archconservatism on *National Review*. Neither White nor Rusher nor many of the other leading Drafters had been inspired by the stolid traditional approach of Robert Taft, and most of them supported Eisenhower against "Mister Republican" in 1952. In fact, it was later disappointment with Eisenhower, his colorlessness and lack of political awareness and spirit, that began in the minds of many of these men the ferment which ultimately led them to believe only a true "conservative" could revive the Republican party and make politics exciting and meaningful for them again. They wanted a new kind of candidate for 1964—a conservative who would not compromise and vacillate, a "true" Republican, politically sagacious but anchored to principle.

Within the next year, White—the political pragmatist turning missionary—and Rusher—the ideologue turning realistic political strategist—combined to make their ideal a project. As publisher of *National Review*, Rusher, long before White, had become alienated from more moderate Republicanism and he had refused to support Nixon in 1960. White was more recently and less deeply disaffected, but he too was dedicated to "conservatism." Together they now turned for help to their old political associates, the former members of the YR syndicate, many of whom they kept in touch with over the years. Dispersed to various and sometimes influential positions, within and outside the Republican party, these men were well situated to sustain a national political operation such as White and Rusher envisaged.

The composition of their initially nameless committee as it was expanded into a full-scale Draft Goldwater operation reflected the regional composition that the movement ultimately assumed, but it did not have the extremist complexion of other Goldwater groups. Almost half the Drafters came from the South and were influential in ineffectual state parties, while most of the others, like White and Rusher, were ineffectual in relatively strong state parties in other regions. The leading Southerners were Peter O'Donnell, a Texas millionaire with contacts among other Texas millionaires, who soon became state chairman, and later titular leader of the entire Draft Committee; and John Grenier, a young Alabaman with the demeanor of a Marine drill instructor, who so eclipsed his Mississippi competitor Wirt Yerger, that Yerger left the Draft movement to work through the national apparatus. Also connected with the Draft movement were a variety of right-wing money sources like the Millikens of South Carolina, Charles Barr of Illinois and Standard Oil of Indiana, Jeremiah Milbank of New York, J. D. Stetson Coleman of Florida, and William Mittendorf of Connecticut.

Most of this group came to Goldwater from a context of assumptions and experience far different from that of the Courtneys, Everinghams, and Manions who had managed his national operations in 1960, and were preparing new campaigns for 1964. The veteran extremists were conspicuously absent from the 1964 Draft organization. Only a few of the Southerners, like the soon-discredited Yerger, were animated by the strange demons of fear and hate that characterize the true extremist. Only a very few, Roger Milliken most notable among them, were closely tied to the John Birch Society. Among the rest, Rusher and White represented the polar positions in the leadership group, and Grenier and O'Donnell, the Southern front. Between White and Rusher, moreover, it was White, committed to right-wing views under Rusher's tutelage but essentially a sensible and pragmatic professional, not Rusher, the perfervid ideologue, who set the tone of the Draft operations—which turned out to be almost the only part of the Goldwater campaign where ideologists of "conservatism" were not ultimately supreme.

The initial obstacles to the nomination of Goldwater were redoubtable. At the time of the committee's inception Rockefeller was considered an almost certain nominee and Goldwater was disinclined to offer himself as a meaningless sacrifice. He told White that he would not become a candidate "until and unless he sees adequate financing and the energy of a full-scale professional operation." He indicated repeatedly that he did not endorse the Draft efforts in his behalf. "I don't think the convention would buy me," he said candidly to Mary McGrory during his interview in February, 1962. "I've walked up that hill too often with fellows like Taft and come down too often with fellows like Willkie, Dewey and Ike." At one point in 1963 he ingenuously advised the Drafters to suspend operations altogether while he pondered his future. But the Drafters, though discouraged, were undaunted. Fortified by optimistic memoranda from White, and the high hopes of clandestine meetings, they went ahead with their program of money raising and delegate gathering, determined, "if he won't let us draft him," to "draft him anyway."

The late spring and summer months of 1962 were the hardest the group underwent, both politically and financially. Rockefeller seemed to be recovering the popularity he had lost by his divorce, and with Nixon running for governor of California it was assumed that one of them would be the nominee. The right-wing money that had not gone into various election campaigns had been dissipated in a series of unsuccessful primary races against progressive Republican incumbents, such as the impregnable Manhattan city councilman, Stanley Isaacs, and Senator Kuchel in California. And of course, over $10,000,000 had gone to extremist groups, many of them directly or indirectly working for Goldwater. But it is safe to say that White, Rusher, Grenier, et al. with their $60,000 in 1961 represented more of a threat to progressive Republicanism than Robert Welch with his $1,500,000, or the Courtneys with their estimated $150,000.[5] The Courtneys, in fact, almost stopped helping Goldwater altogether. They had detected a "socialist" taint in their hero in 1961 and had turned to organizing a third-party movement, until the senator won them

[5] Forster and Epstein: *Danger on the Right* (New York: Random House, Inc.; 1964).

back with fulsome praise in a magazine interview for *U.S. News and World Report.* Asked about his "odd ball supporters," he said he had to check every invitation to speak "to be sure they're OK." Then he added gratuitously: "Some are first rate, like this fellow in New Orleans, Kent Courtney. He publishes a magazine down there. He's quite a guy." The senator did not show such approval of the Draft Committee.

After the 1962 election things began looking up for the committee. Nixon's defeat, Rockefeller's failure to improve his margin of victory, James Martin's close race in Alabama, and the election of the five Southern Republican congressmen raised the Drafters' spirits as they prepared to convene in Chicago in December. Moreover, the movement had continued to advance on the state level. White distributed a memorandum in August which cited the election of committed Goldwaterites as county chairmen in Chicago (Hayes Robertson) and Pittsburgh (Paul Hugus), and revealed that the Draft organization had acquired representatives in forty-one states. The elections of Robertson and Hugus were examples of the right-wing practice, so evident in the South and crucial to Goldwater's ultimate nomination, of infiltrating the party in areas where it is weakest. Pittsburgh Republicans failed even to run a candidate for mayor in 1961, and though Mayor Daley's hold on the Chicago electorate had been weakening appreciably because of his blundering on the racial problem, his hold on the venal Republican officials in Cook County remained strong.

But of course the fact that Goldwaterism is the worst possible therapy for crumbling city Republican parties did not reduce the value of Robertson and Hugus to the Draft operation. Both represented city parties which might normally have led the resistance to the right wing. Scranton's belated interest in the national party prevented Hugus's presence on the Pennsylvania delegation in San Francisco, which nonetheless contributed four votes to Goldwater. But Robertson was a leading member of the Illinois delegation, which went almost totally for the senator in defiance of the obvious interests of Illinois Republicanism, not to mention Republicanism in Cook County. This phenomenon of right-wing usurpation of weak Republican city organizations also gave delegates from Boston and St. Louis to Goldwater, and is a richly deserved indictment of the irresponsibility of progressive Republicans in many urban areas.

At the December convention of the Draft organization, its leaders divulged their full plans to the committee and a public announcement of the movement was projected for March. Held in secret but sketchily covered in the press, the meeting was first fully reported, with a list of forty-five of the fifty-five people present, in a long exposé of the Draft movement in the spring issue of *Advance*. The article's accuracy was attested to by Clif White himself, who, according to Robert Novak in *The Agony of the GOP: 1964*[6] thought that someone had planted a tape recorder. Actually, *Advance's* source had attended all the Draft meetings and, contrary to White's belief, did not leave the committee after the story appeared.

By the time of the meeting, the Draft Committee seemed to have overcome its financial problems. Over $285,000 was pledged at the meeting itself, most of it from the South, Connecticut, and New York, and over $300,000 more was anticipated before the March unveiling. A total campaign fund of $3,200,000 was projected, with $1,300,000 to be spent in the Presidential primaries.

The Draft Committee's approach, revealed at the meeting, covered almost every aspect of the nomination process, from research to public-opinion polling, and every part of the GOP, from the National Committee to the Young Republicans. The group discussed gains made in Women's Federation elections in September and made plans for the Goldwater takeover of the YR's in June. Several subcommittees were established: one to deal with Republican leaders with influence among particular delegates; one to maintain liaison with other potentially useful organizations, like the NAM and the Southern Industrial Council (an organization of anti-union and pro-segregation businessmen which was well represented on the Draft Committee); one to develop cam-

[6] New York: The Macmillan Company; 1965.

paign issues; one to develop slogans ("Crusade for American Freedom" was suggested at the meeting); and one, comprising the heads of the other committees, to decide on strategy. William Rusher, moreover, was named as a one-man committee in charge of liaison with the lunatic fringe, with the nearly impossible job of keeping them busy but out of the papers.

Such was the Goldwater Draft organization as it mobilized for public emergence in March, 1963, in Washington. It was the only pro-Goldwater organization with minimal involvement with extremists and with a clear concept of the political realities of the nomination process. On April 9, just a little behind schedule, Peter O'Donnell and Mrs. Ione Flynn Harrington, National Committeewoman from Indiana, announced the formation of the Draft Committee at a press conference at the Mayflower Hotel. The group was out in the open and there was no turning back. Until this point, it was clear that Clif White had played the determinate role, ensuring that the committee would be respectable and authentically Republican. His role had been crucial in reinforcing the reputation of Goldwater as a responsible Republican leader, and this reputation in turn was crucial to the acquisition of support among traditional Republicans outside of the South and California, who made his nomination possible. But from then on the ascendant figure in the Goldwater movement was not White but John Grenier.

Grenier's responsibility was to deliver the South immutably to Goldwater at the convention. He delivered 271 out of 278 available delegates, and he claims that 260 of them were "rock hard," which is to say that they would have stayed with Goldwater even if he had lost the California primary. Although it is true that the South was exceptionally arable territory for Goldwater, many Southern right wingers were not yet Republicans, and many Southern Republicans were disposed to remain neutral to maximize their chances for patronage. Moreover, there was the overall problem that many of the potential Goldwaterites were embarrassingly racist. Grenier's success in providing monolithic support, with minimal representation of conspicuous kooks, remains impressive testimony to his energy and ability. Only the members of Yerger's Mississippi delegation (who unanimously insisted to reporters that the disappearance of the three civil-rights workers in 1964 was a NAACP plot) were markedly more retarded than the average Goldwater delegate from California, for instance. Grenier could not have managed this through polite long-distance inquiries on the telephone. He earned his National Committee office on the front lines.

The non-Goldwaterites who managed to elude the Grenier ax were predominately from Arkansas and Florida. In the other states which were not automatically Goldwater's, the right-wingers had begun, two years before the convention in most cases, the process of invasion and takeover familiar in California but easier and less violent in the South because of the great popu-larity of Goldwater and the lesser strength of the incumbent Republican moderates. The moderates were undermined in 1961 and 1962 by the National Committee's right-wing Operation Dixie, by the crescendo of concern with the race issue, and by the possibility of nominating a Republican opponent of civil rights. At the time of the December plenary meeting of the Draft Com-mittee, Grenier reported resistance to Goldwater only in Georgia, Florida, Virginia, North Carolina, Tennessee, and Arkansas (where Winthrop Rockefeller was running for governor). Both Virginia and North Carolina soon fell without a struggle and the rest succumbed to well-prepared programs of infiltration.

In Georgia, for instance, Goldwaterites led by Fuller Earle ("Bo") Callaway, Jr., a textile millionaire, now a congressman, organized in the counties to take over the party from the bottom up. Their success was almost complete, even in Atlanta (Fulton County), despite the fact that they were fervent segregationists and the incumbent leadership there regularly elects two moderate Republican aldermen with a majority of the Negro vote and now has elected at large a GOP state legislator, Rodney Cook, who may run for mayor. The Atlanta Negroes even gave Nixon a majority in 1960 despite Kennedy's call to Mrs. Martin Luther King, who lives in the city. Grenier's contention that Negroes were excluded from delegations only because they were vendible or ineffectual Republicans is preposterous in Georgia. They have long been the most reliable Republicans in the state. Like the moderate Republican leadership, they were considered unreliable and ineffectual only as supporters of Barry Goldwater, and it was because of this that they were deliberately and ruthlessly driven out.

Such Southern delegations were committed to Goldwater more than to the GOP. If Clif White's decline marked the increasing irrelevance of the politics of blandishment and compromise in the Goldwater campaign, John Grenier's vaulting ascent marked the triumph of the politics of high-handedness and narrow sectionalism.

Just as important to Goldwater's nomination as the successes of Grenier and his associates in the South, however, were the successes of an improbable young Californian who did not receive much public recognition at all from Goldwater—John H. Rousselot, the coordinator of the massive John Birch Society effort that contributed indispensably to Goldwater's only significant primary victory. In fact, it may be argued that Rousselot's contribution was more important than Grenier's since even moderate delegations from the South would have gone to Goldwater after the California victory.

Rousselot's Birchers comprise a formidable political force in California. The Birch Society has fourteen full-time organizers in the state and an estimated ten thousand active members, concentrated mostly in Los Angeles County, the largest center of Birch activity in the country. It was Birchers in Los Angeles who provided the overwhelming organizational effort that gave Goldwater the primary victory despite the fact he lost all but three of the fifty-eight counties. The finances of the California group have never been divulged, but it may be assumed that as well as their statewide income they are given a substantial proportion of the some five million dollars[7] reported by the national office in Belmont, Massachusetts over the four years before the conven-

[7] Forster and Epstein: *Danger.*

tion. Rousselot himself reportedly receives a salary of $30,000 dollars a year, and he is undoubtedly worth every penny.[8]

On first encounter, John Rousselot does not seem the kind of man to lead an underground movement of political extremists. A short, stooped, and boyishly good-looking man with Christian Science views and a pronounced limp caused by polio as a child, he gives a first impression of diffidence and uncertainty. It is not until he begins to speak that his strange intensity begins to work its spell on even the most ideologically hostile listener. Elected to Congress as a moderate in Richard Nixon's old district, he veered rapidly to the right and joined the Birch Society soon after its foundation. But unlike many right-wingers, who are inaccessible and defensive, Rousselot welcomed all comers to his office and was known to debate earnestly for hours with progressive Republican visitors. He always seemed to care deeply about their views and arguments, and unlike most congressmen would intently listen, assenting eagerly or dissenting in reasonable, deferential tones, always giving the impression that he regarded his visitor as both salvable and worth saving. Leaving his office loaded down with anti-Communist pamphlets and bibliographies, speeches and legislative proposals, even the most knowledgeable opponent found himself momentarily entertaining doubts about his whole political philosophy.

Then as the spell weakened, the visitor was struck by the realization that this man; so earnest and engaging and reasonable, held views on the edge of political lunacy. He had defended Robert Welch against William F. Buckley's vehement attack in *National Review* and even intimated that Welch's characterization of Eisenhower as a Communist was not altogether preposterous. He had argued that our defense programs could be maintained by the sale of government enterprise after abolition of the income tax. He had argued that the civil-rights movement, though pursuing noble goals, had been captured by the Communists. One recognized then that the ideas were ridiculous. But one was

[8] Raymond R. Coffey: "Birch Society Turns on the Charm," *Chicago Daily News*, February 2, 1965.

aware, too, how beguiling they had seemed when voiced by this appealing young man. It was easy to imagine the impact he could have on a confused and impressionable youth like Bob Gaston, disillusioned with Eisenhower Republicanism and looking for a more incendiary cause. In 1962 Rousselot was defeated for re-election after the California legislature had reapportioned his district. This defeat, cited as a repudiation of the Birch Society, was actually a boon for the organization, and ultimately for Goldwater, because it released Rousselot for full-time work as the Society's Western states' governor.

The Society could not have found a better man for the job. For the next two years he devoted himself with phenomenal success to proselytization and organization, focusing on California. Although the original goal of complete control of the California Republican party was not fully achieved, in two years the Birchers and their equally extreme allies controlled the two top amateur Republican organizations in the state: the 15,000-member California Republican Assembly formed by Earl Warren as a vehicle for progressive Republicanism, and the 10,000-member State Young Republican Federation. At least six known Birch Society members, sympathizers, and financial contributors even managed to get on Senator Goldwater's special twenty-three man advisory council, designed specifically to dispel the notion that his campaign was heavily infiltrated by extremists. Among the six were Joseph Shell, who had often praised the Society and was its candidate against Nixon in 1962 primary, and Walter Knott, a heavy contributor to various Birch activities and an adviser to the Christian Anti-Communist Crusade. In the spring of 1964 as the primary approached, the Society, under Rousselot, despite its relatively small membership, had clearly emerged as the single most important influence in California Republican politics. Militance, money, and Rousselot all contributed to their ascendancy, but as in the Young Republicans, the right-wingers also distinguished themselves from their moderate opponents by a tactical ruthlessness rarely seen in American politics.

One of key Birch operations in their drive to power was capture of the California Republican Assembly. Following the pattern of their seizure of the Young Republicans months before and including many of the same people, the rightists had spent the year before invading, disrupting, infiltrating, and commandeering local assemblies and then fragmenting them into smaller units, thus multiplying their votes. The story was the same all over the state. Between fifty and one hundred strangers would appear at a perfunctory business meeting of a local assembly, plunk down their money, and acquire membership. Often they were members also of other local assemblies. The capture of the assemblies in Berkeley, West Berkeley, and Oakland, for instance, turned out to have been a well-coordinated operation organized by Birch Society personnel and conducted by many of the same persons. At the assembly elections in each locality, the invaders would disrupt the meeting until much of the membership left, then vote in a bloc exclusively for their own candidates, and in effect establish a new local assembly. Their capture of the State Assembly was consummated at a riotous convention in Fresno in March, 1964.

Combined with the earlier seizure of the Young Republicans, the capture of the assembly gave the Birch Society and its allies control over most of the party's organizational manpower as the June confrontation drew near. As it turned out, it was organizational manpower that won for Goldwater. Goldwater's official representative in California, Richard Kleindienst put it this way: "Those little old ladies in tennis shoes"—as Governor Pat Brown had once characterized the Birchers—"turned out to be the best political organization you ever saw."[9]

Thus Goldwater arrived at the convention with an insuperable lead for the nomination and with a disparate and unmanageable following across the country, led by men with their own views and purposes which Goldwater himself had little influenced or directed. There were the mutually contemptuous Southern

[9] David Broder, Washington *Star*, July 16, 1964.

politicians Grenier of Alabama and Yerger of Mississippi; the Eisenhower financiers Humphrey and Summerfield; the Senate parochials Curtis and Tower; the manqué potentates Knowland and Jenner; the political debutantes Gaston, Lukens, and Baumann; the *National Review* New Yorkers Rusher, Bozell, and their associate and ideological protégé, Clif White; and the various extremists, Rousselot, Milliken, Welch, Manion, Loeb, and the Courtneys—all working, with widely disparate effectiveness, for a candidate whom few of them knew, but all of them, according to their varying fancies, wishfully imagined was theirs at heart. The fact that the extremists played a decisive role at every crucial juncture in his national ascendancy—in the publication of his book *Conscience of a Conservative*, in his demonstration and speech at the 1960 convention, in his emergence as the champion of youth, in the acquisition of his most stalwart delegate strength, and finally, and most important, in his triumph in California—does not mean that Goldwater himself was deeply committed to extremist views and purposes, though he was at least acquiescent toward them—but that the extremists were strategically situated to move into the vacuum created by Goldwater's "pooping around," refusing to accept the responsibilities of political power.

The organizational role of Barry Goldwater himself in the capture of the Republican party could not have been very much smaller if, like Eisenhower in 1952, he had spent most of the preceding four years in Europe. His own major contributions reduce to the book and his Senatorial Campaign Committee speeches. He was a catalyst or stimulus, and occasionally—as when he discouraged it—even an opponent of the Goldwater movement, never before the convention its active and commanding political leader. As John Grenier said after the campaign: "Goldwater never understood or enjoyed the exercise of political power. He liked to think of himself as the conscience of the party." In this role he seemed unconscious of the fact that it was his own undirected right-wing following, often hateful and authoritarian, not the Republican party, which most sorely needed a conscience. He allowed his movement, even its most ruthless and racist elements, to proceed in their unconscionable way without his guidance and often with his active encouragement. Goldwater invited them, come as you are, to the Republican party, and he did not seem much embarrassed even when some of them showed up in sheets.

◇◇

CHAPTER 14

The Loyalty Test

MANY PARTY officials grant that the progressives were right about Goldwater in 1964, but now argue that the party should move toward its vacuum center, to a compromise candidate, one acceptable to Goldwater, in 1968. They are willing to be understanding both toward the right wing (after all, most of the party was somewhat intrigued with the idea of nominating a "true conservative" for once) and toward the progressives and moderates who refused to campaign for the party's nominee (after all, you have to understand their constituencies). But it is widely agreed that neither element can be given power in 1968. Most Republicans are inclined to accept the argument adduced so frequently by Arthur Krock during and after the campaign, and adopted so fervently by Richard Nixon—that Goldwater's nomination was a legitimate expression of majority sentiment at the convention and that, therefore, Republicans who refused to support him were betraying their own party and the two-party system.[1]

[1] The most prominent defectors were Governors Romney, Rockefeller, and Hatfield; Senators Keating, Javits, Case, Scott, and Kuchel; and Con-

Goldwater's nomination, however, was not an ordinary event in American politics, achieved by traditionally legitimate methods. Individual responses to it cannot be judged by the ordinary criteria of partisan loyalty. Goldwater's reliance on the tactics of infiltration and conspiracy in California and the South; his dependence on supporters who violently opposed many of the party's most eminent incumbents; his support by leading segregationist Democrats in several states, despite his party's deep commitment to civil rights; his abandonment by many Republican incumbents, Republican newspapers, and normally Republican voters; and his overwhelming defeat, running behind local Republicans almost everywhere, together signified a breakdown of the democratic mechanisms of the convention system. With the exception of the nominations of William Jennings Bryan by the Democrats, it has been the genius of the American two-party politics over the last century to produce invariably two consensual national candidates, relegating extremists to fringe or sectional influence. In 1964, however, the extremists infiltrated one of the major parties, captured it, and attempted a revolution within it and in the two-party system. This is a most extraordinary and portentous event in a country whose democratic processes are depended upon to provide leadership for the entire free world. It is thus important to understand how it happened, not only to vindicate fully those Republicans who resisted but also to show how such dangerous breakdowns can be prevented in the future.

The most important difference between 1964 and other years

---

gressman (now Mayor) Lindsay. But in fact a great majority of the lesser Republicans who ran successfully for office outside the Deep South in 1964 came finally also to disavow Goldwater or at least to ignore his existence. Since the Presidential-quality candidates who *were* "loyal"—notably Charles Percy of Illinois and Robert Taft, Jr., of Ohio—were defeated, the only potential Presidential candidate for 1968 who matches the Nixon-Krock standard is Nixon. And Nixon's stand in 1964 was not inconvenienced by a candidacy of his own. It might be noted, too, that though the progressive Republicans refrained from endorsing Goldwater, they did not explicitly oppose him or praise Johnson. Goldwater, on the other hand, supported Buckley in his campaign against Lindsay in 1965.

was that the San Francisco convention majority was assembled partly by deception and did not represent majority sentiment in the party—whether considered as rank-and-file voters or incumbent officeholders. In fact, the majority which nominated Goldwater was dominated by delegates with no allegiance at all to any national Republican party that existed at the time, and with no real commitment to any state Republican party that actually held important office or governed anything but itself. Most of the hard-core Goldwater supporters—which is to say, most of his pre-convention support—were committed only to a Republican party they envisaged in the future, purged of progressives and transformed by Goldwater into a radical-right organization, resisting integration, and controlled by themselves. The new party would be composed of incumbent right-wingers, right-wingers newly elected or newly converted from the Democrats, and the lemming neutrals in the party willing to follow the leadership, whatever it is, into hell or high water. In moving toward this new party, defeat in the national election could be considered a manageable misfortune; defeat in state and local elections in areas controlled by traditional Republicans was considered triumphantly desirable.

Goldwater did not try to disguise his strategy except by making claims, ritualistic and ridiculous, that it would help the party everywhere. Even as announced, the strategy was utterly oblivious to the needs of a great national party seeking election in the United States in 1964—the time and place that Barry Goldwater, to his great inconvenience as a right-winger, found himself as a Presidential nominee. The appropriate strategy for 1964 had been repeatedly indicated after Republican failures in 1958, 1960, and 1962 by the research division of the Republican National Committee. According to the National Committee's own figures, the party clearly needed to improve its appeal in the metropolitan areas of the North and West, critical to carrying eleven of the nation's largest states which, together with Lyndon Johnson's Texas, comprise 259 of the 270 electoral votes necessary to elect a President. Although it is often difficult to separate strategy from stupidity in the Goldwater approach, it can be safely averred that he did not show any solicitude for the interests of the existing Republican party, as calculated in the Committee's arithmetic. No matter what one counts, electoral votes, popular votes, or marginal districts, one concludes that Goldwater's campaign, like Mr. McNamara's Edsel, was streamlined to lose.

One cannot assume, however, that Dean Burch, John Grenier, Clif White, and the other Goldwater master hearts cannot count. They counted very well, but they were counting delegates not votes. The Goldwater strategy, conceived to exploit a flawed democratic process in order to win a nomination, and the Goldwater strategists, adept at capturing a party by conspiracy, infiltration, and subterfuge, were together confounded by a real democratic process, where all the people can vote and the majority wins.

The delegate counting began in the South, where the party was weakest and the counting was best. Right-wing Southerners made the most militant and dependable Goldwater delegates, for they festered with resentment toward the federal government and lacked any connections or loyalty at all to the traditional Republican party. Most of them, moreover, were unscathed by any contact with practical political reality such as they might have risked if they had held office, served a constituency, met a political payroll, or conducted a campaign. They were more impervious to the usual logic of political discourse—of consensus and compromise, of national issues and voter distribution—than any other group to reach a national party convention in recent years except the Freedom Democrats of Mississippi.[2] No matter what effect his nomination would have on the national party, the Dixiecans were all out for Goldwater, and what they knew in their hearts could not be shaken by so insignificant a force as their minds.

[2] The Freedom Democratic Party came to the Democratic convention in 1964 and attempted unsuccessfully to unseat the regular Mississippi delegation on the grounds that it was elected illegally, i.e., through exclusion of Negroes from the voting rolls.

The leaders of these Confederate Republicans, with the exception of Peter O'Donnell of Texas, were from the most far right, most intensely segregationist, and most unsuccessful of Southern Republican parties, those in Mississippi and Alabama, whose state chairmen, Wirt Yerger and John Grenier, respectively, had never conducted a Republican campaign in their lives before 1962. The attitude of the Southerners was symbolized by Goldwater's exultant embrace of Strom Thurmond, a racist and militarist and champion of the Southern filibusterers, who soon after swearing allegiance to what he called "the Goldwater Republican party," was claiming it for his own and asking all "liberals" to leave. The Confederates all agreed that if the progressives would not switch they should be defeated.

Along with his some 270 hard-core supporters in the South, Goldwater had about a hundred delegates in the North and West who were similarly committed, not to the existing Republican party, but to a rightist Republican party which they would create with Goldwater's help. These delegates, too, were immutably his, and were unshaken by the argument that Goldwater would disastrously lose their states and jeopardize incumbent Republicans in them. For example, Massachusetts contributed five Goldwater delegates, including Lloyd Waring, former campaign manager for Robert Welch, despite the fact that virtually every incumbent in the state had to divorce himself from the Goldwater campaign to avoid defeat in 1964. New Jersey contributed nine delegates even though Goldwater was certain to be an albatross for New Jersey Republicans. Michigan gave ten hard-core Goldwaterites, although Republican Governor Romney would have to repudiate the national ticket to avoid defeat. Illinois contributed forty delegates in spite of the similar problem of its Republican gubernatorial candidate, Charles Percy, who had demolished the Goldwater candidate in the primary, and had run 200,000 votes ahead of the senator's total in the Presidential primary. Maryland produced four immutable Goldwaterites despite the fact that the three leading Republicans in the state, Senator Beall, Congressman Mathias, and Mayor Theodore McKeldin are all progressives; despite the fact that both Mathias's and Beall's seats were jeopardized by the Arizonan's nomination (Beall lost); and despite the fact that Mathias swamped well-financed Goldwaterite Brent Bozell in the primaries.

These Northern dissidents gave Goldwater a further increment of support as adamant as the Southerners. Their presence on delegations from states whose Republican parties were preponderantly progressive should be contrasted with the complete absence of progressives on most Goldwater state delegations. These right-wing Northerners, many of them from states committed to progressives on the first ballot, gave Goldwater a great advantage at the convention. For instance, because of the presence of seven Goldwaterites on the Oregon delegation Rockefeller, who had won the Oregon primary, was prevented from releasing the delegation to Scranton. In fact, so many of the Northeastern and Western delegations were infiltrated by rightists, committed to Goldwater and indifferent or hostile to the interests of the Republican party in their states, that even if Rockefeller had won in California, Goldwater might well have been able to win the nomination by fragmenting putatively moderate delegations.

To these 370 unalterable delegates from the North and South, Goldwater added over 100 more in primaries in Indiana and California. Most important, both psychologically and numerically, were the 87 delegates from California. Goldwater won through a great organizational effort energized by extreme-rightist groups— although he was the first choice, according to the Harris poll, of only 28 percent of the state's registered Republicans, even after the primary, and although he was opposed by almost the entire established Republican party in California, led by the National Committeeman and Senator Kuchel, the state's top vote-getter.

Goldwater's leading supporters included William Knowland, who had lost a race for governor by over a million votes six years before, and Joseph Shell, who had received just a third of the vote in losing to Nixon in a gubernatorial primary in 1962. Goldwater's victory only revealed Rockefeller's personal weakness, not his own strength. The 87 delegates he won were virulent opponents of almost the entire California Republican hierarchy. They had been losing primaries and elections for years, and seemed suspicious of any Republicans who could win them, as if such an affinity with the voters were presumptive evidence of disloyalty to the party—if not of some Faustian pact.

So here among the Confederates, the Northern dissidents, and the California extremists were the "four hundred and twenty-five hard-core" who, Goldwater declared, assuming a victory in the California primary, "will stay right to the end and march out the back of the convention if they don't get what they want. This is how hard these people are."[3] Over half of these delegates came from states which elected only 7 percent of the Republican congressmen, 9 percent of the senators, and which elect no Republican governors and control no state legislatures at all. Most of the other 150 were deeply antagonistic to the leading Republican incumbents in their states. One hundred of the delegates represented Southern state parties which had elected virtually no Republicans to anything—and which had a much closer affinity with the Democratic parties in their states than with Republican parties outside them. These hard-core Goldwater delegates were divided among the Northerners using the Arizonan's campaign as a vehicle for their own advancement in existing state Republican parties controlled by others, or Confederate Republicans exploiting Goldwater to make the Southern Republican party a bastion against integration. Thus, they had no loyalty at all to the existing Republican party and its traditions.

However, 450 delegates, no matter how militant, cannot win a convention, and Goldwater at the end had some 400 more. These, for the most part, were ordinary, loyal Republicans, sensible and pragmatic in approach, disposed to support the Lincolnian traditions of the party, uninterested in grand schemes of party realignment, unintoxicated by the fevered conspiratorial

[3] American Broadcasting Company Television News Reports, 10:30 P.M., May 14, 1964; quote taken from transcript by Graham Molitor. Contrast the Goldwater address, given at Madison Square Garden, New York City, on May 12, two days before: "I am sick to death of this rule or ruin talk that demands loyalty to a faction above loyalty to the party."

visions of Phyllis Schlafly and John Stormer,[4] solicitous for the interests of incumbent Republicans in their states—and gullible. Primarily, as far as Goldwater was concerned, they were gullible, for they were to be won by deception and sophistry.

In charge of Goldwater's overtures to the traditional Republicans were former Nixon associates like Clif White, former Eisenhower officials like George Humphrey and Arthur Summerfield, and senatorial colleagues in secure seats like Norris Cotton of New Hampshire and Carl Curtis of Nebraska. Most of these respectable, if still ultraconservative Republicans were shunted aside after the convention or relegated to subordinate positions; but in the nomination campaign they were indispensable, and continually on display. This was one of the more obvious indications that the objective of the movement was primarily to secure party control for the right wing: unlike any other recent national candidate, Goldwater embraced a wider range of supporters and selected high-level advisers from a broader circle in the party before he was nominated than after. During his nomination campaign Goldwater continually appealed to all Republicans, yet his first utterance as candidate contained a whoop for extremism ("in the defense of liberty," of course) and a defiant declaration that he did not ask or expect the support of those Republicans who disagreed with him.

By that time, however, his traditionalist supporters had done their job well, and most were thought to be no longer needed.[5] Goldwater had been championed across the country as a conventional conservative Republican, like Taft or even Eisenhower; he was said to be opposed by the same conspiratorial group of Eastern liberals who had deprived Taft of the nomination in 1952. This appeal to the thwarted sentiments of more than a decade ago was reinforced by a Goldwater posture as the representative of the West against the alleged long dominance of the East in party

[4] John Stormer, former president of the Missouri Young Republicans, is author of *None Dare Call It Treason*, a foreign-policy tract which urges readers to join the John Birch Society.

[5] Some early supporters, such as Senator Norris Cotton, were already disillusioned by the time of the convention.

affairs. This new image was as serviceable as it was false, and it successfully mollified many Republicans who would have stubbornly resisted Goldwater as the intraparty revolutionary he actually was. These men came to believe that Goldwater was a loyal, dedicated Republican, with a few kooks around him but essentially reasonable and sound, and as many liberal columnists predicted, sure to moderate his positions as he moved closer to national power.

Softened by misrepresentation, the traditional Republicans who supported Goldwater were captured by sophistry. Many of them were persuaded not only that the paramount objective of the Goldwater movement was party victory, not party purge and control, but also that Goldwater had the best chance of the prospective nominees to win.

There were three main schools of thought maintaining Goldwater as a winner: the "Dixie-" whistlers, who represented a kind of strategic division for the Dixiecans; the backlashers, who played a similar role for the Northern dissidents; and the necromancers, or gravedigger Conservatives, who served the traditional conservatives around the country. Their theories were developed alone, but they often appeared in various combinations.

The "Dixie"-whistlers argued that Goldwater, as a "states' rightist," would sweep the South, and with the South won everything else would fall into place. Almost all the "new" Republicans in the South took this point of view, along with some members of the Republican National Committee under Bill Miller. With Confederate flags and "Dixie" more in evidence at Goldwater rallies than the American flag or the national anthem, the "Dixie"-whistlers gave the disturbing impression that as far as they were concerned the South was the nation, and that if Barry lost it wouldn't really matter; they would secede and make him President of a new and Republican Confederacy.

The blacklashers were more cynical and realistic in their covert racism. They made a national extrapolation from their own hearts, and argued that a preponderance of the voters were white, that a preponderance of white people were bigots, and that if

Goldwater could divide the electorate along racial lines, he would win overwhelmingly. The "law and order" and "violence in the streets" issues were based on this theory. Many Republicans who prided themselves on their "realism" took this position in private during the early part of the campaign.

The necromancers, or gravediggers, were more a chiliastic religious sect than a school of political thought. They believed in a vast underground majority of conservative voters who had been avoiding elections since the days of McKinley, preserving their ideological chastity for a "true" conservative. Goldwater, according to this theory, was a kind of Second Conservative Coming who could resurrect the conservative majority and bring it to the polls. In accordance with the religious nature of their faith, the necromancers—led by Phyllis Schlafly—were undaunted by Goldwater's "so-called" defeat, attributing it to too much liberal echo in the choice. They will still be waiting for a conservative who is really true in 1968 and beyond. Their theory, moreover, was perhaps the most useful of the three, since unlike those of the backlashers and the "Dixie"-whistlers, it could be discussed in public. It was the necromancers, for instance, who provided not only the slogan "a choice, not an echo," but also endless newspaper speculations on the "silent" vote and the unreliability of the polls. The most serious flaw in the theory, of course, is that most of the conservatives who voted for McKinley are now dead and will still be dead, barring the unforeseen, in 1968. Moreover, the concern for the underground conservative voters distracted the party's attention from the warm-bodied electorate and its concerns.

Thus Goldwater acquired the needed conventional Republican delegates to put him over the top: (1) through the cultivated deception that he was a principled conservative, loyal to the Republican tradition of Taft and Eisenhower; and (2) through the argument speciously corroborated in the California primary, that he could win by circumventing the Democrats to commune with some private right-wing majority of backlashers or nonvoting conservatives unknown to the pollsters or practicing politicians. The fact, however, was that Goldwater represented not at all the traditional strain of Republican conservatism, but a reactionary fabrication designed to purge and remake the Republican party and bring about a realignment in the American two-party system.

Moreover he was not even interested in winning in 1964 for the traditional Republican party. Though he vaguely hoped to win the Presidency himself through some miracle of demagoguery, he was not willing to adjust his campaign for moderate Republicans in order to preserve incumbent party strength in Northern and Western states, and facilitate moderate campaigns against the nineteen Democratic incumbent senators up for re-election. Goldwater was far more ardent in his appeals for the conversion of Dixiecrat extremists like Strom Thurmond than for the return of moderate Republicans abandoning the national ticket. In reference to businessmen defectors to Johnson Dean Burch told the *Atlanta Journal* on August 10: "As far as I am concerned, he can have them ... they're not leaving the party. They're going home." Goldwater's campaign, in fact, seemed designed to defeat, weaken or isolate moderate Republicans and thus debilitate potential opposition for the future.

The course of the 1964 campaign is well symbolized by its contrasting role in the careers of White and Grenier, one an alienated New Yorker, the other a militantly sectional Alabaman, both crucial to Goldwater's nomination but representative of different elements in his support.

White, though a strong conservative by temperament and deeply committed to Goldwater, was a Republican politician by trade and, unlike many of Goldwater's top advisers, he rarely forgot that in American political parties, political realities take precedence over ideological fixations. One of the few top Goldwater leaders never associated with any extremist groups, he quickly saw the danger that association with the far right posed to the Goldwater candidacy. It was he who asked John Rousselot to stop attending Draft meetings because of his Birch Society ties.[6]

6 Richard Dudman, St. Louis *Post-Dispatch*, December 5, 1964.

White also was quick to see the practical political impotence of Young Americans for Freedom, and remarked ironically during the night of the New Hampshire primary: "I guess the YAF vote hasn't come in yet."[7] White's orientation, unlike that of most leading Goldwaterites, was primarily to the Republican party and to traditional political values and approaches.

Yet largely because of this relatively conventional orientation, which constituted his chief value to the Draft movement and to Goldwater (who was to be drafted, after all, by the GOP), White was regarded with suspicion by most of Goldwater's inner circle. After the public formation of the Draft Committee, his star began a precipitous decline. In November, 1963, according to a story in the Detroit *Free Press*, Goldwater expressed his dissatisfaction with the Draft operation and toyed with the idea of giving Denison Kitchel control of it. The senator was reported as saying that he had not established a satisfactory liaison with White and the Draft people. After Goldwater won the nomination he neglected to give special credit to White, and then he upset the widespread expectation of a White appointment as chairman of the National Committee by naming his Arizona crony, Dean Burch.

At the end White must have felt the same feelings of frustration and unfulfillment that he experienced after the Nixon-Lodge campaign. It was as if, after the bitter determination in 1960 that next time it would be different; after the precarious clandestine months of organization; after the public emergence into a world of doubters; after the long dual courtship of the delegates and the leading doubter himself, who was, it seemed, the candidate; after the shocking, providential fall of Rockefeller and the surge to a commanding lead, with thrilling intimations of victory; after the crack of disaster in Dallas; after the long, cumulative return; after the despair of New Hampshire and the enigma of Illinois; after the state-by-state garnering of delegates; after the portent of Oregon and the miracle of California; it was as if after all this— what seemed a cresting tide of vindication—with Goldwater delivered, drafted as planned, and White there for the triumphal

[7] William K. Wyant, Jr., St. Louis *Post-Dispatch*, December 7, 1964.

union, deferred by the candidate until the moment of victory, but surely his, White's moment now; after all this . . . only betrayal— as at the convention the candidate moved away and adopted what seemed a different, defiant, factious politics, and the union of White's ideal and his candidate never came.

White worked hard during the campaign, suspended anxiously in the gap between ideal and candidate. He watched as Goldwater made continuous errors of political judgment; and then at the end he had seen even the candidate's honesty and principles slip away. "Conservatism," White said afterwards, speaking of a betrayal he never understood, "was never an issue in this campaign." But White's betrayal was that of the Republican party, and of traditional American politics, by a candidate, driven by a vision of realignment and purge, who never understood conservatism, or American politics, or the Republican party. And perhaps for White there was not only the awareness of betrayal but also an intimation that he himself was an agent—often a conscious one—in that betrayal, of his ideal, and of himself.

White's role in the campaign symbolized the moral problem of Goldwaterism. Here the responsible Republican, free of extremist associations, took control of National Citizens for Goldwater-Miller, designed as the vehicle for the unaffiliated extremists and widely known within and outside the Goldwater movement as the "backlash committee." Here the proponent of principled conservatism, who felt Goldwater's campaign was betraying his principles, prepared a film, *Choice*, which became the prime example of that betrayal, and was repudiated by Goldwater as "nothing but a racist film."

The Citizens deserved their repudiation for the film, and White disqualified himself, one would have supposed, from attacking anyone for abandoning ideals or principles. The Citizens involvement with the extremists, moreover, was so indiscriminating as to include Allen Zoll, associated with a number of notorious anti-Semites and a leader in American Patriots, Inc., cited by the Attorney General as a "fascist front." Zoll was on the Citizens payroll for a month and a half and, according to Richard Dudman in the St. Louis *Post-Dispatch,* served as a liaison with far-right Texas billionaire H. L. Hunt. After the Jenkins exposure, Zoll was assigned to the Citizens' attempt to pin morals charges on another White House official.

Thus White's commitment to "conservatism" and to Goldwater in the end led him from a respected position as a promising party leader to a role outside the party, trafficking with extremism (although White denies knowledge of Zoll) and resorting to desperately conceived demagoguery. After the election White certified his departure from significant Republican politics by releasing the Citizens lists to the new "Conservative Union," headed by former Congressman Donald Bruce of Indiana and designed to appeal again to those unaffiliated "conservatives" whom Goldwater had worked so long and so fruitlessly to bring into the party. And in October, 1965, White along with Bill Rusher and some of the other original Draft-Goldwater Committee members held a meeting in Chicago to discuss the possibilities for another conservative candidacy in 1968. White's ideological tiger in the end devoured both his Republicanism and his sense of political reality.

The rise and fall of Clif White was as mysterious to the press as it was to him. However, the mystery is not difficult to penetrate if one remembers that the Goldwater movement, regardless of its appeal to many naïve Republicans, was largely sustained by the extreme right. White's role in expurgating its image for traditional Republicans was important. But most of the traditional Republicans did not commit themselves to Goldwater until he had taken a commanding lead in delegate strength and appeared a likely winner. His delegate lead was the sine qua non, and it was acquired primarily through the operations of John Grenier and Peter O'Donnell in the South and the John Birch Society in California—not through White's long-distance phone calls from the Draft headquarters in Washington.

Though White had remained executive director after the committee's public unveiling, and though for some time he felt he was running the show, his main contributions were already over. The nomination battle moved to the Southern and California fronts, where others were in command, and where most of the time White did not even know what was going on. It was typical that at the convention White should be credited with the crucial role (and indeed he did play a leading technical role in charge of the master switchboard at Goldwater's control center) when, according to Robert Novak (*The Agony of the GOP: 1964*), he had no idea who would be named Vice-Presidential nominee, National Chairman, or what Goldwater would say in his acceptance speech written a week earlier.

John Grenier, who with O'Donnell had early supported Burch over White for National Chairman and whose ascendancy paralleled White's decline, knew long before that White would not be selected. Although he was not much noticed by the press until he was named executive director of the National Committee, Grenier had become the most important man in the official Draft effort soon after it was publicly announced. Only John Rousselot, Western director of the Birch Society, excluded from the Draft by White but crucial to the victory in California, was of comparable importance to Goldwater's nomination.

"A typical Marine," says one of Grenier's closest Republican associates. A graduate of Tulane in New Orleans and New York University Law School, with three years in the Marine air wing ending as a captain, Grenier is an able and resourceful politician with a somewhat cavalier manner. But politically he is a sectional figure. His years in the North at law school and with a Wall Street firm have conditioned his attitudes to the extent that they are not as crude and parochial as those of his Alabama "Big Mule" and senatorial prospect, Representative James Martin. But his views of political priorities are straight from the South. He has never developed a national perspective, or even, it may be charged, a broad Southern perspective. To the end of the campaign, he was completely indifferent to the needs of the party in the North. He was representing the interests of the Republican party in Alabama, and its paramount interest was the nomination, come what may, of Barry Goldwater, known throughout the South as an opponent of civil rights, and the transformation of the national party in the Goldwater mold.

In Grenier's view, expressed without irony several months after the election, the crucial question of the nomination campaign had been: "What are you going to pay for the South?" "Some of the liberals," he said, "were not willing to pay anything at all." He cited George Romney particularly as a politician who had let his own "ambitions" prevent him from supporting the necessary sacrifices.

This reproach from the young state chairman of Alabama to the Republican governor of Michigan is deeply revealing. In the attitudes it implies lie the causes of the party's debacle in 1964. For the ambitions of the governor of Michigan and most of the party's incumbent officeholders in the North and West were clearly in conflict with the ambitions of Mr. Grenier and a group of rapidly growing but still, in national terms, insignificant Republican parties in the Deep South. Moreover, the hopes of many of these Republican incumbents, including Romney, had been reduced by the Goldwater insurgence to mere survival. Yet the state chairman of Alabama, who until 1962 had still not conducted a successful Republican campaign for anything but was then reaching for a leading role in the control of the entire party, was not embarrassed to pass off as an unseemly "ambition" the concern of the governor of Michigan to keep his job.

The remarkable aspect of Goldwater's 1964 approach both before and after he captured the party was the fact that the interests of the state chairman of Alabama always took precedence over the interests of the governor of Michigan. It is not unusual for a local politician like Grenier to identify his own interests with the interests of the party and the country; but it is unusual for a national candidate to agree with him. Grenier had made a major regional contribution to the nomination of Barry Goldwater; Goldwater repaid him by devoting much of his national campaign to the regional political interests of Grenier.

Goldwater's conduct as nominee was an abuse and exploitation of the American two-party system, which is based on consensus, inclusiveness, and consistency. Acquisition of the nomination of a major party confers the prestige and authority of the party on the candidate and his views and gives him large numbers of votes won through the performance of the party in the past; in turn, the candidate is expected to maintain faith with the traditions of the party and to serve the interests of its incumbent officials. Goldwater and his supporters, however, not only failed to maintain faith with the traditions of the party, but they directly and sometimes deliberately undermined the campaigns of many of its incumbents in 1964. And because most voters acquire their image of the two parties in Presidential campaigns, his performance made a successful moderate Republican appeal much more difficult in the future. Goldwater thus sacrificed the immediate and long-range interests of the party to enhance the power of a faction and to lend prestige and publicity to his extreme views.

Goldwater not only exploited the two-party system and abused the confidence of his party, he also attempted to exploit and exacerbate already dangerous racial tensions for his own political advantage. Although there is enough fear and misunderstanding between the races already to endanger the future of many American cities, apparently there was not enough to suit the strategy of white backlash. Goldwater's attempt to exacerbate these tensions by associating violence and crime in the streets with civil-rights demonstrations and even with the Civil Rights Act itself was an unscrupulous and deeply reprehensible act of demagoguery. It was not as if Goldwater had some remotely promising program for urban regeneration. He had nothing but a freely associated montage of images designed to evoke racial antipathies.

In the end, Goldwater was reduced to wrapping himself in the American flag and hoping for national disasters. Race conflict in the United States, American rout in Southeast Asia, death or incapacitation of the American President—this is the nightmarish stuff that right-wing dreams were made of. Stripped by voter antipathy of most of the rightist proposals that he used to arouse his followers, he was left with no programs of substantive issues at all, nothing that he or anyone else could "put his finger on." Just demagoguery focused on arousing racial fears. This alone was enough to relieve conscientious Republicans, conservative or moderate, of any obligation remaining after the convention to support their party's nominee.

Part Four

IMPERATIVES
FOR REFORM

◈◈

CHAPTER 15

Organization for Change

N O MODERN precedent exists for the revival of a party so badly defeated, so intensely discredited, and so essentially split as the Republican party is today. The Democrats after 1952 and 1956 did revive rather quickly, but they were neither so confused nor so abject as the GOP is now. To turn to overseas comparisons, the British Conservatives recovered from defeats in Parliament in 1945 and in subsequent local elections that were as severe as suffered in recent years by the Republicans here. But the Conservatives had lost with Winston Churchill, a leader well worth fighting for again, and the Tories did so in a spirit of reform that is more than just geographically foreign to the current spirit of the GOP.

To revive itself in the sixties, the Republican party must borrow from the lessons and ideas of other parties, wherever they are applicable; learn from its own lesson of failure; experiment with new ideas and proposals; and be as united as possible without imperiling its new vitality. Such a program of reform should be initiated by the national organization, centralized in it for a quick impact, and aimed at the three most neglected and decisive targets: the metropolitan voter, youth, and the intellectual.

The first two of these targets—youth and the metropolitan voter—stand for what is new and growing in America. If the Republicans are really "to go hunting where the ducks are," as Senator Goldwater advised a few years ago, they will travel to the cities and suburbs—the centers of the Negro, the nationality voter, and the laborer, all of whom need to be shown that the Republican party does have answers for their problems. The party will visit anew the independent suburbanite, who reads his newspaper and interprets his interests broadly. It also will travel to colleges and new homes, and involve itself with the ideals and futures of young people and seek to show them a party both lively and responsible. The intellectuals (and the communicators) will be approached not with contempt or fear but with respect and a request for cooperation, for they will help the party reach the others.

Such a program means changes in party structure and outlook. It does not mean neglecting other concerns. The rural communities are not to be forgotten, for their stake in the nation should not be separated from the more dynamic political development of the metropolitan areas. Indeed, a change from regarding rural and small-town America as an ideal to be re-created will help the party address itself to the more appropriate tasks of re-integrating the small communities into the progress of the larger so that their distinctive character might be protected by change rather than obliterated by it. A falsely conservative party that preached hold-the-line and social resentment lost support in the rural and small-town countryside; a party that promises to shape change to old values—a truly conservative party, that is—might succeed.

An emphasis on the metropolitan man, youth, and the intellectual also does not necessarily mean a de-emphasis of Republican appeal to the South. It does mean a sharply different emphasis, however. From 1960 to 1964 a large part of the GOP in the South hitched its wagon to the falling star of segregation. It tried, with some success, to relieve the Democrats of their racists just as they were no longer needed. The Negroes were registering faster than the white bigots could convert to Thurmond's "Goldwater Republican party," and the Republican nominee of 1964, running on a plank that proclaimed "states' rights," the traditional wink to the racists, managed to do no better in the South than the 1960 candidate who gave civil rights tangible, if lukewarm support. Locally, the party that rode Goldwater's coattails gained ten seats in thirteen Southern and border-state legislatures, but lost forty-one, for a net loss of thirty-one. The reservoir of future Negro votes is bursting its walls. The old swamp of racist votes is drying up.

Of course the political strategy of "holler 'Nigger'" will always appeal to the simple-minded, and its inefficacy will require repeated demonstration at the polls before it is finally given up everywhere. The new Republican leadership nationally and the responsible leadership in the South must now prepare itself to confront a new attempt of the rebel rousers to tap their mythical spring of insurrectionist votes. According to reliable evidence, this effort might well take the form of a drive to transfer tax collections and law enforcement from local and county governments to the state. With increased Negro registrations threatening to establish a black majority in some localities, whites (they hope) may become exceedingly nervous about the possible election of Negro mayors and sheriffs. Nowhere is there a statewide Negro majority, the Republican rebel rousers will point out: Help us therefore to move the power of government to safety in the state capitols. Of course, it is on the state level, free from competition with Dixiecrat courthouse cliques, that the GOP has been most successful politically. The new crusade would damage the local-based hold of the Democratic party and give the post-Goldwater Southern Republicans an issue on which to outbid the Democrats for the rednecks.

This feint, following as it does the last four years' systematic ouster of all Negroes from Republican organizations in most Southern states, will seek to delude the Southern GOP into opting further for segregation as a way to power. What they will not know until it is shown them conclusively is that the white resistance to civil rights comes after the change itself, which could not have occurred without widespread adjustments of attitude. It was not, and is not, a movement of growing numbers but the alarmed intensification in feeling of the dwindling number who still care. That the racists would embrace a minority party is evidence of their desperation; they are going down, and they will drag down with them the inopportune opportunists of the "Goldwater Republican party."

The reformer on the national level must oppose this strategy which would jeopardize the future of both the party in the South and the national party. The national party should be outspokenly pro-civil rights and fiercely inhospitable to segregationists, including seated officeholders and their chief spokesman, Senator Strom Thurmond of South Carolina, former Dixiecrat Presidential candidate, notorious heir to the mantle of Theodore Bilbo and Pitchfork Ben Tillman, consort of the radical right. For every vote the departure of spurious Republicans like Thurmond will cost the young Southern GOP, doors to a half dozen new votes will be opened.

But the reform Republican appeal to the South must go beyond a disavowal of the fading cause of racism. Realistically speaking, it cannot simply echo the party's proper appeal in the urban North. It can, however, renew the development it began as early as 1948 and maintained as late as 1960: that of an economically conservative, socially and racially inclusive, modern party, representing the New South and speaking for its needs for more honest and efficient government at local and state levels, for soundly financed state services, for improved schools, medical and correctional institutions, and for the creation of new jobs through recruitment of new industry. Such a party offers the possibility of durable gains in the South. It is not a party that will inspire jubilant emulation from Northerners, but neither will it continue to inspire their disgust. Coupled with the progress of a progressive national GOP, it is a formula that suits the party in most of the South and it will work. Southerners in the GOP who truly comprehend the long-run interests of their region and their party will not hesitate to join the cause of Republican reform.

The main thrust of reform, appealing to the metropolitan man, youth, and the intellectual, requires a conscious overhaul of party machinery as well as party policy on issues.

There is a near-universal agreement in the Republican party that it is weak organizationally and that an improvement in organization will immensely help prospects for future victories. Although this line has been fashionable for decades, GOP politicians, including most of the progressives, continue to confide it like a revolutionary insight. Actually, few party politicians understand organization except in its narrowest sense—the practical procedures of putting one worker in charge of a larger group of workers who in turn direct the army of volunteers who ring the doobells in the precincts, stuff the envelopes, and watch the polls. No wonder everyone can agree on the value of such an enterprise; superficially it is the most non-controversial and most productive activity of the party.

In 1962 this attitude was codified in Raymond Moley's book *The Republican Opportunity.* Two years later the *Newsletter* of the Republican Congressional Committee, a frequent promoter of the Moley opus, looked back on the devastation of November 3 and concluded that what the party needed was better organization: a voter-registration campaign, "rebuilding . . . in each District from the ground up, instead of the top down," and getting the GOP voters to the polls (noting that many Republicans did not vote in 1964).[1]

Precisely that simple-minded approach has lost the party votes for years and will continue to do so if not changed. It worships the grass roots but has no concept of how to plant and nourish them, apparently believing that they grow themselves. It sees the problem of recruiting workers as wholly apart from the questions of party position and leadership, and dotes on numbers. There have never been more Republican volunteers than

[1] Republican Congressional Committee *Newsletter,* November 6, 1964.

came out for Citizens for Goldwater-Miller, the crabgrass roots of the 1964 campaign, yet six million Republicans did not vote in 1964 and many who did go to the polls voted for Johnson.

Moley's book, though not so simplistic as the dogma of the party professionals, is almost more misleading for its seeming plausibility. Moley's great example of organization is the Conservative party in England. It is true, as Moley says, that the Tories did not change their principles after their defeat in 1945, but they did set them out in the garb of new and more fashionable policies. It is also true that improved organization was the "foundation" of the party comeback, but it was a foundation, not the whole building. However well constructed, as a foundation alone it would have left the Conservatives out in the cold for good. The Conservative comeback of that period, indeed, is an especially exemplary one for Republicans, just for the reason that it was put together with changes in not just one but every sphere of partisan endeavor: organization, research, propaganda, and policy.

Organization, to genuinely assist in the revitalization of the Republican party, must be undertaken in concert with the other elements of partisan operation and, moreover, must be viewed more widely than it is. Much of the party's organizational deficiency derives from its lack of recruiting in non-Republican areas, and this work requires more than calling for extra effort from the Republican workers already active, for often none *are* active. Similarly, organizational work among youth requires contacts with the groups and individuals who form opinion among young people, but today the Young Republicans are neglected in the party structure and the YR leaders themselves are often far removed from the main currents of youth activity in the country and hostile to them. While primary responsibility lies with the party at the local and state levels, the national party does have powers of initiative, incentive, and prestige with which it can encourage reforms. The Republican National Committee may be weaker than the collective state and local party structures, but it is stronger than any one or group of them.

Full-scale organizational reforms should begin in the makeup and operations of the Republican National Committee itself. Most political scientists and a few practicing politicians are aware that though the national committees of both parties choose and empower their National Chairman, they little influence either him or his staff. What's more, the committee memberships are largely unreflective of the political importance of the various states. Thus the big states, under-represented and frustrated, are inclined to ignore the committees as much as possible. In the Republican party the membership is made up of a committeeman and a committeewoman from each state plus the state chairmen of states which went for the Republican Presidential candidate in the previous election or which have an incumbent Republican governor. The state chairman addition was an Eisenhower innovation intended to decrease the relative power of the numerous but Republican-poor Southern states. This system does not especially help the populous states, however.

A further obstacle to a meaningful role for the National Committee is the fact that it meets only twice a year, with the members responsible for travel expenses unless the state parties reimburse them. The membership is detached from the day-to-day operation of the national organization, and serious politicians in the states are discouraged from seeking so expensive and uninfluential a post. Hence, in both parties, a disproportionate percentage of committee members are simply wealthy party figures whose influence at the state level is not considerable. Sometimes National Committee membership serves as a way station to political retirement, or is a state party's method of compensating a well-heeled patron for not being allowed to run for office on the state ticket. Women in politics, at least at the higher levels, are seldom as influential in the party as are men, and the appointment of a committeewoman for every committeeman still further prevents the national committees of both parties from reflecting reality. In several Republican state parties (Minnesota and New York, for example) the quality of representatives, their degree of interest and participation, and their real power in their own states is very high indeed, but these are exceptions.

Many structural reforms have been proposed for the Republican National Committee in order to make it truly representative of party power and truly influential in party activities. (The Democratic Committee membership is just as unrepresentative and just as uninfluential, but as the agency of a party in power, whose operations are naturally directed from the White House, this weakness is not so debilitating.) Two eminently desirable reforms were proposed even as the party and the National Committee stumbled into the organizational debacle of Goldwaterism. In their study of the national party committees, *Politics Without Power*,[2] Cornelius P. Cotter (a Republican) and Bernard C. Hennessy (a Democrat) recommend that the present membership standards of the national committees be radically revised, that no national committee men and women be elected at all. In their place on the national committees Cotter and Hennessy would place the chairman (by custom a man) and the vice-chairman (by custom a woman) of each state party. These individuals would better represent the true power structures of the party and from their daily involvement in state politics be better judges of national policies.

Among the face-saving recommendations made by Chairman Miller after the 1962 defeat was the appointment of a study committee to review the operation of the Republican National Committee and make suggestions for change. To Miller's surprise, and perhaps consternation, the committee, unlike his other recommendations, did see fruition largely because of its determined and energetic chairman, former National Chairman Meade Alcorn of Connecticut. Alcorn's committee by no means considered all the problems of the national party structure, but it did break ground, and its confidential report was delivered in closed session to the full Republican National Committee in January, 1964. Most

2 *Politics Without Power: The National Party Committees* (New York: Atherton Press; 1964).

of its proposals were not implemented. Among those only par-
tialy implemented was a plan for the division of the RNC into a
number of standing subcommittees to supervise party activity in
regard to state and local organizations, public relations, campaign
planning, voter groupings, and affiliated organizations (Young
Republicans and Women's Federations). It also called for closer
cooperation and elimination of overlapping functions among the
Republican Congressional (Campaign) Committee, the Republican Senatorial Campaign Committee, and the National Committee itself, and that they all be housed in one building.

To abet the Cotter-Hennessy and Alcorn committee reforms,
the Republican National Committee should pay the relatively
small amount of money for expenses of committee members and
have them meet at least four times a year, as well as in regional
conferences. All new members should be officially briefed on
their jobs and serviced with committee progress reports. Greater
frequency of meetings and operational briefings would afford
greater familiarity with party operations and a greater sense of
responsibility for planning them. To make sure, finally, that a
National Committee actively leading the national party headquarters was also reflective of the party's national interests, the
votes of the members should be weighted in the same propor-
tions as delegations to national conventions. Now Mississippi and
New York, for example, have the same representation (i.e., three
votes each), though one is large and dominantly Republican
and the other is small, dominantly Democratic, and in a state
of virtual insurrection against the leadership of both parties
and the law of the land. Moreover, to provide a still more accurate echo of true power in the state parties, we recommend
that each state chairman should cast two thirds of his states'
votes and the vice-chairman one third (although we recognize
that given the uncommon ferocity of Republican women, the
execution of this humble reform might prove the most difficult
of all).

Barring a reformation of the National Committee, the most

significant potential influence toward reform in the party today is the National Chairman. Meade Alcorn once described the typical National Chairman as "the least appreciated, most abused and most harassed party official in the country."[3]

The truly great national chairmen, the Mark Hannas and Paul Butlers, were pros, although the unstable nature of national politics in America precludes any professional training for the job. It has been only recently that Republicans have realized that a chairman must give full-time to his job if he is to do more than serve as a caretaker and that, for a minority party far out of power, caretaking is hardly a formula for success. But if there is at last a growing appreciation of professionalism for the party's official head, it has yet to extend to the whole realm of Republican organization. Few states and fewer localities have a truly professional party organizer, and at the national level there are no more than two with any notable competence. Here again the Democrats are in nearly as bad shape, but the Democrats compensate for their weakness through the Committee on Political Education (COPE) of the AFL-CIO.

In the torpid view of most party leaders, the problem is a lack of money to train and hire professionals. But behind that difficulty is an inane lack of business sense; the party refuses to invest today for results tomorrow. The same party leaders who decline to allocate funds in January for hiring and training of professional organizers, desperately rush about in August looking for qualified men to manage campaigns in the fall.

In Britain the Conservative party maintains a professional cadre of political agents, one to each district of 70,000 people, hired and trained by the central office, though responsible to distinct party leaders. Each agent begins his career with an extensive education not only in the techniques of political organization but in every facet of national and regional law that pertains to political operations, as well as in party history and philosophy. Swinton Conservative College, operating in a con-

[3] Lecture at University of Massachusetts, November 13, 1962.

verted castle, was established in 1948 and partly serves today as a headquarters for the training of agents and volunteers.

The Republican party urgently needs such a system, adapted, of course, to our own particular demography and politics. The Young Republican Federation's program of training a half dozen field workers to campaign in selected marginal congressional campaigns is one of that organization's few successful enterprises (inaugurated before the federation became the ideological sounding board of the arch-right), and it ought to be expanded. Certainly young people just out of college, who can be trained for a few hundred dollars, perhaps with state party scholarships over the course of a summer, and paid the $4,500–7,000 they would earn in business, would provide vigor, ideas, and expertise to the party organization. It also would engage the enthusiasm of young Republicans for future party service and expand the party store of candidate talent. Strictly professional and centrally controlled in training and hiring policies, the program would discourage exploitation by the Rasputins of the radical right or any other group.

Simultaneous with structural reform of party organization should begin a reorientation of it toward increased emphasis on metropolitan voters, youth, and intellectuals.

When Barry Goldwater was nominated, a near-total reorganization of functions, as well as a usurpatory Reign of Terror, swept through the National Committee's floor of offices on Eye Street in Washington. While a person might return from lunch to find someone else sitting at his desk, he nearly as often would find the desk gone, too—not only *his* job, but *the* job. The already skimpy Minorities Division, for example, was simply abolished. For a while, a former staff man of the division served as Goldwater and Miller's chauffeur. Later he received publicity as the man who was put up to organize the devious campaign to persuade Negroes to write-in Martin Luther King rather than vote for Johnson. There was enough money available to pay in advance for 1.5 million King-for-President leaflets and on another occasion to track down and stop circulation of a District of Columbia Republican party pamphlet proclaiming Goldwater an integrationist. But there was no money available at national headquarters to make special appeals to Negroes in behalf of any level of the Republican ticket. Four full years after the unmistakable lesson of 1960, the Republican party entered its new era with less support among metropolitan voters of all racial, religious, nationality, and economic groups than anytime since the Depression. Most of the failing stems from hostile or inadequate policies advocated and poorly expressed by Republicans nationally. But some of the problem is traceable simply to the Republicans' continued lack of personal contact with metropolitan voters.

After the election the obvious first step toward reform, besides giving attention to policy and propaganda, was to dust off the Bliss Report and put a meaningful effort behind it at party headquarters. Almost as obvious was the need to reopen and expand the staffs of the Minorities, Nationalities, and Labor divisions. Over a year after the election, with Ray Bliss as National Chairman, the obvious was still not accomplished.

The mandate of these divisions should hardly be too broad. They should represent the party to their special groups and represent the special groups to the party. When a Negro or labor or nationalities conference is held, a Republican representative should be present to listen and explain. When an event occurs that is favorable to the Republican cause among Negroes or labor or some nationality group, it should be publicized in press releases, mailings to opinion-molders, and speeches. When a law of importance to Negroes, labor, or nationalities is in Congress, the appropriate division chief of the RNC should explain to Capitol Hill Republicans its political implications for the party. When a union member or a Negro Republican or a Republican of recent immigrant stock runs for political office, the National Committee should send special help—in the knowledge that the party needs such leaders who can carry its message back to their people.

A major reorganization is also needed in the party's youth

activities. The National Young Republican Federation, so lively and relevant in the early fifties, has become in the sixties a mere extension of the intraparty debate at its most strident, uninformed, and meaningless level. This organization, the logical instrument for the party's appeal to youth, has deliberately severed ties with other youth groups, such as the Young Adult Council and the National Student Association, and failed to establish ties to the Negro student movement and other special groups. Fearful of contamination from the predominantly liberal majority among youth, the YR's have been afraid to convert among it.

The result of this strange political isolationism has been to keep most of America's youth away from the Republican party, and most thoughtful Republican youth away from the Young Republican Federation. The growth of Republican research and political-action groups at Harvard, MIT, Columbia, Yale, in Los Angeles, and elsewhere, testifies to a trend among the most active and articulate young Republicans against involvement in the party's official youth program.

Sadly, the groups that form outside the party structure cannot speak for the party and are not coordinated, while, on the other hand, the failure of the Young Republican National Federation to appeal to such young people (let alone to young independents and Democrats) orients that organization toward still further parochialism. Unable to fulfill its purpose of bringing young people into the Republican party and bringing the party to young people, the YR Federation turns inward and finds excitement in infighting. Each National Convention (every two years) brings new leadership, and most important, new staff, to national headquarters. Just as the leadership and staff begin to develop competence and a long-term perspective, there is another shake-up, and, as in some banana republic, the old revolutionaries are replaced by the new.

The senior party, watching the Young Republicans' antics, decided some years ago that the movement had stagnated and was of little use to the national party and that to meddle in it would simply cause greater inconvenience and personal antipathy than the group is worth. This was a mistake, for the decision simply contributed to the YR Federation's decline. The group now typically encourages the participation in its intragroup politics of men and women far past anything resembling "youth"—generally people who cannot succeed in the senior party, but whose experience gives them advantage in a movement that has a high turnover in membership. One former Young Republican, Biehl Clarke of Washington, D.C., observes: "the principal value of the YRNF appears to lie in producing leaders who are 'ring-wise' in winning intraparty scraps," but who do little toward training or inspiring young people to win elections.[4]

The Alcorn study committee reported that the increased autonomy of the Young Republican movement "has resulted in inefficiency, lack of coordination and unnecessary expense." College Republicans, who are a branch of the regular YR's but elect their own chairman, were found in even greater disarray. To remedy the structural and operational flaws, the Alcorn committee called for a full-time, permanent staff to persist through all changes of elected leadership and provide continuity, a college chairman who is appointed rather than elected, and a strictly enforced age limit of thirty-five. Moreover, the study committee urged that the Republican National Committee take a larger role in the overall direction of the YR's policy and programming.

Perhaps the most propitious innovation in the Young Republicans would be to abolish the biennial national conventions, the pathetic-comic imitations of the worst aspects of a senior-party convention. About the only serious business these expensive and indecorous conclaves accomplish is the election of a new national Young Republican chairman. The rest is puerile enough to make a Shriner blush. If the senior-party chairman himself simply would appoint the YR's national leader the YR Federation's internecine obsessions could be much deflated. The un-

[4] *Political Intelligence*, Washington Newsletter of Civic Affairs Associates, July, 1963.

graduated alumni whose Young Republican bulletins arrive with their Medicare checks would be left with the prospect of interfering in the YR politics of fifty states or joining their fellow senior citizens in retirement. Some useful party building might then be undertaken.

Such reforms may seem picayune, but they might well energize the whole Young Republican movement. The trend of the next few years, in any case, should be toward greater senior-party guidance of the party's appeal to youth, until such a day when the Young Republican Federation is representative of young people in America (or at least, of young Republicans) and has a program suited to winning their allegiance.

Six weeks after the defeat of Barry Goldwater the Young Republicans' executive director perhaps realized that new voters had given his man's arch-conservatism less support than had any other age group (36 percent to 64 percent for LBJ). The new approach of the Young Republicans was to be "practical, not philosophical . . . We have to stop appealing just to the white-collar young businessman and go after the blue collar worker and the no-collar worker" [*sic*]. Something "practical," the young pro thought "might be a bowling league or a baseball team."[5] His answer is not "Organization!" but wild-goose chases. Both approaches, however, share a conspicuous aversion to appeals based on issues.

This concept of party philosophy as antithetical to practical politics is analogous to the idea that the national party organization has no business concerning itself with such "impractical" matters as party policy and program. Officials at the National Committee and their counterparts on the House and Senate Republican campaign committees have long maintained that policy is outside their purview, which is organization and public relations. Whether or not these men are sincere, they are wrong, even in describing their own activities. The organizational and publicity functions of the committees have a profound influence on policy. When William Miller rejected a proposal to expand

[5] Interview, December 14, 1964.

the National Committee's program in issue research, the effect
was to abet the negativist record being compiled by the predominantly Old Guard congressional leadership. His alleged
neutrality again verged on policy-making when he opted to build
party strength in the segregationist South rather than among the
minorities in the cities of the North and South. This "organizational" decision both aided Goldwater and obstructed the overwhelming support for civil rights in the party, even among the
Old Guard in Congress, at a time when civil rights was the key
domestic issue. Organization and public relations unavoidably
interact with policy, and must be considered in that light.

But the National Committee also takes *direct* policy positions. Not only does the chairman speak out on those issues on
which there is putative unanimity within the party, but he also
often testifies for a mere majority view; and, sometimes, he takes
the minority side, though seldom on issues before Congress itself.
When the chairman speaks for the party on a foreign-policy crisis
or a government scandal, he takes a policy stand. When reporters
on "Meet the Press" or "Face the Nation" ask him his views and
the party's on a housing bill before Congress, his answer is not
just public relations. He may sometimes try to evade the question,
or even the interview itself, but evasion is often a sort of party
"policy."

Barry Goldwater, after his defeat, declared that all party
organizations should defer to the Republican congressional delegation in the making of policy. The irony of this stand is that it
came from a man who had seized party policy from the congressional leadership, as well as everyone else, and ran on his own
exotic issues of morality and crime on the streets, rather than on
the party's congressional record—not that this record would have
been helpful either. Moreover, any such dependence on Congress
for policy initiatives would just deepen the party's ideological
stagnation. As long as the congressional leadership is reduced to
tactical maneuvering, and as long as the so-called Republican
Policy Committee of the House remains moribund and the so-

called Senate Policy Committee contents itself with tabulating legislative business, most of it Democratic, there will be no rebirth of Republicanism in Congress and the Congressional Republicans will only look good in comparison to the Presidential Republicans when, as in 1964, a Barry Goldwater is the Presidential nominee.

The question of who properly makes policy for the party is, in any case, largely misunderstood. Since decision-making within America's weak-party political system is extremely complex, the policy followed by any individual congressman, for example, is merely *influenced* by such agencies of his party as the congressional leadership, the Congressional party conference, the party's national and state platforms, the advice of non-Congressional party leaders and the National Committee. Some of these party agencies do exert greater influence on decision-making than others, and that is what the argument is really about: To whose attempt to formulate a "party line" should the party as a collectivity lend its official prestige?

There has been much agitation in many corners of the party for a "party conference" representing all major spokesmen. Given the proper research facilities, such a body, essentially the All-Republican Conference proposed by Senator Keating in 1961, might become a primary source of "policy" influence in the party.

Traditionally, the congressional leadership has opposed such an organization for the obvious competitive reason that under the present system, when the party is not in control of the Presidency, the source of influence best organized and most conspicuous is the congressional leadership. A vigorous party parliament would end the monopoly.

It was a surprise in early 1965 when Senator Dirksen and Representative Ford made the seemingly uncharacteristic proposal for a Republican Coordinating Committee, to be composed of eleven leading members of Congress, the five living Presidential candidates (Landon, Dewey, Eisenhower, Nixon and Goldwater), and five governors, with the Republican National Chairman presiding. This group, they said, would speak out on national affairs. But soon it became clear there was no intention to build a real party conference or "shadow cabinet."

The Coordinating Committee is really an adivsory board which meets infrequently and does not "make policy." Its research staff is inadequate, essentially the five men who serve full time on the research division of the National Committee. The faces are those of the party's big names, but the voice is still the voice of the Congressional leadership. The Republican Coordinating Committee is a mouth without a head, a collective constitutional monarch for the GOP—impressive, elegant, innocuous.

Even when issue research is not the problem, the Coordinating Committee is timid. An attempt of the governors to have the John Birch Society repudiated led to an attack by Melvin Laird, carrying the banner of "unity" Bill Miller has dropped, and the final resolution was so vague that Birch spokesman John Rousselot promptly telegrammed his support for it.

So far the Coordinating Committee is a failure. Its existence lulls the party into thinking it has a real parliament when it does not. It distracts attention from the salient need for reform of Congress. Without proper research facilities and an attitude of innovation regarding research, the window display of prominent Republicans is largely a waste of time for all concerned.

Far preferable would be a real party parliament, an all-Republican conference with extensive staffing and policy roles for talented younger Republicans as well as the prestigious but often unproductive headliners.

The responsibility for developing such a conference lies not primarily with the congressional leaders but with the National Committee, the central party headquarters, whose sole interest is to build a party capable of winning elections. A reformed National Committee should adopt party policy as a legitimate, overt concern and integrate it fully with organizational objectives, and with the party's public relations program.

Such integration, too, will mean exorcizing another prevailing misconception. It was testimony to the incompetence as well as the direction of the National Committee in the years 1960–64 that the Research Division was considered the flunky of the Public Relations Division, rather than its equal. Widely considered in Washington to be the best research staff in town (before it was turned out by Goldwater), the Research Division was constricted and neglected in the National Committee. Its functions were limited to statistical compilation and analysis, and even that work was largely ignored. The Research Division head did not sit in on most major staff planning sessions, and his offices were as physically distant from the chairman's office as possible while the Public Relations directors participated in all the sessions and had an office within shouting range of the chairman.

If the research function atrophied through neglect, and finally almost expired under Dean Burch, the public relations function failed in a more grand and noticeable manner. Without proper market analysis, for example, a series of fund-raising advertisements in national magazines in 1963 not only failed to raise funds but within a few months went $75,000 into debt.[6] The party's official publication, *Battle Line,* vied with the Republican Congressional Campaign Committee *Newsletter* for bilious and extraneous prose. It never said anything newsworthy or new; it was a graceless and tiresome partisan tirade that inspired contempt even from party officeholders. Governor Bellmon of Oklahoma, for example, told an *Advance* interviewer that he considered such publications "junk" and pined for a few "brief memos of sound, objective analysis." *Battle Line's* successor under Bliss reads like a trade journal.[7]

Unlike research, the value of public relations is understood by the tacticians of the Republican apparatus, but only in the abstract. Often sharing the right-wing antipathy toward the news media and the lobbies, they continually fail to "make" favorable

[6] A different fund-raising program, based on direct-mail solicitations, was later attempted and proved extremely successful and is today the sustaining source of party headquarters revenue. Bliss' best appointment, General Lucius B. Clay, is the party's best Finance Chairman in years.

[7] Interview, July 23, 1963.

news or mobilize allies with public followings. Their idea of popularizing a position is to present it in the most extreme form through the Congressional Committee *Newsletter* or the National Chairman's virtuoso harangue of a Republican Women's Federation conference. When the right-wingers who get the *Newsletter* and the matrons who attend the meeting write or exclaim their appreciation, the party tacticians in Washington—less those in Congress—think they have an issue. They do not research their stands very deeply or think about them very long. They paraphrase what they hear in a Capitol corridor and parody what they read in the papers.

The Republican party, which was accused only six years ago of being Madison Avenue's slickest client, does not have to be so awkward in public relations now. As a party in opposition the GOP does face the disadvantage of lacking Theodore Roosevelt's "bully pulpit," the Presidency and the rest of the resources of national leadership. It also cannot easily take credit for good legislation that it influences but that the majority passes—such as the civil-rights bills. Nor can it exploit the successes of national institutions under federal administration—such as space feats.

But these limitations need not be incapacitating; the opposition simply must play a different game. It has the advantage of escaping conspicuous blame for national misfortunes and now, as a near-negligible minority in Congress, it cannot be called obstructionist. Moreover, the party has time, potentially, to stand back from the issues and think them through with relative dispassion. It can experiment with new proposals without much risk that they will be implemented before they meet the tests of time and criticism. If the proposal is a bad one, or if the incumbents solve the problem without using it, the suggestion usually will be forgotten. If, on the other hand, the incumbents fail to solve the pertinent problem, the opposition—right or wrong—can make a persuasive sounding case of the fact that its own proposal would have worked. Churchill calling for preparedness in 1938–39 is the classic example of such development of an issue. A more recent, and perhaps reprehensible, example was the "missile gap" issue of the 1960 campaign. A false position, but one with veri-similitude, it was prepared by the Democrats to exploit increased anxiety over Soviet advances in space in the latter Eisenhower years. It was useful in the election, and while its proponents still claim they believed in it at the time, it was quietly dropped after the campaign.

The opposition's advantage is decreased at least by half if, like the Republicans today, it does not bother to research and develop new proposals but merely attacks those of the incumbents. What is the Republican proposal for the faltering Alliance for Progress, European unity, or the farm problem? Although every Democratic position does not justify provisions of an alternative, the Republicans would be greatly strengthened if they contributed more than partisan invective to the political debate.

On many issues, particularly during the seed-planting time between elections, it is possible for an opposition to experiment with proposals which begin with criticism of the incumbents but do not end there. A well-balanced portfolio of issues, like one of stocks, should contain some that will produce mediocre but safe returns—and also others with the possibility for rapid growth. The "farm problem" may not be a good "growth" issue to develop, while Latin-American policy may turn out, as the result of a revolution or coup, to be a profitable investment.

This balance and experimentation is not typical of Republican research and propaganda today. Even where the party, or a few people in it, has presented a new proposal, it is often half-baked, as, for example, the 1960 platform's endorsement of international "confederations" of free-world countries. Or it is not produced when it is timely. "Nine tenths of wisdom," said Theodore Roosevelt, "consists in being wise in time,"[8] and a good example of bad timing was the Republican proposal in 1964 for reformation of the draft, successfully anticipated by President Johnson just two days before it was released, and promptly neutralized by the appointment of a Presidential study committee. Or it is not pushed hard or dramatically or widely enough

[8] Speech in New York City, October 30, 1912.

to become identified in the public mind as a distinctly Republican program. It does the Republicans little good when a Democratic program founders, if the voters are not made aware of the Republicans' alternative. A good example of this is the House Republican poverty bill in the Eighty-eighth and Eighty-ninth Congresses, virtually unnoticed despite the foundering of the "War on Poverty."

Representative Thomas B. Curtis of Missouri criticizes the press for not reporting the Republican side of issues before Congress. If reporters would only read the official, government-printed testimony before congressional committees, he says, they would know the GOP position. But whether or not hard-pressed reporters should pore over volumes that most congressmen themselves do not read, the fact remains that it is the Republican party and not the reporters who are hurting and it is the party that will have to reform—at least to the extent of recognizing that the U. S. Printing Office is not a sufficient propaganda facility for the congressional opposition.

The mere acceptance of responsibility for its own reputation with the public would represent a substantial gain from 1964, when the party's unpopularity was explained by a conspiracy of the press. Then may come the reform of the party itself and especially a redirection of its message toward the metropolitan voter, youth, and the intellectual.

Then a new leadership will have brought the Republican party a good part of the way to its promised land, the tantalizing political paradise where most voters are Republicans, most elections are won by Republicans, and history is shaped by Republicans. A reform program, however, must go beyond organization and publicity if it is finally to succeed.

◇◇

CHAPTER 16

A New Republican Establishment

T HE REPUBLICAN party must now face the need for reform. The party can no longer sustain its optimism with self-deception, its unity with vacuity, and its organization with a tolerance of the extreme right. Elections are usually won or lost in the years that precede them. By that measure the party has been compromising its future since the late Eisenhower years.

It is ironic that just as the Republican appeal was being impaired by the uninspired handling of several domestic and foreign crises of 1958–60 (the 1958 recession and the U-2 incident, to name two), the Eisenhower Administration was at last beginning to see the wisdom of making reforms in the party structure. The Percy Committee report was a start toward informed citizen participation in the setting of party goals—but just a start; and like other initiatives of the Eisenhower years, it was not followed through. In early 1959, moreover, able men like Dr.

Malcolm C. Moos from the White House staff and Charles Mc-Whorter from the Vice-President's staff had been put to work on the problem of improving the party's relations with intellectuals. By election time the next year, they had made a start, but it, too, was just a start; and Nixon did not extend it into his campaign.

Similarly, the Administration was always interested in making Republican voters out of the new generation of young Americans. But this interest never went beyond exhortation. The President himself talked about youth, in public and in private. He told his assistant, Sherman Adams, that he felt the party organization was not attractive to most young people because it was too conservative. But the arduous, beleaguered path from preachment to reform was more than the President could negotiate in those last years of his Administration. He preferred the global sweep of jets and the smooth passage of his convoy through cheering foreign throngs to the problematic domestic matters of party reform and legislative preparation. Failure perplexed him. "What happened" he asked Adams in 1960, "to all those fine young people with stars in their eyes who sailed balloons and rang doorbells for us in 1952?"[1]

What happened, of course, was that many became disillusioned and inactive; some became active for the Democrats; and some turned to Goldwater, then moving into the breach of Eisenhower's recumbent "crusade" with a new crusade, full of trumpeting alarms and pied-piping rhetoric.

Republicans in the second half of the 1960's cannot allow another breach to open in the party's commitment to responsible politics or another vacuum to open in its ideological address of the future. The far right is prepared to enter again, and the Democrats are prepared to decimate the party further in future elections. As the next election approaches the signs are not encouraging. Retreating from the politics of the far right, the party seems to be adopting again the politics of the vacuum center.

[1] *Firsthand Report* (New York: Harper & Brothers; 1961).

The National Committee under the careful chairmanship of Ray Bliss is no longer in the hands of right-wing exclusionists as it was for eight months in 1964 and early 1965. It represents a coalition of all those Republicans, including a few chastened Goldwaterites, who comprehend now the unsalability of arch-conservatism. It is another attempt at compromise within the GOP, a transitional directory run by technocrats, commanding wide but tepid support because its ideology is organization, the lowest common denominator of Republicanism. Reform comes only to the degree it is noncontroversial, i.e., it does not outrage the arch-right. At its very origins, the coalition showed its neutrality. The choice of Ray Bliss, the personification of organizationalism, showed a determination to avoid ideology; the successful effort to persuade Barry Goldwater himself to bless, however reluctantly, the new order, showed an unwillingness to affront the old. The mandate was mainly to keep peace in the party.

This compromise coalition in the National Committee is echoed in the new leadership team of Dirksen-Ford on Capitol Hill. Dirksen is Dirksen, and Ford, whatever his intentions, is beholden to a congressional majority which also elected Melvin Laird as chairman of its conference and cherishes Leslie Arends as its whip. The coalition includes party progressives, but it is not progressive. It can bring at least a semblance of harmony to the party, for a while, and it is potentially capable of winning back Republican congressional seats lost in 1962 and 1964. However, since it does not fully face up to the great swath of reforms that the party needs, it is not capable of electing a Republican Congress or a Republican President. It partially solves the immediate internal problem of the Republican party in the Congress, but it does not solve at all the party's problem in its confrontation with the Democrats or with the nation's problems.

Reform remains urgent, and only the progressives have sufficiently stripped themselves of illusions about the party situation to show the way. But unhappily, though they have few illusions about the party, progressives have many about themselves. Hence, the place for reform to begin is within the progressive Republican movement itself.

In April, 1964, the final communication of *Advance* magazine said: "As a long-range political movement, progressive Republicanism is in terrible shape." It still is. While the right of the Republican party and the various shades of modern liberalism within the Democratic party have an array of self-conscious and purposeful political organizations, the Republican progressives, collectively, have only a common commitment to a relatively amorphous body of opinion which has proven itself popular with the voters from time to time. The GOP progressives should stop defending themselves from the charges of "Establishment" and actually build one. It would be good if this real Republican establishment possessed some of the coordination, money, resolution, and perhaps even a mite of the ruthlessness which the Goldwater movement sometimes showed and which Phyllis Schlafly imputed to the feckless group whose default allowed Goldwater to take command. Such an establishment should be based on the following five elements:

1. Articulate and movement-conscious public spokesmen and leaders.

2. A vigorous intelligentsia—with lines to leaders and key supporters of the movement and to the communications media.

3. Action organizations.

4. Conscious "followers" who not only identify with the movement, but work for it and finance it.

5. Coordination.

Measuring progressive Republicans one finds a small band of persuasive spokesmen who accept the movement's overall philosophy. However, not one of the major leaders in the party since 1960 has thought in terms of remaking the Republican party and set about doing so. There is still no Hubert Humphrey or Barry Goldwater of progressive Republicanism—no one who actively initiates, participates in, and supports national organizations to promote that philosophy. That the most qualified men for that role, Rockefeller and Nixon, each opted against it is the saddest indictment of their party careers.

Similarly, there are few progressive Republican columnists, not because of some press conspiracy, but more because of the neglect of the GOP moderates and their failure to develop a distinct and relevant approach to the issues. There is now no special organ of communications among progressives, and only a few of the movement's sympathetic intellectuals, chiefly Henry C. Wallich of Yale and Malcom Moos of the Ford Foundation, now attempt even rarely to think and write in terms of the progressive Republican dilemma. It is still impossible to say whether the various embryonic and poorly financed progressive Republican organizations will develop into an effective force in the party. But so far the outlook is cloudy.

Financially, the situation is similar. Some money is available to progressive Republican candidates, but, with a few exceptions, such as the John L. Loeb family in New York, the contributors give little to operations of the movement as a whole, and what they give is not proportionate to the gifts of their equally wealthy rightist and liberal counterparts.

Nonetheless, whatever the errors of the past and the deficiencies of the present, there are a few current sources of progressive Republican initiative, and the reservoir of public sentiment is as large as ever. Rank-and-file Republicans, in the Gallup poll of January 13, 1965, cited "unity" (29 percent), the replacement of Goldwaterism in party leadership (28 percent), and a more moderate platform (12 percent) as the top criteria for reviving the party. Only 2 percent suggested the party "stay conservative but change its tactics." The moderate mandate from independent voters was even stronger. Subsequent polls have corroborated this rejection of the right, and it was substantiated by election results in both 1964 and 1965. Progressive congressional candidates in 1964 universally ran ahead of the Goldwater ticket, and most ran well ahead of the Republican average despite the fact that many came from marginal rather than safe districts. In 1965 progressives won impressive victories in Philadelphia, Louisville, and Atlanta, while in New Jersey, using a right-wing "soft on Communism" appeal in the gubernatorial race, they suffered a catastrophic defeat, including loss of both houses of the state legislature for the first time since 1914.

Moreover, interest in preventing another 1964 was manifested widely among progressive party workers and backers after the election. Many of them—joined by converts and young people becoming active for the first time—dedicated themselves to constructing an inclusive and progressive Republican apparatus. Established groups like the Ripon Society, the Republican Governors' Association (avowedly non-factional), the Wednesday Club of House GOP progressives, the Negro National Republican Assembly, and a Republicans for Progress Committee (essentially concerned with legislative research) all stepped up their ambitions and plans as a result of the Goldwater campaign and defeat. A Council of Republican Organizations, with Ripon Society staffing, took up the task of coordinating the various old and new initiatives.

In such a fluid situation it is almost certain that the shape of some developments will turn out quite differently than anticipated. What is also certain is that the progressive Republican movement, to succeed over the years, must employ a whole galaxy of organizations, spokesmen, information outlets, campaign committees, and issue-research operations, each reflecting and strengthening the others. One essential is greater staff assistance for Capital Hill progressives trying to develop reasoned and researched Republican legislation. The Democratic Study Group, a professionally staffed association of liberal Democrats organized in 1959, has shown the efficacy of institutionalized cooperation among like-minded partisans. While progressive Republicans are a small minority within the minority in the House, they can multiply their influence manifold through shrewd public relations and through a monopoly on new Republican ideas—a market fairly easy to corner.

Unhappily, the Wednesday Club began its highly publicized new program in the Eighty-ninth Congress by disintegrating over the question of Ford versus Halleck for minority leader. The Wednesday members failed to use their united strength effectively as a bargaining tool simply because they could not agree upon whom to support. After that humiliation they still failed to agree on the relatively more simple matter of how to go about hiring even one staff member. Although the group was put together out of frustration with the inability of the whole House GOP caucus to act dramatically for moderate causes, it would seem that the Wednesday Club itself is similarly frustrated. The need remains for at least one clarion voice for a group of progressive Republicans in the House of Representatives, whether on behalf of 140 members, 24, or 14.

Progressives in the Senate are relatively a larger band, led by Senators Kuchel, Javits, and Scott. With the governors, the moderate GOP senators have the potential for a historic role in the revitalization of progressive Republicanism. Not only do they compare favorably with arch-conservative colleagues (Nebraska's Carl Curtis is the Senate's leading Goldwaterite) but they are physically closer to national developments than progressives outside Washington and individually enjoy the political glamour and power that accrues, in and out of Washington, to the position of U. S. senator. Whether or not they exploit their advantages may depend on their willingness and ability to informally and inclusively associate and build a joint political-legislative staff.

Another priority is the recruitment and assistance of progressive candidates in party primaries and general elections. This is the job of the House and Senate progressives and any progressive Republican campaign organization that is established.

Many of the House seats lost by the party in 1964 were in normally Republican districts. Almost all of them were represented by rightists whose voting records had never been examined by their constituents until the Democrats compared them to that of Goldwater's. It seems likely that the Republican party can recapture many of those seats—if not in 1966, in 1968. By historical precedent, the party should win back also a few of the seats lost in 1962 and 1958 (although under the direction of the Republican Congressional Committee, the GOP has been breaking such precedents for years). The party has now sunk so low in both houses that its margin can be increased just by winning existent *Republican* votes. These nearly inevitable "new" GOP seats afford the progressives a chance to take their message to the voters and add significantly to their own ranks in the next Congress.

A third priority is the establishment of at least a newsletter as a means of communication among all the progressive Republican activists in the country. The splintering of effort during the last four years is largely traceable to inadequate contact and rapport among progressives. As a long-term goal, progressives must look forward also to establishing a magazine of intellectual thought, topical opinion, and information to compete with the several on the oppsite sides of the political spectrum.

As well as expanding existing organizations and creating new ones, the progressives must turn also to the general organizational problem of bringing new recruits into the movement and into the party. As the rightists found new workers in the radical right, the progressive Republicans should look for them in church and fraternal groups, and especially among minority groups and youth.

Plans and master plans will come and go, evolve and expand, and for a while the progressives' characteristic lack of coordination will continue. But given sustaining enthusiasm for individual projects, this weakness can be turned into a strength. From experimentation will come new techniques and a broad base of experienced leadership for the time when the various efforts will, by general assent, have to be brought into intimate cooperation—and made a bona fide Establishment at last.

It is probably even preferable for this cooperation to evolve from natural associations, rather than be imposed by some artificially stratified super-organization set up by a few individuals. After 1952, the liberal Democrats, in a somewhat similar situation (they were never as abject as the GOP today), attempted to form various overall coordinating committees. Although their organizational blueprints and constitutions were models of perfection, carefully worked out, and fought out, over months and months, these efforts outside the party structure did not succeed. The liberal Democrats did not actually cooperate effectively until after 1956, when liberal National Chairman Paul Butler brought them into active participation in the party structure itself, largely through the creation of the Democratic Advisory Council. The lessons for the moderates in the GOP— if the lessons of four years of their own folly were not enough— seem obvious; their effort must be concentrated within the official party.

Finally, the rebirth of progressive Republicanism will rest on the attitudes of the activists in the movement—toward their commitment to it, toward each other as individuals, toward the party and the right wing, and toward the Democrats.

The first principle of conduct for new and old progressives might be an attitude of humility and forgiveness toward each other. Since few among the progressives were clairvoyant, altruistic, or persistently active in resisting the right-wing danger, few, if any, have the right to assume a mantle of righteousness.

Moreover, all should accept the challenge ahead as lengthy and difficult. The new progressive Republican organizations show the mistakes that amateurs often make. But full-time amateurs can become "pros" very quickly, while their dedication need not slacken with experience.

Perhaps the geratest threat to any revitalized progressive Republicanism is the false, debilitating call of "unity" (read: surrender or at least compromise). Unity based on a mutual examination of agreements and disagreements can be productive, and this process ultimately will be necessary in the Republican party. But, as evidenced repeatedly over the last five years, unadorned "unity" appeals are usually the ruse of the self-seeking or the reflex of the befuddled. Progressives should be skeptical toward any in their number who engage in public displays of pique or in any other form of personal angling at the expense of the cause. As for who is or is not a worthy leader within the movement, is it not sound to assume that the man who leads is the leader? While progressives have endlessly debated who *should* be their leader, few active leaders have actually emerged. The best test of who deserves the favor of conscious, committed progressives is that of who does the most in advancing the whole movement.

In no case does it behoove the progressives, who have problems enough, to split up the next two years over prospective Presidential candidates, for that is the most sure means of re-creating the nightmare of 1964, or almost as bad, the nomination of a compromise mediocrity whose defeat, like a rightist's, would not even have the beneficial side effect of building the party for the future.

The progressives should eventually look for a Presidential nominee who has unequivocally faced the party's need for reform. No other candidate could gain the confidence of the mass of American voters, nearly 75 percent of whom are non-Republicans. Such a candidate does not need experience and longtime familiarity with the voters (which may actually be a handicap for several of the more prominent possibilities) so much as an informed and credible approach to the issues, in turn displaying originality of thought and expression. The man, and not the office from which he runs, should be the main focus of the progressive search come 1968 and 1972. In other words, mayors, congressmen and distinguished private citizens, as well as governors and senators, should be considered. The wrong man running from the right office, if he is a Republican, will lose. The right man running from the wrong office will build the party, and might win.

It may be asked if these proposals for progressive Republicans do not represent just a moderate version of the Goldwater movement, a manifest attempt to promote a narrow range of opinion, even at the expense of the party. This easy interpretation would be wholly incorrect, however. It is the Republican party, as an organically evolving political instrument, that holds the chief political allegiance of progressives. That allegiance can be strained, as it was in 1964, only when the party foolishly prostitutes its heritage, not in the name of honorable compromise, but on behalf of doctrine traditionally alien to it. The organization that party progressives envisage is broadly inclusive, welcoming and not just tolerating controversy, knowing that vitality is often the product of debate and that vitality is the party's overarching need. They would exclude from the party only the zanies and segregationists of the radical right, whose presence in it today is indefensible in the face of the party's unmistakable heritage and in the face of political reality. They represent a wall against the entry into the party of thinking independents and Democrats, whose conversion is elementary to the party's construction of any new political majority.

This position of firmness, however, should not preclude extending an open hand of understanding to right-wingers in general and even some individual "kooks." There are a few fanatics in every movement (probably even an "extreme moderate" somewhere), and they are a burden for any responsible leadership. But as Dr. Louis Levin, professor of psychology at San Francisco State College urged in a 1964 speech, responsible Republicans should "keep the lines open," even to the radical right, in hopes that through personal realtionships the veil of aloofness that often creates unreasoning suspicion might be lifted. "Some knowledge of analytical psychiatry would be helpful," said Levin, "but lacking that be sure of your facts and good luck."

None of the radical right, of course, are immediate prospects for progressive Republicanism. The responsible right-winger is another matter. Much of the internal Republican conflict—that which derives from the old Taft-Eisenhower, "conservative"-"modern" split—is superficial and subject to negotiation. Here is where the dialogue must take place, over time and in depth, if real Republican unity is to evolve. The meeting of the professed "conservatives" and "progressives" is propitious if for just the two reasons that they both view reality without illusions about the nature of the electorate or the patriotism of the other participants in the political system and because they both share a primary political devotion to the Republican party. Indeed, the 1964 experience converted many an individual arch-rightist to a more moderate stance, and the process of regeneration is, in this sense, already underway. If the party can develop a coherent, responsible, and distinctive approach to the issues, the progressives and reasonable conservatives may in fact be able to unify behind it.

Part Five

‹‹

PRINCIPLES
IN PRACTICE

◇◇

CHAPTER 17

Needed: An Ideology

THE PRIME need of progressive Republicanism today is a distinct ideological identity. This need is dramatized by the strange impotence in party councils of two leading Republican vote-getters, Senator Thomas H. Kuchel of California and Mayor John V. Lindsay of New York. Any number of others are similarly blighted, but Kuchel and Lindsay are more striking in their manifest qualifications for leadership and their practical incapacity to lead their party.

Senator Kuchel, as minority whip in the U. S. Senate and the leading vote-getter in the most populous state in the country, should have been—by conventional political logic—a leading contender for the Presidential nomination in 1964. Yet he was barely considered. In the end he found himself at the head of the losing California primary campaign of Nelson Rockefeller against the junior senator from the neighboring expanses of sand to the East. Mayor Lindsay has as great personal appeal and charisma as any other Republican. He is as well endowed intellectually, and as articulate, as any officeholder with the possible exception of his New York colleague, Senator Jacob K. Javits. But Lindsay, too, is a Republican leader only in a selective, *ad hoc* way. He does not lend his party anywhere near his full potentialities for leadership.

Lindsay was perhaps the most valuable U. S. congressman. He was valuable because he was unique, and he enacted his uniqueness frequently on the floor of the House—by standing alone, with the constitution, and building in the end a majority on the conscience of a true conservative. In fact, John Lindsay was probably the only congressman often to have given substance to that old and optimistic maxim about the power of one man and the truth. The power of his truths was their frequent ability to animate the conscience of the Republican party.

In particular instances, Lindsay's truths were rarely popular. Where a determined majority in 1959, swept with brush-fire indignation, saw a needed attack on pornography, Lindsay found an unwarranted grant of arbitrary power to the Post Office Department. He voted alone in opposition, and the bill was finally revised in the Senate according to his recommendations. In August, 1962, an overwhelming congressional majority was ready to support an Administration request for extension of security regulations to private university and industrial personnel working on national-security projects. Lindsay assailed the measure as an unwarranted and unprecedented invasion of the rights of individuals and private businesses. Arguing that the bill would give the federal government the power to deprive up to five million private citizens of their jobs without due process, Lindsay first objected, alone, to its passage on the unanimous-consent calendar. Then he objected again with five others (the requisite six), including Republicans Curtis of Missouri and MacGregor of Minnesota, and again succeeded in blocking passage of the bill by unanimous consent. Finally he mustered 128 congressmen against the bill—including such a right-wing Republican as Alger of Texas—just over the third of the membership necessary to require submission of the bill for amendment on the floor of the House. Thus the Democratic Administration was effectively thwarted in a new attempt to pry into the personal lives of employees at colleges and businesses across the country.

These initially lonely, but later vindicated stands, ostensibly in behalf of pornography and communism (Lindsay is said to have said jokingly to Charles Halleck that these were big industries in his district) are typical of the former congressman's record. His 1959 pornography vote won him a personal tour, guided by Postmaster General Arthur Summerfield, through the chamber of pornographic horrors which Summerfield kept in the basement of the Post Office Department to titillate visiting lobbyists into supporting anti-pornography legislation. Lindsay was nauseated by the experience (by all reports it would nauseate any sentient human), but he does not think with his guts when constitutional rights are at stake. He left unpersuaded that Summerfield (who later became a leading Goldwaterite) should have the right to stop and frisk any mail he pleases.

Other vanguard positions taken by the New York Republican included his attack on the anti-poll tax amendment to the Constitution (a "bad precedent"—"tinkering with the document for trivial purposes" when a statute would suffice); his fight to transfer the functions of the inquisitional House Un-American Activities Committee to the Judiciary Committee, a body which is aware of the First Amendment; his innumerable efforts in behalf of artists and writers; his early advocacy of a Department of Urban Affairs; his support for the creation of an Atlantic Parliamentary Assembly; and his advocacy of a congressional committee to oversee the two-billion-dollar operations of the CIA.

On most of these issues Lindsay was defeated. But the stands he took were valuable and he can expect many of them to be accepted in the future.

But if Lindsay was sometimes known as "the representative from the Constitution," he was also the representative of the Seventeenth Congressional District of New York, extending along the East side of Manhattan, from Greenwich Village through fashionable midtown and on to Spanish Harlem. In his devotion to the interests and dispositions of this, the nation's most sophisticated constituency, Lindsay came close to parochialism. He allowed himself to be confined by his district as much as any congressmen from downstate Illinois. One Republican legislator from California, so tied to the particular prejudices of his own suburban constituency that he opposed the 1964 Civil Rights Bill, answered a Lindsay speech about the mainstream of the Republican party with the comment: "John's idea of the mainstream is at the bottom of a well in Manhattan." The charge has some validity. Although Lindsay's services to his pullulating district made him one of the most widely active, constructive, and knowledgeable of all the members of the House, he was rarely inclined to transcend his district to make the contributions to the national Republican party which his talents would have made possible. He did not become a national party leader; and his failure is not satisfactorily explained either by his militant efforts in behalf of civil liberties, or his long confinement to the position of congressman from New York by Republican control of the higher state offices.

The larger problem is ideological. John Lindsay, like most progressive Republicans, is ideologically adrift. Although many of his specific positions on the issues, separately considered, seem to identify him with the Democratic liberals; although he would have been welcomed exultantly by the Democratic party in New York where some Republicans still look on him with sullen skepticism; and although as a Democrat, Lindsay would undoubtedly have been a national leader with no trouble escaping from the Seventeenth District, he categorically rejects the Democratic party. But like most progressive Republicans he has yet to develop a distinctively Republican identity; he has yet to develop a Republican ideology which offers a comprehensive critique of Democratic liberalism, a Republican ideology oriented to the city but nonetheless recognizable and appealing to members of his party across the country. He *has* made efforts. His testimony before the Platform Committee was a start; so was an article in *Harper's Magazine* on the Republican responsibility on civil liberties.¹ His position papers in the New York mayoralty race, though in most cases avoiding identifiable Republican rhetoric, contributed to his ideological development, and a book, collecting his past writings, will also be helpful. But he has not gone far enough; nor has he gone nearly as far as he could go without compromising any of his principles. So he has not been an effective leader in the national party, despite the fact that his party, and particularly the responsible majority in it, desperately needs the urban leadership which he almost uniquely could give, particularly in the primaries and in the election of 1968.

Now, Lindsay's immersion in the microcosmopolitan tangle of New York City politics has been deepened by his election as mayor. Lindsay retains an intense concern for the plight of his party nationally; but he has been cut off still further from its partisan ideological development. Although his victory inspired Republicans across the country, Lindsay himself was forced—by the Democratic preponderance in the city and by William F. Buckley's kamikaze dive² upon him from the right— to renounce all the partisan implications of his approach. Pointing out that "there is no Republican or Democratic way to clean the streets," he proceeded with a campaign ostensibly devoid of Republican ideology. Yet, obviously there was a Republican-Liberal way, for example, to use the park land in the city; to encourage the emergence of new businesses; and to bring back from the suburbs some of the departed members of the middle class, with their heavier proportionate tax contribution and more independent view of the city's politics. And above all, there was the Republican-Liberal assertion of the transcending claims of the city as a whole against the special demands of the strategically placed interest groups and ethnic blocs which dominate the New York Democratic party.

1 September, 1963.
2 For this phrase, the authors express their gratitude to Barry Goldwater, who used it at the 1965 *National Review* Fund-raising Dinner held in New York the week after the election.

The Democratic conception depends on the group-con-
ciousness of the blocs, and thus, to a degree, on maintaining
antagonisms among them. Lindsay promised a reorganization of
the political process, offering access to a greater citizenship for
millions of New Yorkers previously bound to a narrow conception
of their interests and affiliations by the ward-boss mentality of
the Democratic leadership. The Republican approach was
founded on a vision of the New Yorker as a responsible individual
citizen of the greater urban community rather than as a pawn
to be bought with the favors and patronage of a political "power-
broker." Such an approach has obvious partisan ideological
implications in a country where most of the biggest cities are
dominated by Democrats with the computing-machine view of
politics.

Lindsay believed there was still more to his Republicanism.
But it was so much a part of him, so deeply ingrained in a
temperament fundamentally but complexly conservative, that it
could not be expounded in the midst of a campaign in an overwhelming Democratic city. However, if Lindsay ever wishes to
move beyond New York, to communicate with Republicans across
the country, he must make explicit and coherent his Republicanism and present it as an ideology for an urban America.

Senator Kuchel's situation is somewhat akin to Lindsay's
and perhaps even more illustrative of the debilitating effects
of ideological failure, since the Californian, as senior senator
from his state and minority whip, occupies far more important
official positions in his party than does Lindsay, and was little
more effective in stopping the Goldwater movement.

In fact, Senator Kuchel's relative impotence on the national
scene is as remarkable a political phenomenon in its way as
Senator Goldwater's strength. There is no obvious reason for
the Californian's weakness. Unlike Lindsay, Senator Kuchel is
not a New Yorker, anathema to the presently buoyant know-nothing and bigot wings of his party. Also unlike the former congressman (and incidentally, Senator Javits), Kuchel is not associated
in the public mind with Eastern urban liberalism and its am-

bience of immigrants, minority groups, and left-wing radicalism. Senator Kuchel's ADA and ACA ratings are somewhat to the left of the mean of Senate Republicanism, but not prohibitively so, and he is well to the right of most Senate Democrats and several Republicans. His voting record, that is to say, places him in that position slightly left of the Republican center shared by the last four Republican Presidential candidates before Barry Goldwater, and well within the American political consensus as reflected in public-opinion polls and national elections over the last quarter century.

The ostensible superiority of Senator Kuchel over Goldwater as a Presidential possibility goes well beyond geographical location and voting record. Kuchel is respected in the Senate as an attentive and hard-working legislative leader; Goldwater enjoyed little respect from his Senate colleagues. Kuchel has a distinguished academic record; Goldwater is an early college dropout. Kuchel is circumspect and responsible in his public statements; Goldwater is impulsive and volatile. It is true that Goldwater is considered a more colorful and ingratiating political personality than the somewhat saturnine Californian. But personality alone, though it might bear on Kuchel's failure to acquire the nomination, cannot explain the enormous disparity in national and party influence between the two men. For Kuchel's influence on the national party over the years when Goldwater took it over was small in proportion to his status and ability.

The key, of course, lies in a further element of contrast between the two senators. Barry Goldwater is the proponent of a distinctive Republican ideology that carries a wide-ranging critique of the prevailing approach of Democratic liberalism. Senator Kuchel, it is hardly unfair to say, offers no coherent ideology. He is a distinguished and responsible senator, with a remarkable knack for assisting and pleasing his heterogeneous constituency. But his ideology reduces to amorphous moderation, combined with vehement opposition to the most virulent extremists and with strong support for civil-rights and pro-labor legislation, reflecting his strong minority-group and labor backing. These attitudes fail to distinguish him from many Democrats. Nor do they contribute to a Republican critique of the opposition.

Kuchel and Lindsay are by no means alone in their dilemma. But their exceptional potentialities make their failures most conspicuous. Their dilemma is shared by most responsible Republicans. The problem can be stated simply. The progressive Republicans—individually and collectively—have failed to produce a distinctive political ideology to meet the needs of opposition after the Eisenhower years. A political ideology may be defined as a systematic statement of ideas or doctrines designed to justify and rationalize the pursuit or possession of political power—a statement of goals and programs. Progressive Republicans, to a degree almost unique in world politics, lack an articulated ideology. This deficiency severely hampers them in the pursuit of national power. But more than just an ideology— for many progressive Republicans do have an ideology of sorts, which might be called "amorphous moderation"—they need a distinctively Republican ideology, one that can acquire general support within their own party as well as among the American people. The ideology of Hubert H. Humphrey will not do, nor that of Lyndon B. Johnson.

The attempts that have been made to develop a progressive Republican ideology have so far been inadequate. At best they have had a synthetic quality, smacking of contrivance; at worst they have been directly imitative; and most of the time they have been aimlessly eclectic—a selection of positions and postures without thematic coherence.

In its synthetic form, progressive Republicanism is best represented by Senator Javits, who is perhaps the most knowledgeable and articulate man in either party in the Congress, and is to be commended for his awareness of the ideological problem and for his energetic attempts to solve it. But he has not yet succeeded in propounding a satisfactory progressive Republicanism. His book, *Order of Battle*[3] has an air of synthetic rationalizing which is not dispelled by his invocations of Repub-

[3] New York: Atheneum; 1964.

lican platitudes or his sound and constructive proposals. *National Review's* assertion that it could have been written by a liberal Democrat is substantially valid. Indeed, just months later, Hubert Humphrey brought his lesser intelligence to bear on the subject and wrote a book, *The Cause is Mankind,*[4] almost identical in its ideological premises. But it is a measure of the gravity of the problem that *Order of Battle* remains the best published statement of progressive Republicanism since Arthur Larson's *A Republican Looks at His Party,*[5] an eminently satisfactory effort at a time when the Republicans controlled the Presidency, but inadequate now, with moderate Democrats in command.

Javits bases his argument on the notion that the Republican party through most of its history has been the party of the "national interest," seeking an accommodation between individual freedom and the collective welfare. However, the attainment of such an accommodation is the purpose of the American Constitution and in fact of all democratic politics. Javits cannot develop a distinctive Republicanism by stating unexceptionable truisms as Republican dogma. Humphrey's book makes the same claim for the Democratic party: that *it* is the party of the national interest, seeking a similar accommodation between the freedom of the individual and the needs of the collectivity. So did Dean Acheson, in his *A Democrat Looks at His Party,*[6] published some years earlier. In terms of history Javits is simply making a partisan assertion—one with which we would agree—but not one which offers much guidance to the progressive Republican, whether responding to the issues of the day or to a pugnacious right-winger asking how he distinguishes himself from the Democrats.

The imitative approach lacks the intellectual sophistication and political self-consciousness of *Order of Battle* but ends up in substantially the same position: me-tooing the moderate Democrats. The imitative Republicans do not even try to offer an

[4] Frederick A. Praeger: New York; 1964.
[5] New York: Harper & Brothers; 1956.
[6] New York: Harper & Brothers; 1955.

ideological rationale. They are liberal because that is the way to win; they are Republicans, as both Clifford Case and William Scranton have argued at times in the past, because the party needs bright young liberals like them. Case fulfills his role as a member of the opposition by attacking the Democrats on non-ideological issues, like corruption and legislative inefficiency. Scranton has recently adopted the pragmatic-eclectic approach, interspersing his me-tooism with the more sensible right-wing positions, while taking a pragmatic conservative approach as governor. Senators Scott and Kuchel and Governor Rockefeller are also eclectic and pragmatic, though Rockefeller has come closer than any other Republican, which is not close enough, to the development of a sound and distinctive Republicanism. Since none has succeeded, it is difficult to blame anyone for failure, but Rockefeller's is the most poignant because he has shown the greatest promise of success, and because it is possible that if he had been nominated he would have developed a coherent progressive Republicanism before discrediting it in a defeat brought on in part by irrelevant personal factors.

The main lines of Rockefeller's ideological approach, never fully developed or prosecuted except on the state level, were a regenerated federalism, a more ideological and coherent foreign policy, and a more inventive and resourceful use of the private sector in solving national problems. Whether because of occasional staff resistance and the pressures of campaigning, or because of his long experience as a Washington administrator, Rockefeller never stated in full the ideological implications of his positions. At the time of his defeat in California, he had still to fulfill the promise of his book, *The Future of Federalism*,[7] written three years before. But his speeches represent the best attempt so far to produce a progressive Republican ideology. He had shown the way.

It will be objected that many of the most successful American politicians have lacked a systematically articulate ideology. This is true. Dwight Eisenhower, for instance, never expressed

[7] New York: Atheneum; 1963.

a coherent ideology, though some of his supporters developed "modern Republicanism." Nor did Johnson, until after his accidental accession to the Presidency and to a new constituency, when he moved to espouse his own variant of Democratic liberalism.

It will be objected further, that the Democrats as a party also lack a coherent ideology, and it is true that both American parties are inclusive and pragmatic, particularly when they command the Presidency. However, the collected speeches of John F. Kennedy in 1960, as well as recent Democratic platforms, constitute an eloquent statement of what has become most emphatically the Democratic ideology. In its essentials it is managerial and centralist, committed to the use of federal power for the solution of social and economic problems. Urban decay, racial discrimination, poverty, unemployment, agricultural imbalance, educational inadequacies—all are to be abolished in the liberal agenda through the managerial activities of the federal government. Democratic liberalism goes on to project itself, with scarcely tempered optimism, to the international arena, where it would negotiate peace and again eradicate poverty. The outline is sweeping, but little more than the liberal ambition and its ideological expression. Lyndon Johnson has not diminished, but extended, the compass of the ideal, embracing the business community and state and local governments in the grasp of its benevolence. His grand scheme with its historical inspiration in the myth of the New Deal, saving the country from depression and civil turbulence, and with its vision of a Great Society, transfigured by benevolent government and technology—this is an ideology and it has served its party well; this is an idea infused with a will, expatiated in detailed programs, evoked in lilting rhetoric, and projected with a sure sense of political theatrics. This is the kind of ideological style which Barry Goldwater shares with the Democrats, minus the detailed programs, and which the more responsible Republicans lack.

Of course there are many ways of gaining political power in the United States beyond ideology—personality and technical

political skill among them—and there are many constructive
roles in American politics where strong ideological commitment
or reputation may be a hindrance—chairman of the National
Committee, majority or minority leader of the Senate being pos-
sibly among them. Yet it remains nonetheless true that an
ideology, preferably not rigid or extreme, but one which offers
an alternative to and a critique of the opposition party, is an
enormous advantage both in intraparty competition and in effective national leadership or legislative action. It is moreover
true that, though an individual politician can sometimes do
without an ideology, a national political movement cannot, for
it needs an ideology to identify itself and hold itself together.
The lack of an ideological posture, critically distinct from the
Democrats, is one of the crucial reasons for the relative
impotence of nationally prestigious men like Kuchel and Scott
and for the absence of an effective progressive Republican movement.

This ideological problem had its roots over three decades
ago in the party's failure to find an adequate response to the
New Deal and the Democratic coalition it created. In the Congress the party has long been divided between those who attempt
a defeatist and self-defeating imitation of the Democrats, and
those who try a stultifying holding operation against them. In
Presidential campaigns ever since 1940 Republicans have avoided
ideology as if it were a criminal offense, punishable by four years
of confinement in high political office, beset by national problems
best left to the Democrats, who believe in them. Republicans
have sought unity not in a new, distinctively Republican program,
but in resort to non-ideological issues like communism, corruption, and Korea—a retreat from ideology which at times, under
Dewey in 1948 and Eisenhower in 1952, seemed a retreat from
partisan politics itself. The party's platforms were usually as
controversial and as inspiring as the Boy Scout Code.

The one exception to this pattern remains instructive. In
Wendell Willkie's campaign in 1940 the party offered a constructive alternative to the increasingly irrelevant and reflexive cen-

tralism of the New Deal. Willkie rejected the advice of most
party leaders and refused to make an important partisan issue
out of the increasing American involvement in the European
war. Instead, he concentrated his attack where the Democrats
were considered strongest, on economic issues. Proudly accepting
the Republican association with the business community, he
denounced the then-fashionable leftist prejudices against it, and
bluntly demanded "a completely new attitude on the part of
government." "We want no more epithets. We want no more
attacks on the men who make money. We want more men who
make money."[8] Willkie's appeal was exhilarating for the party
because it provided for a direct and dramatic confrontation of
the Democrats without resort to demagogic posturing or sterile
dogmatism. Willkie accepted most New Deal reforms and made
a practice of attacking the Democrats only in those areas where
he could provide alternative programs. Yet he was in no sense
an ideological me-tooer. He rejected emphatically the Fabian
precepts of the Democratic program; his program was distinctively
progressive Republican, and effectively conservative in its skepticism toward centralist planning and in its celebration of the
potentialities of the private economy if emancipated by a sympathetic government. This approach afforded the party its best
chance for victory, and its best guide for effective national leadership. Despite the international crisis, favoring the incumbent
Roosevelt, and despite sometimes inept personal campaigning,
Willkie received a greater popular vote than any Republican
Presidential candidate between 1928 and 1952.

By 1944, however, the party returned to its haven if ideological banality. The platform and the candidate equivocated on
ideological issues. Thomas E. Dewey had made his reputation as
a swashbuckling attorney general in New York, bringing numerous
underworld leaders to justice; he argued during the Presidential
campaign that his understanding of the "gangster mentality"
well equipped him to deal with the gangsters then at loose in

[8] Carl Joyner: *The Republican Dilemma* (Tucson: University of Arizona
Press; 1963).

international politics. The rest of his campaign was shrouded in the clouds of Republican ambivalence toward the New Deal. Dewey spent part of his time in lame attacks on Democratic radicalism, and part in answering Democratic charges that he opposed the New Deal and, like all Republicans, enjoyed seeing poor people suffer. The idea of a new, distinctively Republican synthesis apparently never occurred to him.

The ideological retreat became a deliberate strategy in 1948. Dewey had spent almost a decade in politics without asserting strong positions on the issues. Without ideological entanglement he had been an effective attorney general and governor of New York and had been nominated twice by his party for the Presidency. He was not impressed by Harry Truman and his ideological aggressiveness, which managed to split his party into three factions. Dewey did not like the heat and he would stay out of Mr. Truman's kitchen. Truman's unexpected victory was achieved largely through his clear assertion of Democratic liberalism against an opponent attempting to avoid the issues; it well demonstrated the utility of clear and emphatic ideological commitment in inspiring party morale and effectiveness.

In 1952 the Republicans were preparing to turn to the only coherent ideology they had: Robert Taft's conventional Republican conservatism. They were weary of the politics of foggy ambivalence, and there was no progressive Republican in view who could provide an emphatically Republican approach. The party had twice nominated the paladin of Eastern progressive Republicanism, Thomas Dewey, and he had conducted campaigns which were not only ideologically vapid but also practically ineffectual. The instinct that inclined the party toward Taft in 1952 thus was readily understandable, even sound. The progressives did not seem to have anything better to offer. The Republicans, for better or worse, seemed about to deal in ideology in a Presidential campaign for the first time since 1940. Although the ideology was a sterile reprise of the microcosmic economics of the National Association of Manufacturers, it did offer an alternative to Democratic liberalism.

At the last moment, however, the Republicans were saved again from the perils of ideology. A barrage of polls showing that Taft could not win led to the nomination of General Dwight Eisenhower, who seemed to have few clear political views at all beyond a visible distaste for politics itself. Like Dewey before him and Nixon afterwards, he was not clearly identified with distinctive positions on the issues. In the absence of a cogent progressive Republicanism, the Republicans again showed their preference for banality as against a right-wing dogmatism which however inspiring it was to many of the most active party members, portended defeat.

It is one thing, however, to win an election as Eisenhower did, and another to assume management of a national administration faced with numerous and complex national problems. Soon after he took office Eisenhower began to develop a modern Republican ideology, reflected in Arthur Larson's book, *A Republican Looks at His Party*. Larson, Undersecretary of Labor, writing before the 1956 campaign, argued that Republicans had created a new national consensus founded on the creative practical application of the traditional Republican approaches. Most important were faith and confidence in private enterprise and in local and state government; the use of the federal government to regulate and free, not control or appropriate, the private sector of the economy; acceptance of New Deal reforms; and firmness in foreign policy based on a belief that the fundamental cold-war issues could not be resolved in summary negotiations.

This ideology was a significant new element in the 1956 campaign. Eisenhower's massive victory, with a popular-vote margin nearly twice as large as in 1952 when he was a military hero with no apparent ideological convictions at all, seemed to support Larson's view that the Republicans had formed a new national consensus. Adlai Stevenson, the Democratic nominee, was forced to resort to the proposals of the far left—unilateral suspension of nuclear testing, abolition of the draft on fuzzily argued humanitarian grounds—and finally to unbecoming innuendos about the President's health. Campaigning for Congress across the country, it was the Democrats who adopted the baldest me-tooism, arguing that they would give more consistent support to Eisenhower than members of his own party.

Modern Republicanism lost its ideological impetus during Eisenhower's second term when the President subsumed the party's national image into his own and absorbed himself in defending his military policies and maintaining the cold-war detente with the Soviet Union. In domestic affairs the President's leadership consisted of a holding operation against the congressional Democrats. His public statements rang with platitudinous celebrations of free enterprise, fiscal integrity, and peace—all suffused with his own personal magnetism. The people did not seem to mind that he lacked coherent ideological commitment and that his domestic policies after 1956 had become a series of negative reflexes. Eisenhower's Administration ended as it began—inarticulate domestically—and with the President traveling around the world to bring his goodwill to bear on international politics.

The year 1960 called for a vigorous and emphatic revival of the modern Republican ideology and the consensus around it. As in 1956 the Democrats should have been forced to make a choice between me-tooism and the proposals of the doctrinaire left. The Republican candidate, however, was not inclined toward ideological politics. Like every Republican Presidential candidate since Wendell Willkie, Nixon had gained his national reputation without dealing in controversial political ideas. Dewey had distinguished himself in the war against crime, Eisenhower in the war against Axis imperialism, and Nixon in the war against Alger Hiss. This background of nonpartisan crusade, common to all three, gave them no preparation for ideological combat. In the cases of Dewey and Nixon, the weakness was fatal.

When Nixon was put on the ticket in 1952, the issue of internal communism still retained a residual impact.[9] However, with

[9] Communism had become a political issue in the U.S. through allegations that members of the Communist party were holding high positions in the government. Since neither party *advocated* Communist appointments, the dispute concerned the validity of the charges of infiltration not its desirability, and thus was not an ideological issue but a question of fact.

the election of Eisenhower and the censure of Senator McCarthy, it became academic at best. Yet during his eight years as Vice-President, and his campaigns for the Presidency and the governorship of California, and even his campaign on behalf of the New Jersey gubernatorial candidate in 1965, he never developed another issue. He *trafficked* in other issues: civil rights, states' rights, free enterprise, international firmness, and big government. But he never committed his political personality to them and attracted support as the best vehicle for a particular political program. Nixon always gave the impression of an aimless tactician.

The 1960 campaign provided him and the Republicans with their last chance to build on the ideology and consensus championed by Dwight Eisenhower in 1956 but allowed to languish during his final three years. At first Nixon seemed to sense the opportunity, and he adopted much of Rockefeller's program for the platform. But he never fully committed himself to the progressive Republican approach he professed to adopt at the convention. If he had prosecuted his platform positions resourcefully in the campaign—in civil rights, welfare, economic growth, federal-state relations, and foreign policy and defense—he would have driven Kennedy to the defensive, and compelled the Democrats to adopt a posture of me-tooism, or far-left critique, like Stevenson in 1956. But, instead, most dramatically in the television debates, Nixon allowed Kennedy to take the offense. Nixon assumed postures in response to Kennedy's programs. Never did he project a systematic ideological commitment, asserting his own goals for the American future. Kennedy stated the goals; Nixon offered marginal comments and criticism on his opponent's choice of means.

His failure in the 1960 election was a disaster for the Republican party. Soon after the election the Democrats moved to form a new political consensus. No longer were they relegated, as in 1956, to the insular provinces of the doctrinaire left; the Democrats moved to the center and proclaimed that their solutions to the problems facing the nation were the only solutions. In the absence of a constructive Republican alternative, the Democratic claim assumed a surface plausibility. It was then the Republicans found themselves as isolated as the Democrats in 1956, by the command and articulation of the American consensus by an incumbent Administration. Under Goldwater the Republicans attempted to go outside the consensus and appeal to covert prejudices and fears, and the result was abysmal defeat. Progressive Republicans chose to work within the consensus and thus reinforce it and American unity at the same time. But with the Democrats in control of national power, attempting at once to reflect, affirm, and influence the consensus, the Republicans had difficulty identifying themselves with it without identifying themselves with the Democrats.

Barry Goldwater's campaign against Lyndon Johnson in 1964 bore a significant resemblance to the Democratic campaigns against Dwight Eisenhower, particularly in 1956. In both instances a dearth of politically promising issues led in the end to an unreflected call for termination of the draft, to promises of a tax cut, and to the issue of the President's health, and the political views of his prospective successor. In neither case—the Stevensonian Democrats against Eisenhower or the Goldwater Republicans against Johnson—was the opposition capable of the ideological creativity necessary to unsettle a popular incumbent President astride the moderate national consensus. In both races the challenging candidate found himself moderating his views as the campaign progressed. Although Stevenson, more moderate to begin with, did not have to change as much, he fudged his position on the draft, and his bold call for a unilateral suspension of nuclear testing diminished into an appeal for a temporary moratorium to allow for negotiations. Goldwater compromised everywhere except on civil rights. His advocacy of voluntary social security became a proposal to strengthen the program, his categorical appeal for suspension of diplomatic relations with the Soviet Union became a conditional suggestion for reconsideration of all our relations with the Communist world, and Victory in the Cold War succumbed to Peace as the paramount purpose of our military strength.

Of course Goldwater's approach, even though somewhat veiled, was more ideological than any other Republican campaign in recent years. Goldwater had hoped and promised to win through ideology, and he did appreciate far more than most Republicans its value in arousing somnolent party workers and supporters, and in capturing the idealistic imagination of youth. But Goldwater's stands were too extreme and uncompromising, too radically different from the traditional views of his party, too unresponsive to the real problems of the people to gain fully even the advantage among party regulars and youth. Moreover, he sacrificed almost entirely the other advantage of an ideological appeal: its potential usefulness in attracting intellectuals, apathetic Democrats, and independents into the party. His ideology worked well only among a small minority of intellectuals and young people, among a substantial minority of party workers, and among radical-rightists and segregationists. But these successes, though significant, were dwarfed by the failure of his attempts to attract a national consensus, if only the consensus against atheism and crime, and he was engulfed by the consensus for a temperate foreign policy and for civil rights. In his belated and half-hearted compromises, he only managed to impair his reputation for honesty. And so, like Stevenson before him in 1956, he lost his crusade and the election, too.

Thus Democrats and Republicans alike work under the sway of the moderate consensus, commanded and defined by the incumbent President, whether Eisenhower or Johnson. Under Eisenhower the consensus was couched in Republican terms and shaped by a Republican ideology; under Johnson it is oriented to the liberal Democratic ideology. But in neither case is it bound to doctrinaire precepts which strongly alienate great segments of the electorate. Eisenhower was more conservative than Johnson, but he increased the minimum wage, raised the national standards for unemployment compensation, increased social-security benefits, established a Department of Health, Education, and Welfare, opposed a national right-to-work law, and sent troops into Little Rock, Arkansas, to enforce the Supreme Court's desegregation rul-

268 / THE PARTY THAT LOST ITS HEAD

ing. Kennedy and Johnson were more liberal than Eisenhower, but they supported passage of a tax cut of unprecedented size and so advantageous to business that it was bitterly attacked as a regressive measure by several militant liberals in the Senate. Moreover, Johnson's general attitude toward business has been so favorable that he received the support of the National Chambers of Commerce. Through its victory in 1964 the Democratic party finally has succeeded in eschewing its anachronistic hostility to business, assailed by Willkie in 1940 and once the most serious weakness of its ideological position. In sum, Johnson has been allowed by the Republicans to usurp much of the Eisenhower consensus and make it his own and his party's. Even the Democratic division on the race issue, once so damaging, has been mitigated by the passage of the Civil Rights Act, the loss of Strom Thurmond to the GOP, and Republican obtuseness and prejudice on the issue of self-government for the District of Columbia.

The all-encompassing sweep of the new Democratic ideology poses an agonizing problem for the Republican party, and especially its progressives. It makes the failure of party leadership of men like Kuchel and Lindsay both more difficult and more imperative to overcome. The problem will not be solved unless its essential nature is recognized. Potential leaders in the party must recognize that unless they take a new creative approach to ideology they may find themselves, like the moderate socialists of the thirties, superannuated as a partisan force at the very time many of their views are being vindicated in acceptance by the national administration. Goldwater showed in 1964 the appeal of an ideological crusade to many Republicans. All but the racists and right-wing extremists can be equally attracted to another Republican crusade, aimed not at the prejudices of the past but toward a regeneration of the best in the Republican heritage.

CHAPTER 18

The Relevance
of Conservatism

I N DEVELOPING a new ideological approach of their own in domestic policy, the progressives must begin by recognizing the fact that the Republican party during this century has become the conservative party in the United States. Although it may not be politic after the Goldwater aberration for the party to emphasize its "conservatism" as such, and although the Republican party is by no means exclusively conservative, its prevailing leadership and the majority of its members impel it to take a dominantly conservative approach—both to most of the initiatives of the Democrats and to the radical forces of change in the modern world. The Goldwater approach has been at least nominally rejected. But the party will cling long to its identity as a defender of the Constitution, the role of the states, and the realm of private enterprise and individual opportunity against the encroachments of the federal government and other officious intruders.

Progressive Republicans should not imagine that they can or should transform the party into a vehicle of centralist liberalism of the kind which the Democrats have sporadically advanced over the last decades. By adopting such a position the progressives would only increase their own isolation and widen the party split. Rather, the objective of the progressive Republican should be to transform the Republican party into a responsible and effective conservative party and thus unify it, and make it into a party which advances its principles not only in rhetoric but in fact.

The country greatly needs a sound and constructive conservative party. It does not have one now. Rarely before in history have the principles of American conservatism been so truly in jeopardy. These principles assert as primary and interdependent goals of policy the maintenance of individual freedom, private economic opportunity, and decentralization of political and economic power. These comprise the most reiterated concerns of Republican philosophy. All are endangered by the dominant forces for change and progress in the country and in the world today: technology, industry, government, and military nationalism. Joined in a great bureaucratic complex, well developed in the more advanced countries and an aspiration in most of the rest, these forces pose a dire threat to conservative values. This is the real "alliance for progress" today. Its emphasis is on size, predictability, surveillance, and control; individual freedom and privacy, individual economic initiative, and political and economic decentralization all seem awkward and retrograde in the schemes of its servant bureaucrats.

In recent years those who proclaim themselves "conservatives" in the United States have done little to promote their principles against this new concert of opposition. The Democratic liberals, with their commitment to big government and federal planning, barely recognize the threat at all. If anything they advance it. But contrary to the usual conservative assumption, they advance it not so much by acts of commission but by acts of omission, by negligence in the defense of liberty. It is not so much high government spending, or expanding welfarism, which threatens liberty. It is undirected technocracy and bureaucracy in the private and semi-private, as well as the public, sectors of the economy; it is the degeneration of local and state government; it is the general confusion of the private and public, of the federal, state, and local, and of the economic and social spheres. In this confusion functions and responsibilities become dislocated—the private life of a worker becomes "socialized"; civilian defense is considered a local or private responsibility; individual farm planning becomes a federal concern; the income-tax law is employed to harass individuals who affront the government; and the military draft is used as a punishment for political dissent. Technocratic and bureaucratic values prevail at the expense of democratic and libertarian values. But conservatives, in their often justified efforts to limit federal power, have failed to develop programs to discipline and reorient the other forces in the society which threaten individual freedoms and opportunities; and they have failed to provide for the regeneration of local and state governments, necessary if a more rational and balanced division of labor between them and the federal government is to be achieved. These last few years of alleged "conservative revival" have in fact been years of conservative abdication.

Conservatism today is a more difficult and challenging political philosophy than the liberalism of the Democrats. It was to some degree the party's frustration with the difficulties of the conservative role that led the Republicans to their recent debacle. The agenda and prospectus of the conservative will rarely seem as inviting, his vision as utopian, or his triumphs as majestic as those invoked in the liberal melodrama. The liberal President proceeds from crisis to crisis, on an ideological "wave of the future," cresting in a foam of exalted oratory, the proclamation of national purposes, and the summoning of collective energies—all in military imagery, for wars on disease, poverty, crime, and other manifest evils. The conservative will use rhetoric, too, in a crisis, and he will summon the country to collective response when the threat is grave. But his triumph is to avoid conflict and crisis, not to invoke them; to guide and modulate change, not to command it. By the time a crisis erupts and the people clamor for federal action, the conservative has already failed in his initial cause. He has failed to anticipate the crisis with action to prevent it. He has failed to maintain the traditional institutions and processes of the society in sufficient order and responsiveness to manage the problem without new federal programs.

A considerable proportion of Democratic legislative proposals reflect real problems in the society which, for some reason, often a compelling one, have not been adequately alleviated or solved at the local or state level or in the private sector of the economy. Defeat of such proposals in Congress will not necessarily impel the solution of the problems locally or privately. Rather, it is likely to defer their solution until the need is so extreme and pressing that adequate treatment is impossible except through the blunt use of federal power; and legislative palliatives offered by the Democrats—irresponsible and ineffective though they sometimes are—gain wide support. The absence of constructive Republican proposals affords the impression that the Democratic approaches are the only alternative to neglect of the problems and thus almost ensures their passage.

This sequence can be illustrated by the farm problem and consequent attempts to plow it under with federal funds, by unemployment and its federal compensation and occasional promotion, by the emergence of slums and the unsuccessful efforts of federal housing programs to bulldoze them away, and by protracted failures of collective bargaining and the imposition of compulsory arbitration. In each instance, early attention to the source of the problem—the failure of the established private and local procedures to operate effectively—might have obviated extensive federal intervention later. Failure to act resulted in federal measures sometimes offensive to the true conservative. Yet the offensive measures in each instance were as much the result of the early failure of the conservatives as of the irresponsibility of the liberals.

The failure of the conservatives has been most dramatic in the field of civil rights and it bears important lessons for the future. Both the Southern diehards and the Northern gradualists have rationalized their positions with reference to "conservatism."

Yet "conservatism" as it is conceived by those who use the term most insistently in America, was no longer relevant, and its prescriptions no longer applicable to this problem by the time it erupted into crisis in the late fifties and early sixties. By obstructing change, the conservatives could only intensify it.

Over a decade ago, when the Supreme Court outlawed segregation in the schools, appeals for changes in "the hearts and minds of men," appeals for law and order, cautions about the inefficiency of "bundles of laws," might have been relevant and important. But at that time many conservatives, and almost all those in the South, attacked the Supreme Court ruling. Far from undertaking a campaign to "change the hearts and minds of men" by educating them in the new realities, Southern "conservatives" exploited and reinforced the prejudices of their constituencies. They deceitfully prattled "states rights" and "property rights," engendering Negro contempt for both. Asked about court-ordered desegegration, they said "never," thus mocking their own appeals for "law and order." Even many non-Southern conservatives like Barry Goldwater and magazines like *National Review* indulged and propagated the Southern fantasies.

But even if Southern politicians were inclined to undertake the task, it soon became too late to change hearts and minds without new laws—some of which indeed overrode the traditional boundaries of federal responsibility, some of which did indeed seem objectionable in the abstract, did seem to distend the constitutional mandate of the federal government in such areas as voting requirements and public accommodations. By the late fifties and early sixties the point of no return had been passed; if the federal government had not intervened, even more extreme federal action, perhaps comparable to the Civil War Reconstruction period, would have become necessary.

Of course this familiar pattern of local and private negligence and ultimate federal usurpation did not bother the liberals. It is the conservatives who suffer ideological pain. But by the time of the crisis, conservatives and liberals alike had no valid choice except to support comprehensive legislation to provide the Negro with an alternative to civil disobedience or humiliating submission to injustice.

As it was, the "conservatives," in the course of their obstruction, alienated the large body of Negroes who had previously identified themselves with the Republican party, and estranged another large proportion of the Negro community from the very values and institutions of American democracy. As many radicals clearly see today, their most numerous and militant allies and potential allies are Negroes, and they are radical not only in their purposes—often the dissolution of the rights of the states, and a basic restructuring of the economy, for instance—but also in their methods—direct action, and among a significant number, civil disobedience. These attitudes and techniques, adopted by much of the new generation of young Negro leaders and intellectuals, promise in the future to make them an important force for radical change in American society.

But there was little inherently radical about the civil-rights movement. Its original objectives were unexceptionable, even "conservative." The established civil-rights organizations have shown persistent concern for traditional American principles of justice, democracy, and orderly change. American Negroes have dreamed and sustained the American dream of equal opportunity for everyone to reach the top. It has been an American Negro, James Baldwin, who has perhaps most clearly diagnosed the American sickness—our inability to come to terms with our identity as a racially mixed nation—and most eloquently envisioned the new American promise—as the first nation to achieve a full multi-racial reconcilation within a constitutional democracy. The civil-rights movement became radical primarily as the avenues for orderly, institutional change were foreclosed by misguided and self-defeating "conservatives."

Those who regard the conservation of balanced federalism and individual freedom in its economic as well as political aspects as prime values bear a heavy responsibility. They must be vigilant to succeed. They must anticipate problems and mobilize against them before their symptoms require expedient treatment. They must not reject programs of judicious governmental attention or they often will find themselves faced with the necessity for extreme governmental action.

The validity of the true conservative position depends upon the essential health and versatility of the political and economic structures. When either fails gravely in some respect, as both have failed on the racial question, the federal government usually must subvene. The responsibility of the conservative is to prevent the original failure rather than the later subvention. The constructive conservative attempts to anticipate the crisis with legislation or private action which remedies its causes and obviates the need for abrupt and usurpatory federal intervention. But when, as in the case of civil rights, it becomes clear that extensive federal intervention will be necessary to prevent social disruption and conflict, or simply to achieve justice, the conservative should be the first to advocate such intervention. Delay will only exacerbate grievances and polarize opinions, making the problem more intractable and increasing the severity of the government action that ultimately must occur. The first lesson which American conservatives should learn is the fact that time is often against them, and that obstruction and delay in a situation of marked grievance will often intensify the grievance and the ultimate change it may impel.

The far right of the Republican party and the Democratic left converge in rejecting this conservative, preventive use of government intervention, particularly in relation to the free-enterprise system. Both are implicitly skeptical of the versatility and resilience of free enterprise. Haunted by Depression memories, many Democrats advocate continuous federal intervention. Fearful that the system is so fragile that even moderate federal programs will destroy it, the right-wing obstructionists want none at all.

The constructive conservative is not thus stultified by the prospect of federal action. He would use it judiciously to preserve and improve the existing political and economic institutions against the radical forces of change in the modern world. He will be alert to threats to liberty coming from outside of the federal government. He will observe closely the development of technology, urbanization, industry, and local government in an attempt to appraise their effect on the preservation of free-enterprise opportunity, individual liberty, and balanced federalism. He will be suspicious of proliferating investigations, controls, and "emergency" powers, which invade individual freedom and privacy, whether in the interests of "national security" or in the interests of bureaucratic efficiency, private or public. Confident of the essential vitality and utility of American free institutions and safeguards, he attempts to accommodate them to necessary change without damaging them. He recognizes and accepts the conservative burden of provident anticipation.

The party's position as a minority makes such vigilance more difficult than it is for a party in power. The majority party is compelled to face the problems of the society. The minority can more easily deny they exist and obstruct government action. This path of least resistance (obtuse obstruction) has too often been the Republican policy. The future of the party depends on its ability to abandon this path and assume the more difficult and elusive responsibility of facing and treating the problems early and judiciously. The Republican party must master the conservative role in a period of radical change.

◇◇

CHAPTER 19

The Democratic Failure

N ow is a propitious time for new ideological departures.
Many of the most hallowed tenets of Democratic liberalism are coming into question, and many Democratic programs
are foundering before the changing problems of the postwar
period. These failures have proven little political embarrassment
to the Democrats primarily because of the partisan incompetence
of the Republican party, divided between its conservative wing—
intellectually bereft and ideologically sterile—and its progressive wing—intellectually superior, but politically ineffectual within
the party and ideologically incoherent in opposition to the Democrats. Nonetheless, the erosion of the Democratic liberal ideology
over the last two decades and its increasingly conspicuous failures
afford an inviting opportunity for constructive Republicanism.

In the domestic arena, the Democratic ideology favors the
use of the managerial power of the federal government to treat
a variety of social and economic problems formerly considered
in the sphere of private enterprise or of the state and local government. Their approach of the last thirty years has been based

on two main assumptions: that state and local governments are obsolescent in most areas of policy, except as administrative extensions of the federal government; and that free-enterprise capitalism has exhausted its potentialities for contributing to human welfare and economic progress. Both of these assumptions have been refuted by the course of events since World War II.

The fact is that state government has been expanding much more rapidly than the federal government. Over the last thirty years federal expenditures, excluding defense, decreased by more than 50 percent as a percentage of the Gross National Product, while state and local spending have remained almost constant by this measure. Moreover, it is estimated that state and local outlays, now at over sixty billion dollars and six times the amount of federal outlays for civilian functions, will have to double in the next decade. The Supreme Court's recent decisions in the area of reapportionment promise to make state governments more responsive to the needs of urban and suburban centers, where in the past they have been most delinquent, and where federal programs have been concentrated.

Yet the Democratic ideology pays little attention to this vast arena of government activity. In the belief that state governments are almost necessarily corrupt, irresponsible, and reactionary, most Democratic liberals advocate programs which deprive them of current responsibilities, extend federal control over their activities, or bypass them altogether to deal directly with private businesses, individuals, and local governments. These programs do not greatly reduce the responsibilities of state governments, which remain enormous and continue to grow, and which are still protected to some degree by the Constitution. But by giving the impression that the federal government is assuming responsibility, they diminish the prestige and the sense of accountability of the state governments, impede the passage of adequate programs on the local and state level, and make it more difficult for the states to eliminate the very kind of irresponsibility and corruption by which Democrats justify federal intervention and control.

A particularly flagrant case of Democratic confusion on the proper division of labor between the federal government, state and local governments, and private enterprise is its civil-defense program, introduced early in the Kennedy Administration and annually eviscerated in Congress. Although Defense Secretary McNamara continues to give lip service to civil defense, the last major attempt to pass the program was in 1963. (If the United States should adopt a major anti-missile program, however, pressure for civil defense will be renewed.)

The key proposal is the shelter incentive program, offering an allowance of up to $25.00 for each shelter space provided locally. Since McNamara estimated, on the basis of optimistic assumptions about the likely form and intensity of Soviet attacks, that shelter spaces would cost an average of $40.00 apiece,[1] states and localities would have had to spend an average of $15.00 per space. Moreover, the Pentagon estimated that they would have to put up an average of $2.55 (*sic*) per space for food, medical supplies, and radiological equipment, on the evident assumption that these services could be provided during the two-week period underground for less than 17 cents a day. The Secretary also proposed federal incentives "designed to encourage private ingenuity in low cost shelter building." If such private ingenuity is not forthcoming (and there have been no signs that it was anything but a figment of McNamara's irrepressible optimism), the burden on the states and localities would be correspondingly increased. In any case, the total burden on these already overburdened governments would have been at least two billion dollars for the 110 million spaces projected.

This program exhibited utter indifference to the need for a rational division of labor in American federalism. It would have cost local and state governments about five times the amount proposed by the Kennedy Administration for federal aid for school construction and almost twice as much as advocated by President

[1] All these figures are quoted from Defense Secretary McNamara's budgetary testimony before Congress in 1963 and 1964. However, most of the subsequent figures on the prospective cost of the program are estimates calculated from the McNamara specifications.

Johnson. Since civil defense is directly competitive for tax money with education on the local and state level, the shelter incentive program, if passed, would have more than nullified the federal aid in this area.

However there is no reason whatsoever, except the convenience of federal budget-makers, for the state or local governments to help finance civil defense. Civil defense is obviously a federal responsibility. Although the Constitution may be somewhat indeterminate on education, it is quite clear in consigning "the common defense" to the federal government. In no domestic program, moreover, certainly not education, is federal direction so imperative as in civil defense—where much of the scientific data is classified; where all the people regardless of ability to pay, should receive as equal protection as possible; where the absence of national planning would result in panicky and disruptive movements from poorly to well protected areas in case of attack; and where the nature of the program conveys significant information about American intentions to the enemy. Yet in this area the Democrats insisted, and still insist, on state and local participation and individual initiative. If such a program is passed, the effect, of course, will be to increase gratuitously the financial burden on the already overburdened lower levels of government, reducing their ability to cope with growing needs in education, housing, and other fields primarily in the state and local domain. Thus a compelling rationale will be provided for further federal encroachment. Present dislocations in federal-state responsibilities will be exacerbated. Yet the Democrats give no sign that they recognize the implications of their civil-defense program for the federal system. If the program had not turned out to be politically unpopular for other reasons, it would be in operation today.

Civil defense is at present only a peripheral issue in American politics. But maintenance of a rational division of labor between the various levels of government in a revived and balanced federalism will become increasingly difficult and increasingly important as the pressures on all governments increase. The Democrats do not even seem to grant the existence of this problem.

Assuming that the states are obsolescent, they contribute to their decline. Yet the assumption is false, and the decline of state and local government means not the accession of federal panaceas but the deterioration of American government on every level, as the federal government overreaches itself in intervention.

Events since the war also have left prostrate the other original assumption of liberal democratic ideology: that increasing government initiative and control is essential to economic progress because of the exhaustion of opportunities for profitable investment in the developed economies. In fact, this assumption is now so preposterous that it is explicitly maintained in the Democratic party only by moralistic socialists and visceral populists, who represent a small though occasionally influential minority. However, prejudice against private enterprise still influences many leading Democrats—prominently including Vice-President Hubert Humphrey and Senate Majority Whip Russell Long—and Democratic ideology has never fully come to terms with the meaning of the postwar resurgence of private enterprise around the world, and the provisional adoption of some of its methods, like profit incentives, even by Communist countries.

Max Ways has described in *Fortune* what he calls "The Postwar Advance of the Five Hundred Million" (the population of the advanced capitalist countries, minus the underdeveloped segments, such as, for example, much of the American Negro population). These countries have surged forward, adding more to their total product in less than two decades since the war than they had added in the previous fifty. The method of the advance is as significant as its size.

> Within each of the advanced countries there was some degree of postwar liberalization from the state's intervention in capitalist processes, an intervention that had been growing before and during the war; there was a very marked liberalization in international trade among the advanced countries. As a result, competition flourished after 1945, and in the allocation of resources the role of national and international markets waxed.[2]

[2] Max Ways, "The Postwar Advance of the Five Hundred Million," *Fortune*, August, 1964.

The meaning of this phenomenon of growth "is often obscured by a deadly phrase—'of course.' In retrospect, we regard it as 'inevitable' that the industrial production of the seven leading countries should have doubled in 16 years. 'Naturally,' this was done while the average length of the work week was being reduced. 'Of course' they managed to provide more goods and services per capita for an increased population, and at the same time expanded the capital plant that will build tomorrow's goods. 'Of course,' in the U.S. the existing stock of plant and equipment rose nearly 70 percent from 1947 to 1963."[3]

Yet these possibilities would all have been dismissed as quixotic by most liberals after the war, impressed by the achievements of government planning during it, and relishing the prospect of new government management and planning for the economy in the future. The prejudice of the Democrats today for federal-government economic activity and their indiscriminate willingness to support new federal programs is a vestige of their once-articulate pessimism about private enterprise and their advocacy of quasi-socialist controls.

The record of failure of a large number of the most vaunted federal programs does not vindicate uncritical willingness to support them. Federal programs have failed, or promise to fail, in meeting such problems as growing agricultural subsidies, urban degeneration, unemployment, and poverty. If Republicans had often presented constructive alternatives, instead of dividing and neutralizing themselves on the Democratic initiatives, they would be in a good position today to claim a massive vindication of their critical and cautious attitude toward expansion of the federal government. But in many cases they lacked both the initiative and the intellectual resources to perceive the specific weaknesses of these federal programs and to make suggestions for their improvement. The opposition was usually so categorical that it actually facilitated the passage of the bills by lending the impression, again and again, that the only alternative to the Democratic approaches was neglect of the problem. Sentient

[3] Ibid.

Americans could hardly accept Republican denials of the existence of many of these problems: unpredictable and demoralizing fluctuations of farm income; the aesthetic and physical degeneration of many of the nation's cities; the prospect of acceleration in the growth of already excessive manpower unemployment; and the pertinacity of both urban and rural poverty. The problems were obvious to anyone who came into contact with them.

The failure of the federal farm programs—particularly in the field of price supports—is a national scandal. To point out this failure today is not very difficult or constructive. However, the failure illustrates some of the problems to be incurred by ill-conceived and incautious federal intervention in the market economy, and thus provides a useful lesson.

The results of the program mock most of its original purposes and expectations. Price supports and related costs now total nearly five billion dollars. But four fifths of this money goes to the million farm families (under 30 percent) who need it least: those whose farms are affluent and productive and whose problem, in fact, is national over-production. The price supports tend to reduce pressures for quality and efficiency normally exerted on these farmers by competition in the marketplace, and often actually encourage them to produce more, thus increasing the surpluses that depressed the price of their commodities in the first place.

On the other hand, the two and one half million farmers (over 70 per cent) who provide a little over 10 percent of farm production receive only one fifth of the subsidies. Their problem is low income and the government aid they receive is insignificant. Moreover, 35 percent of the "farm families" are actually part-time or part-retired farmers and derive their principal income from off-farm sources. Yet they are treated the same in the subsidy program as full-time farmers living in poverty and the affluent farmers contributing to the swollen surpluses.[4]

The Johnson Adminstration seems to have all but given up on efforts to improve the situation. One of the program's most

[4] Position paper on agriculture, Governor Nelson Rockefeller, 1964.

militant proponents, Hubert Humphrey, is Vice-President, and the party's Southern wing, led in the Senate by Majority Whip Russell Long, is growing increasingly enthusiastic. The Democrats are unlikely to initiate major reforms. The problem may soon deepen into a real crisis, when the Common Market countries close off American farm exports and thus increase the American surplus. Meanwhile, in a bureaucratic enormity, the number of employees in the Department of Agriculture approaches the number of farmers in the United States.

The federal programs for urban renewal have been a similar five-billion-dollar fiasco (though stretched over a longer period rather than spent annually). As in the case of farm price supports, the Democrats recognize the failure but lack the political initiative and ideological creativity to do much about it.

The 1963 report of California Democratic Governor Edmond Brown's Advisory Commission on Housing Problems indicates the failure of the program in our largest state. Present federal housing programs, according to the commission, are "inadequate to California's needs and largely irrelevant to its situation."

> The federal housing program was devised to help prime the country out of a depression. In 1937 it assumed a social purpose, primarily to aid older eastern and southern cities. Gradually, it expanded into a program of many motives—economic and political as well as social—until today it is a melange of programs, some usable in California, others not; some operable in certain situations and not in others; some that can be used but which are not being used; some that might be useful with supplemental state assistance and others that are presently inconsequential but would be helpful if modified.[5]

One of the many ironic aspects of the program is the tendency of those who object to it in their own area to assume it must be working better elsewhere, perhaps in the "older Southern and Eastern cities." But with some exceptions (primarily in the few cities with plenty of vacant housing), the program

[5] Governors Advisory Commission on Housing Problems, California, 1963.

has not worked satisfactorily anywhere, and many observers are reaching the conclusion that, as presently constituted, it will never be a satisfactory instrumentality for the regeneration of the nation's cities and particularly for improving the housing of the poor.

The best and the only comprehensive analysis of the program is *The Federal Bulldozer: A Critical Analysis of Urban Renewal, 1949–1962*[6] by Martin Anderson, an exhaustive and authoritative statistical study sponsored by the Joint Center for Urban Studies at Massachusetts Institute of Technology and Harvard University and based on data from all the country's urban-renewal projects. One does not have to accept Anderson's thesis that the entire program should be abolished to recognize the cogency of his case that, because of the way it has been managed, it has dismally failed to achieve most of its declared objectives.

The figures are by now familiar. In its first decade it destroyed 126,000 homes, of which 25,000 were judged to be in good condition by the local renewal authorities. Meanwhile, it constructed 28,000 homes, of which only a little over 3,000 were public housing, cheaply available to those displaced by the project (after a five- to nine-year delay for its completion). Although few people were affected during the first years, Anderson estimates that by the end of 1962, 1,665,000 persons had been displaced or were scheduled for displacement. By April, 1963, the number actually removed was over 600,000, and William Slayton, Commissioner of the Urban Renewal Administration, has stated that 1,000,000 families (or approximately 4,000,000 persons) will succumb by 1972. With them will go over 200,000 small businesses, of which according to past experience, 25 to 40 percent will be dissolved. At the same time, rents for those displaced (and almost everyone else) will increase, without an appreciable improvement in their housing conditions.

The statistics of the failure, marshaled like the Chinese army in Anderson's book and in adticles by Herbert J. Gans in *Com-*

[6] Cambridge: Massachusetts Institute of Technology Press; 1964.

mentary,[7] can be reinforced by statistics on the incidence of delinquency and crime in urban-renewal buildings, by statistics indicating that urban renewal may often actually reduce the tax revenue available to the cities involved, by the unstatistical but nonetheless undeniable ugliness of many of the projects, by the huge and callous bureaucracy created to manage the program, and by the militant and unappeasable opposition it has provoked from most of its victims. As Nathan Glazer, University of California sociologist, has put it: "One man's slum is another man's home, one man's blight is another man's neighborhood."[8] This point becomes more meaningful when one considers that two thirds of the victims are impoverished Negroes and Puerto Ricans. A sizable number of them were living in housing judged by authorities to be adequate, and in any case inexpensive; after eviction they faced a housing market contracted not only by the destruction of their former homes in the city but also by pervasive discrimination. The "Negro Removal Program," as it has been called even by moderate civil-rights leaders like Roy Wilkins of the NAACP, dislocates the lives and raises the rents but hardly ever improves the housing of the racial minorities dominantly affected. However, the program was continued in 1966 with only minor changes, designed more to increase its political palatability than to increase the availability of adequate housing for slum families.

The urban-renewal fiasco is only one aspect of the concussive impact of federal-government programs on the nation's cities. And it is only one aspect of the abysmal failure of the Democrats in their efforts to solve the problems of these areas, where two thirds of the people live and vote overwhelmingly Democratic, while the Republicans look elsewhere, as Barry Goldwater put it, hunting "where the ducks are."

Federal intervention in the economy over the last decades

[7] "The Failure of Urban Renewal: A Critique and Some Proposals," *Commentary* (April, 1965). See also debate in subsequent issues between Gans and Professor Henry J. Raymond.

[8] "The Asphalt Bungle," *Book Week*, New York *Herald Tribune*, January 3, 1965.

has been growing continuously, and most of the programs affect the cities, often in conflicting ways. For those who manage to avoid dislocation by the urban-renewal bulldozer, there is always the federal highway program to replace them with interstate thruways and more cars, which in most cases the cities need as much as the air pollution they bring, but which are made enormously attractive by the willingness of the federal government to put up 90 percent of the financing. Bernard Weissbourd, the president of Metropolitan Structures Inc., points out that the disproportionate amount of the federal budget allotted to agriculture also adversely affects the cities.[9] By stimulating the mechanization of farm areas, it accelerates the migration of impoverished Negro and white farm labor, imposing new burdens on the cities' welfare, education, and public-housing programs.

A similar conflict between the varying objectives of different federal programs—and one which similarly works to the disadvantage of the cities—provided the background for President Johnson's proposal of federal rent supplements in his housing program for 1965. The President called the supplements "our most crucial new instrument to improve American cities."[1] Their purpose is to stimulate further construction under the hitherto unsuccessful federal middle-income-housing program. This program was designed to bring back some of the middle-income families who have been moving to the suburbs, often leaving the central cities dominated by impoverished Negroes.

Housing experts see little chance that the supplement could succeed in reversing this trend, however, since for almost the last two decades the federal government has been promoting it. Nearly half the total mortgage on one- to four-family houses in non-farm areas is insured by the Federal Housing Administration. Of the rest, a substantial portion is held by savings and loan associations, which are restricted by law largely to invest-

[9] Paper published by the Center for the Study of Democratic Institutions, 1965.

[1] President's message to Congress on housing and cities, March 2, 1965. Text printed in *The New York Times*, March 3, 1965.

ments in home mortgages. Since most of these homes are outside of the cities, capital is artificially directed into the suburbs, and since the Administration persists in its refusal to outlaw bias in homes financed by federally insured mortgages, even middle-income Negroes are artificially restricted to the central city. Along with income limitations on occupants of public housing, this combination of federal programs and policies—some desirable, some not, but few attentive to the real problems of urban areas—encourages the flight of whites to the suburbs and the emergence of the cities as redoubts of segregation and impoverishment.

The Democratic failure in urban areas is exacerbated by the party's failure to provide enlightened local leadership. Many of the largest American cities are run by notoriously corrupt and unimaginative Democratic political machines, based on paternalism, patronage, segregation, and waning ethnic loyalties. It is their ineptitude which, to a considerable extent, has brought about the problems currently cited by the Democrats to justify extreme federal intervention in the cities. It is their ineptitude which has lent credibility to the Democrats' strictures against local government. Yet the inadequacy of these machines should properly be an argument for reform of local government, not for federal programs to control it. The Democratic failure *in* the cities, in fact, can be measured in part by the extent of Democratic legislation *for* the cities at the federal level.

One of the main themes of Democratic ideology over the last several years has been the intolerable incongruity of widespread poverty and unemployment in a society which has overcome the problem of scarcity and acquired affluence even as an epithet. The Democratic ideology of federal expansion and state obsolescence exonerates the party from blame for failure in such areas as the maintenance of a rational and balanced federalism. But the reduction of unemployment and poverty has long been a key objective of Democratic policy and a central commitment of Democratic platforms and campaigns. It is on these issues that they proclaim special insight; it is on these issues that their performance can be judged in terms of their own ideological rhetoric. Of poverty and unemployment, President Johnson says, rhetorically: "We shall overcome." His programs, however, scarcely engage the problems.

To begin with, in rhetoric and in program, the Administration persists in confusing the two problems. But in fact they barely overlap. Less than one eighth of all poverty-stricken families, according to the Administration's definition, are headed by an unemployed person ostensibly capable of getting or holding a job. The rest comprise the disabled, the elderly, and women with children.[2] Unemployment remains a grave and demoralizing problem for millions of Americans, and it is likely to grow more serious in the future as automation advances through the economy and the postwar generation swarms into the job market. But most of the impoverished have jobs. Unemployment could be abolished without helping them. Their problem is that their pay is too little to sustain their families, which are larger on the average than the families of the more affluent. As long as it concentrates on unemployment, the War on Poverty will continue to miss most of the impoverished. Similarly, the campaign against unemployment will miss most of the unemployed as long is it concentrates, as it has so far, on fiscal policy designed to increase demand, without taking major steps to reduce the impact of automation.

Gardner Ackley, the chairman of the President's Council of Economic Advisers, and other Administration officials believe automation to be qualitatively and quantitatively analogous to the general technological advance which has transformed American society over the last fifty years. They believe that, like the previous advance, it can be accommodated by the expansion of demand created by economic growth. Their optimism is based partly on a 1964 manpower report which shows a 4.3 million growth in "non-farm employment" between 1957 and 1963 and on a recent slight decrease in unemployment, to the point where

---

[2] For a discussion of this point, see Eveline M. Burns: "Where Welfare Falls Short," *The Public Interest* (fall, 1965).

it was under 5 percent of the work force during 1965. A few economists believe the reduction is partly explained by the number of unemployed who have given up seeking employment altogether. But even assuming that there was real improvement in the situation during 1964 and the first months of 1965—a period of almost 5 percent annual growth in the GNP—predictions for the future must take into consideration the possibility of recession. Economists who pretend omniscience show only their ignorance of the history of economic prophecy. Moreover, all employment predictions must take into account the enormous projected growth of the labor force at a time when automation is demonstrably accelerating. In 1964 it was estimated that less than 2 percent of all American industry suitable for automation was actually automated. But orders for automated equipment are expanding and the number of computers in use was expected to increase 25 percent in 1966. Meanwhile the labor force, according to Labor Department statistics, is expected to increase by almost 20 percent in the next decade, as the postwar generation moves into the labor market.

Technological change was estimated by the Labor Department to have cost over a million jobs in manufacturing industries alone between 1956 and 1961, and there was a comparable absolute overall decrease in the number of such jobs in the economy, partly due to the 1958 recession. Since then, according to controversial government statistics,[3] the trend has continued but employment of manufacturing production workers has increased nonetheless by an average of almost 300,000 a year because of high economic growth. Almost 65 percent of job growth throughout the economy, however, has been the result of direct government employment or employment generated by government procurement. Nonprofit institutions provided 16 percent, while full-time jobs created by industry's own efforts accounted for only 5 per-

[3] Since it is impossible surely to disentangle technology from other factors in national productivity increases, these figures are presumably very speculative.

cent.[4] Yet there was no increase in the government proportion of the Gross National Product. The fact is that the great expansion of industrial production was generating only insignificant numbers of new jobs even at the very beginning of the automation era. The amount of investment required to create a new job in the five-hundred largest corporations has increased almost three times in the last seven years, to over $70,000.[5]

The Administration's belief in the sufficiency of expanding aggregate demand as a source of new jobs thus implies an assumption that the economy will grow faster than ever in the years ahead. For it will require a steadily increasing increment of demand to justify the steadily increasing increment of investment needed to create each new job. Yet there is little evidence that economic growth can be increased much beyond the present level of nearly 5 percent, attained during these last years partly by heavy tax reductions. If growth does not increase, and *at an unprecedented rate,* the increased productivity level, inevitable in the long run with the progressive application of the new technology, will necessarily reduce the rate of employment growth—during a period when 1.5 million new jobs will be needed annually just to absorb new entrants into the labor market.[6]

Apart from fiscal policy, particularly in the tax-reduction programs, the chief Administration instrument to reduce unemployment has been the Manpower Development and Training Act, largely the product of Operation Employment, a rare congressional Republican initiative which studied the unemployment problem in 1961 under the leadership of Representative

[4] Ben B. Seligman: "Automation and the State," *Commentary* (June, 1964).

[5] Paper published by Research Institute of America, 1964.

[6] Some economists disparage the controlling importance of technology in increasing productivity growth. Cf. Robert M. Solow: "Technology and Unemployment," *The Public Interest* (Fall, 1965); Charles E. Silberman: series of articles on "Technology and the Labor Market," *Fortune* (beginning in January, 1965).

Curtis.[7] This act is valuable and constructive, but it is not a solution to unemployment. Although a high percentage of those receiving training have succeeded in getting jobs, the totals are insignificant in relation to the need. Moreover, the high percentages are largely the result of careful testing and screening of applicants. This approach alone clearly will not rescue the Democrats from the crisis of the convergence of automation and population growth.

The most formidable effort against unemployment is the War on Poverty. It is difficult to resist pointing out that it is neither a war, nor against poverty. The War on Poverty is in fact a minor skirmish directed primarily against youth unemployment, and escalated into a War on Poverty by the excelsior of Presidential rhetoric. Its educational aspects are difficult to gainsay, but it should be pointed out that there is just as much unemployment among educated youths as among dropouts. The early effect of the War on Poverty was to arouse hopes that it could not fulfill, and to dramatize the disarray of Democratic parties in the cities, where they disintegrated into warring factions over the new offer of federal money.

The war originated as a device to give President Johnson a distinct political identity that would be appealing to liberal Democrats. As such, it reveals as much about the poverty of imagination of the liberal Democrats as it does about the President. Poverty is indeed anomalous in the affluent society. For indeterminate millions of Americans, it means a grueling diet, dilapidated housing, unattended mental and physical illness, and lives of corrosive desperation. It would be good to have a program to attack it. But the President's program, though desirable if it can disentangle itself from the parasitical Democratic urban machines, will not reach the main body of the impoverished. It is in fact strange that the Democrats could not have developed a more respectable effort. As Irving Kristol has observed in several articles in *The New Leader,* the War on Poverty has raised expectations far beyond its capabilities—bearing an incriminat-

[7] Cf. Chapter 5, "Revise and Dissent."

ing resemblance in that regard to President Johnson's ineffable war on Cancer, Heart Disease, and other terminal illnesses. These, too, "We Shall Overcome" says the President, establishing a group of federal research centers and providing still more money for these heavily fertilized but hitherto little productive fields of research.

One of the gravest weaknesses of Democratic ideology is its penchant for creating bureaucracies. The Republican prejudice against bureaucracy is one of the party's most valuable dispositions. A real bureaucratic effort to eliminate the poor would produce a bureaucracy whose members outnumber them. Poverty, today, is different in nature from depression poverty. It is not a generalized enemy against which one can mobilize a vast national campaign on the federal level; poverty is a diverse and multiple phenomenon, found in farm areas despite massive federal subsidies; found in the big cities despite federal programs and paternalistic Democratic urban machines; found among the young and old in myriad individual circumstances. This kind of poverty can only be alleviated by programs which use the multiplicity of private and public agencies—those closest to the diverse problems on all levels of government and in the private sector—not by a Medicare program for the slogans of the thirties.

It will not be supposed that this attack on the Democrats can be complemented with a celebration of the Republicans. The Republican party has been at least as derelict. Neither party has shown an intimation of the ideological creativity of the Conservative party in England. However, the Democratic failures indicate that the mood of ideological defeatism which infects most of the Republican party is completely unjustified. The fact is that the Democrats have looked good only because the Republicans have assumed that their choice was me-tooism or obstruction, because they have succumbed to the banal dogmatism of the far right, and because the Democrats have had the sense to cultivate intellectuals while the Republicans have almost deliberately affronted them.

CHAPTER 20

An Ideology
for Republicans

CRITICISM and obstruction of Democratic programs can rarely succeed in ultimately stopping them. Republican opposition to Medicare was crumbling even before the party nominated a right-wing Presidential candidate and caused election of a Congress almost completely amenable to the President. Moralistic opposition to "the welfare state" continues. But the arguments aimed against this alleged monster usually miss it entirely—either soaring off into clouds of platitude or striking in the dirt with aspersions on the morality of the poor. Sizable welfare programs exist in the United States, but they are less comprehensive and use a smaller proportion of the Gross National Product than those in any other advanced country. Revisions are desirable, but it is fatuous for Republicans to expend energy attacking welfare programs collectively, particularly with reference to such billowy generalities as "self-reliance" and "free enterprise." Welfare programs in themselves have little to do with either.

Sweden, for instance, is often cited as a "welfare state" and thus "socialistic." Yet private enterprise controls a much higher proportion of the Swedish Gross National Product (90 percent) than the American, and Swedish corporate tax rates are substantially lower. As for "self-reliance," the welfare opponents cannot seriously contend that reliance on the state is so much more compromising than reliance on private charity—which, by failing in urban areas, necessitated public-welfare programs in the first place. Or that thrift is encouraged by the probability that old age sickness will wipe out one's savings.

American welfare programs are in chaotic condition today; they are often ineffectual. Republicans could play a useful role advocating specific reforms. However, their empty sanctimony about "individual initiative" represents a self-defeating abdication of this role. As James Burnham has argued cogently in *National Review,* it was the failure of the conservatives to produce a suitable alternative to Medicare that made its passage inevitable. Today it is the role of the conservative to insist that Medicare and other social-security and welfare programs are properly and economically administered. If the Republicans are going to be successfully conservative, they must be specifically and constructively conservative.

A constructive Republican approach in domestic policy could be based on several themes, all consonant with conservatism, Republican tradition, and the national interest. These would be a revitalized federalism based on a rational balance of responsibilities between the states, localities, and the federal government; the regeneration of the nation's metropolitan areas; a more flexible and imaginative use of the private-enterprise system to treat human problems; a new concern for the special problems of youth—such as education and military service; a conservative approach to technological progress emphasizing the primacy of individual liberty; and the conservation of natural resources—their use to enrich the nation's leisure and their protection to enhance its beauty.

The maintenance of a rational balance between federal and state power would be accepted by most Republicans as a fundamental objective of Republican policy. It is a commentary on the party's present condition that it has failed over the last several years to exploit effectively even this area of near unanimity, while some Democrats, particularly former Governor Terry Sanford of North Carolina, and, of course, some high officials in the Administration, are showing considerable interest. Action must begin with the assumption that a revival of federalism is necessary and worthwhile—that the states and local governments are here to stay, and that both contribute to the vitality and creativity of American pluralism and to the meaningfulness of democratic processes.

This view, imposing the burden of proof on the proponent of the essentially "national" character of any particular need, is an ideological position. But its assumptions are demonstrable. The federal government has yet to show any magical competence in solving local problems, and state governments have taken the initiative frequently throughout American history in devising solutions to the problems they face. In fact, much of Franklin Roosevelt's New Deal, including social security, and many of Lyndon Johnson's civil-rights and poverty programs originated in similar measures enacted long before on the state level. The states often can act more quickly, experimentally, and creatively than Washington. The federal government is encumbered by the complex diversity of many national problems and by the diffusion principle—the rarely violated dictate, enforced by legislative politics, that federal programs distribute their benefits as widely as possible among the fifty states. The diffusion principle destroyed the effectiveness of the Area Redevelopment Administration (ARA) and may seriously weaken the Appalachia and the Public Works and Economic Development programs of 1965. ARA, at its height in 1963, had embraced one third of the nation's counties in its depressed-area category but had made little dent in the most blighted regions.

A commitment to states' rights, responsibilities, and potentialities does not imply obstruction of federal programs. A balanced federalism will require the resourceful use of the federal government whenever it is clearly justified by failure on the state and local levels, or by a problem which is homogeneously national in scope and for which a national program affords large economies of scale. Separate state programs of medical insurance for the elderly, for instance, would have been much more expensive and less efficient than federal Medicare. Governor Rockefeller has asserted that use of the Kerr-Mills medical-care program in New York would have entailed politically and economically prohibitive tax increases, or cutbacks in state services.

Financial incapacity on the state or local level, however, is not sufficient justification for federal controls. The idea that federal money must necessarily entail federal controls is currently accepted by both liberals (with relish) and conservatives (with horror). It is nonsense. The fact that the federal government has pre-empted the most remunerative tax sources and, in any case, is the most efficient tax collector is irrelevant to the question of which governmental level can best treat a particular problem. Financial incapacity on the lower levels is in itself justification only for the use of the superior tax resources of the federal government to subsidize the states.

If the federal government does not act, the states are doomed as responsible democratic units of government. For without federal aid their finacial failure is inevitable. In the next decade the financial needs of the states are expected to double. The lowering median age of the population will double educational expenses; the migration of the poor into urban areas, where the cost of public services is greatest, will multiply expenses in housing, community development, highways, public utilities, public health, and sanitation. Borrowing is no answer. State debt has increased six times since the end of World War II—from 15 billion to over 90 billion dollars.[1] In order to maintain anything like the present balance between state and federal responsibilities, major federal abnegation is necessary. Inaction will bring radical change in the structure of American federalism.

[1] Research paper by Richard Nathan, staff economist for Governor Nelson Rockefeller, 1964.

Republicans should commit themselves to the return to the states of certain tax sources now commanded by the federal government; they should review, in terms of possible unrestricted return to the states, all of the some eighty grant-in-aid programs which total over 10 billion dollars and comprise about 15 percent of all revenue received by state and local governments; and they should support the institution of a system of tax credits whereby the states can credit certain specific taxes against specific federal taxes, thus reducing the danger that states which meet their responsibilities will be put at a competitive economic disadvantage in relation to other states. If these measures prove insufficient, Republicans should advocate direct unprescriptive grants to state governments. Such a program should not be designed to reduce present federal resources, which are growing almost 50 percent faster than the GNP; it should be oriented to conserve the system of balanced federalism, which otherwise will be in grave jeopardy in the near future.

Republicans also should pay close attention to the possibilities for interstate cooperation. In 1965 the federal government passed two programs in this area which bear far-reaching implications for federal-state relationships. The first was the Appalachia Act. This measure authorized expenditure of 1.1 billion dollars in some twelve states by an Appalachia Regional Commission composed of the governors or their representatives from the states and a federal official appointed by the President. The second, the Public Works and Economic Development Bill, was passed in August, apparently in concession to the diffusion principle. It provides for the creation of other such regional commissions among consenting states outside Appalachia, and envisages an initial annual appropriation of 60 million dollars. These two programs were passed hastily and their long-range effects are still unclear. Ideally, however, they provide a new institutional vehicle for the fulfillment of state responsibilities through state participation in the planning of federal expenditures for regional economic development. Republican governors should closely investigate the potentialities of these programs for strengthening the states and should insist that the states retain maximum control as the programs evolve over the years.

If these regional commissions are not exploited by the federal government for political purposes or for the extension of federal controls, they may provide the states with a new instrument for the solution of regional economic problems, once left to the inept attention of federal pork-barrels like ARA. It is deeply ironic that as a "constructive alternative" to the Appalachia program the Republican leadership offered a bill almost identical to ARA, which they had wisely opposed when it had been presented by the Democrats. However, it is not too late today for Republicans, particularly Republican governors, to play a leading role in maintaining these new programs as a vehicle for the revival of the states.

Now is a promising time for state regeneration. The enfranchisement of Southern Negroes and the development of the Southern Republican party will ultimately eliminate the one-party system based on racism that has made state government in the South a mockery of American democratic principles. The Supreme Court reapportionment decisions are creating a ferment in all the states which will make them more susceptible to change and more responsive to metropolitan needs than they have been in the past. The Republican party should make it a prime policy objective to guide this change in constructive directions and to publicize achievements of Republican governors and other state officials.

A similar attitude of commitment is needed from the Republicans toward the nation's metropolitan areas. The party's negligence in this area is reflected by the fact that, after continuous metropolitan losses culminating in the debacle of 1964, no member of the congressional leadership specifically mentioned the urgent needs of the cities in his proposals for party revival. Gerald Ford wrote an entire article for *Fortune* magazine on the future of the party without even mentioning the cities.[2] Melvin Laird—

[2] Gerald R. Ford: "What Can Save the G.O.P." *Fortune* (January, 1965).

previously the editor of a collection of "Conservative Papers" which failed to intimate that the United States is no longer a reflection of his own agrarian district—also responded to the defeat without mentioning the special needs of the cities. Later, in one of the party's most abysmal performances in recent years, Republicans in the House, with Ford a significant exception, joined with dissident Democrats to stop a bill giving home rule to the District of Columbia, thus once again flouting the interests of urban voters and, since Washington is 64 percent colored, casting a racial insult to boot. The progressive Republicans excelled the right-wingers in rhetoric, but only a few, such as John Lindsay with his entrance into the New York mayoralty race, showed a full recognition of the party's needs and responsibilities.

The Republicans do not have to imitate Democratic ideology in the cities; nor should they. With the cities seized by a process of near-convulsive and often self-destructive change, the Republicans can usefully adopt a conservative position in relation to them. With the state legislatures growing increasingly responsive and the state treasuries increasingly munificent (presuming passage of legislation to make them so), the Republicans could reject the concept of the city as a ward of the federal government. In general, the Republicans should discourage and impede the Democratic urban alliance, wherein corrupt and sterile but efficient vote-producing city organizations are maintained through the continuous subvention of the federal government, saving them from their own weaknesses.

Apart from resolute and persistent challenge to city governments now dominated by Democratic bossism, perhaps the most important goal of Republicans in relation to the cities should be thoroughgoing reform of the urban-renewal program. Although the cities will need federal aid for some time in even greater quantities than this program now makes available, in many cases new housing projects do not renew the city, but contribute to the inhumanity of the urban environment. These drab, cellular buildings are a kind of vertical petrification of the city's spirit. Not only are they ugly but they also stifle a sense of community and engender new anxieties and frustrations.

Reform should begin with the principle that destruction of existing housing is a last resort. It can be justified only by a demonstration that greater quantities of satisfactory *low-cost* housing could not be produced by expenditure of comparable amounts of money to construct new housing elsewhere or, where possible, to rehabilitate existing homes. The demonstration should be required before the area is condemned. At present the Urban Renewal Administration gazes on city housing with a Medusa's eye. Its mere consideration of an area for urban renewal freezes it in its condition of decay. The entry of new businesses and the expansion of old ones is discouraged. Banks refuse to give loans and mortgages for reconstruction or repair. A true "urban renewal" program would stimulate loans for the rehabilitation of buildings and the establishment of new businesses in degenerating sections of a city. The emphasis of urban renewal must be on renewal, not on destruction, so that its consideration of an area will attract new business to it and encourage its revival.

When destruction becomes necessary, as it often will, it is elementary that the interests of the individuals and businesses to be dislocated take precedence over the economic interests of the project itself. Thus destruction should not occur until the former occupants have been relocated. The whole concept of using federal money for appropriation and destruction of property, not in order to transfer it to public usage but to accommodate other private interests, is of precarious constitutionality unless the rights and interests of the former occupants are scrupulously protected. Urban Republicans should devote themselves to the protection of these rights and interests. Nothing in the record of the urban-renewal program so far justifies its pre-eminent domain in prescribing the interests of the cities. The Republicans should advocate grants of even larger sums to the cities with more flexible federal prescriptions. Some of the money is best used for typical "urban renewal," but much might more usefully be directed toward urban education, medical care, pollution control, and other urban needs, which vary greatly from city to city. As long as the city governments are treated as incompetent and in need of continuous and detailed federal instruction, they will remain that way. But, in any case, the incompetence of many urban governments is no excuse for withholding the massive amounts of money needed by many of the nation's blighted and congested cities.

In taking a conservative position toward the nation's cities, the burden of proof will be on the Republicans, who on the national level have often ignored the cities entirely and on the local level have often defined Utopia as a policeman on every corner. Republicans must recognize that without a full, sympathetic, and intelligent commitment to the regeneration of the nation's cities, conservatism amounts to an abdication before the anarchic forces of urban change and ensures that any urban crisis will be met according to the interests and ideologies of the Democratic urban alliance. The Republican must recognize and act on the premise that the cities have special, expensive needs which must be represented and acted upon by the federal government as long as local and state governments, often underfinanced and malapportioned, refuse.

The conservation and regeneration of American cities is an urgent and challenging task. It cannot, unfortunately, be left to the anarchic forces of a private real-estate and construction market. It is a matter, on the one hand, of conservation—of saving the city's soul, of maintaining the primacy of the individual and asserting his rights against the concert of huge commercial, bureaucratic, and governmental interests that would exploit him, move him, and investigate him; that would destroy his home and his business, pollute his air, invade his privacy, ravish his parks, and desecrate his historical and architectural heritage. And it is a matter, on the other hand, of regeneration—of providing for stable urban growth, which does not end at the edge of the slums; of meeting the great and intractable educational needs of the impoverished, and thus redeeming wasted human lives; and of creating an urban environment of aspiration, excitement, and even beauty, which can bring back many of those who have fled into the suburbs and make life worth living for those who stay. This dual cause of urban conservation and regeneration, if the Republicans commit themselves wholeheartedly to it, could go far toward regenerating the party itself and conserving *its* heritage.

A further area for a constructive conservative approach is technology. This has been the most truly radical force in the world over the last fifty years. When one compares conditions in the United States today with those existing at the beginning of the century, one sees that the most important changes have been wrought not by governments aggrandizing their power, passing new laws, and deliberately changing American institutions, but by the transfiguring thrust of research and development providing new techniques and machines which the American people, their institutions, and their governments together have exploited and accommodated.

Until recently almost all research and development, with the exception of that conducted for the improvement of American agriculture, was done by private industry. It was changes in the private sector of the economy, propelled by business, which effected the transformation of the conditions of life in America. Over the last decade, however, government-financed research and development has vastly increased, to the point where today it is almost four times the five-billion-dollar effort financed privately. Most of the government effort is directed toward space and the military. The amount of economically significant research and development undertaken by private individuals or small businesses has been rapidly decreasing in proportion to the total effort. Technology has become an ally of the leviathans—primarily the military-industrial complex but also the largest industries and institutions outside it, and the federal government.

The conservative role will become increasingly important as the radical onrush of technology continues through the economy and society. The existing federal bureaucracies, many of them created by Democratic administrations, make unlikely a realistic confrontation of the new technology by the Democrats, tied to old improvisations, until it produces a major crisis. So far the Democrats have diverted the thrust of technology into space and to the military, thus mitigating and postponing its impact on the domestic sphere. But as Defense Department economist Charles Hitch has indicated: "There is no reason why technological development cannot have as great an impact in the private sector as it has already had in the military"[3] where it completely revolutionized the nature of warfare. The revolution in military and space technology, however, impinges only peripherally on the freedoms of individuals; it brings higher taxes and it invests new interests. A similar revolution in the private sector could radically threaten traditional American political, judicial, and economic values and institutions.

Such a revolution is in progress. It is only impeded by the diversion of research and development resources—the most scarce and most indispensable being scientific manpower—into the military and aerospace fields. The revolution is gathering force all the same, and the Democrats are inclined to ignore it, or see it as an innately benign and progressive development. Thus they are inclined to allow it to develop anarchically, irrationally. The Republicans, by providing a program to both stimulate and control the new technology in the public interest, could play the most valuably conservative role in their history. They would be conserving their principles, which are distinguished from those of the Democrats in asserting that individual freedom, which the Democrats also plausibly claim to promote in their expansion of federal power, importantly depends on the conservation of economic freedom and political decentralization. The paradox of conservatism today is that only early federal action to discipline and canalize the radical thrust of technology, only early federal action to apply the new technology in ways that promote decentralization and economic

[3] Quoted in article by Edward T. Chase in the *Yale Review* (Spring, 1963).

liberty, can prevent these principles from succumbing to technocracy.

One of the prime freedoms enjoyed by Americans and one which is diminishing under the impact of unguided technology— one which moreover constitutes a prime value of Republicanism —is individual economic enterprise, exemplified by small business. The competitive position of small businesses in relation to larger businesses has long been weakened by the lesser ability of smaller businesses to resist the demands of organized big labor and by their lesser ability to acquire cheap and dependable financing for expansion. Today the new technology further increases the advantages of the larger businesses; for they can best afford to experiment with new techniques and equipment and their size makes it worthwhile to pay the price of expensive new machinery.

The new computers, for instance, not only magnify economies of scale in mass production of goods. They also increase the efficiency of large businesses in processing bills and orders; they facilitate their preparation of tax returns and exploitation of loopholes; and they contribute to the maintenance of appropriate levels of inventory in outlets across the country in response to fluctuations of demand. Small businesses, which benefit hardly at all from new technology even in an absolute sense, find their relative competitive position seriously weakened. As time goes on, they are likely to become weaker still. The larger concerns will grow more sophisticated and discriminating in appealing to special markets, more efficient and perspicacious in circumventing federal regulations and in minimizing their tax burden. For instance, larger concerns have even relocated parts of their operations to take advantage of right-to-work legislation, low state taxes, or other special investment incentives offered increasingly in recent years by states or municipalities seeking new business.

Meanwhile the small businesses find steadily fewer special market opportunities unmet by the leviathans, and small retail outlets encounter new problems as the society becomes increas-

ingly mobile. Many citizens acquire a closer sense of identifica-
tion with the national chains than with the neighborhood
businesses. These trends, largely impelled by technological
progress, show no signs of decline. If opportunities for small-
scale enterprise are to be kept open, government at every level
will have to contribute to solving its problems.

The decline of small business under the impact of automation was statistically verified in 1964 by the Research Institute
of America. For purposes of its survey, a "small" business was
defined as a company with assets up to 5 million dollars; a large
business with assets of more than 200 million. Between 1956 and
1963, the number of small businesses declined, despite the heavy
growth in the population and the Gross National Product. Their
sales grew only one third as fast as the sales of the leviathans;
their investments only 41 percent as fast. Moreover, their profits,
after taxes, actually declined 16 percent, while those of the large
firms were growing by almost 50 percent.

The critical factor in these trends, according to the institute,
was the increasing cost of the equipment necessary to maintain a
competitive position in the economy. Within the seven-year
period, the cost of investment per worker in the larger companies
increased over five times, from $13,000 to $70,000.[4] Although
these statistics may exaggerate the situation in some respects, the
acceleration by the new technology of the trend toward larger
businesses is clear despite the increase in relatively small "service
industries."

If this trend persists, the economy of the future will have
still less room for small business. Most Republicans—indeed most
Americans—believe that small-business opportunities contribute
importantly to the pluralistic freedom of American society. This
contribution is obvious in the economic realm where many Americans experience their freedom most fully in starting and running a small enterprise. But it extends also to the political and
social realms, where small-scale, sometimes idiosyncratic, economic activity affords a livelihood to the nonconformer and the

4 Research Institute of America, New York, 1964. Cf. Chapter 20.

dissenter, even to the crank, who would be rejected for employment in the organization-men bureaucracies of big business. The leviathans, moreover, will be able to coordinate their employment policies much more effectively in the future. It is already possible to construct a computer which could hold information about every employable person in the country. With the increased use of personality and intelligence tests and other standardized criteria, access to the relatively decreasing number of good jobs is likely to become almost impossible for a person with an idiosyncratic record, perhaps marred by youthful homosexuality, by a jail sentence, by controversial political behavior, or by a low "personal-stability quotient." Such persons will suffer most from any reduction in the multifarious opportunities offered in small businesses. Only the conformist bureaucrat will gain.

These predictions are not farfetched. They are fetched in Washington, D.C., in the federal government, where such employment practices already prevail. Employees with good records have been summarily fired for youthful indiscretions belatedly discovered by investigators, and have henceforth been excluded from all other government employment. Talented applicants have been denied government jobs because of abnormal performance in personality tests, because of an unstable private life, or because of former association with a Communist front organization. The federal government, not even counting the FBI and CIA, purchases a quarter of all the mechanical listening and spying devices produced by this booming industry.[5] The use of these devices and other methods for investigating the conduct of employees, even off the job, is endemic in large bureaucracies and represents a major threat to the dignity and privacy of the individual. Although many of these practices cannot easily be outlawed, something can and should be done about the egregious excesses of the mechanical "snoopers," and something should be done to preserve pluralistic free-enterprise opportunities afforded by small business.

[5] See article in *The New Republic* by James Ridgeway, "The Snoops" (December 19, 1964).

An emphasis on small business is essential also to any meaningful program against unemployment. Even though small businesses produce only 34.1 percent of the output of American industry and trade, they provide 44.8 percent of the jobs,[6] and well over half of the jobs for the low-skilled. In general it is the smallest businesses—the businesses which receive the least help from the government and the least help from the new technology—which contribute most to the national effort against unemployment. In general it is the largest businesses, most particularly defense industries—the most heavily aided by the federal government and by the new technology—which contribute fewest jobs per dollar of investment or output. Defense industries, dominantly the aerospace and chemical concerns, have lower value added per manhour (labor intensity) and more highly skilled personnel (mostly technicians and scientists) than any other major sector of the economy.[7] Leading in labor intensity (i.e., providing the most jobs per dollar of investment) are the service industries and such manufacturing concerns as lumber, textile, and leather goods, most of them in the small-business category.

Republicans, therefore, should declare their belief in the value of small businesses and develop a program to encourage research in machines and processes suitable for their use. If the trend away from small business continues, the party should advocate major revisions in the tax laws to improve their competitive position. It is the largest businesses which have benefited most from government-sponsored research and development; it is the largest businesses which have received the bulk of government contracts and which have been able to exploit most

6 Edward B. Shils: "Small Business: Prospects and Problems," *Current History* (July, 1965).

7 It is thus a myth that defense spending is an important weapon against unemployment. Comparable sums spent for almost any other purpose (except space exploration) would produce more employment. Annual tax cuts, such as those proposed by Goldwater during the 1964 campaign, would stimulate the economy far more, provided non-defense public spending was maintained, whether on the state or federal level.

effectively the loopholes and local disparities in our tax, labor, and minimum-wage laws. Yet it is small business which provides proportionately the most jobs and the most opportunities for individual enterprise and initiative, and which contributes most to the variety and pluralism of the American economy and society. Although the overwhelming contribution of big business to the country's economic progress cannot be gainsaid, and while it would be self-defeating to curb its legitimate operations, it is opportune now for a renewed emphasis on the contribution, only quantitatively inferior, of small business. It is appropriate for Republicans to take the lead.

Most economists today predict that the new technology will importantly affect the number and quality of jobs in the economy. Jobs may become harder to find and to hold, and less interesting and challenging than they used to be. Administration economists, however, see it differently. The labor force will need to become more mobile and versatile, they assert buoyantly; henceforth, workers will have to think in terms not of one career but of several, not of a lifetime of homogeneous drudgery but of repeated retraining and new challenges. Technology to them is an unalloyed boon.

This alleged dynamism and fluidity of employment opportunities is presumably the reason for the doubling by the Administration of the percentage of unemployment considered "frictional," and thus an expression not of an objectionable waste of human lives but of surging economic progress. Now 4 rather than 2 percent of the working force is considered to be in transit, moving back and forth across the country, from job to job, from "career" to "career," perhaps orchestrated by new Labor Department computers designed to match men and occupations, much as new computers in large businesses adjust inventories to markets in outlets across the country. The Administration predicts continuous increases in demand and output and acceleration of economic growth to solve the unemployment problem. Presumably "frictional" unemployment will be alleged to increase correspondingly.

It is difficult to deny that technological progress will cause friction. It is unlikely, however, to be entirely as beneficent as envisaged by the Administration. Human beings are not at all like commodity inventories. They have homes and families; they become sentimentally attached to particular communities; as they grow older they are apt to become less adaptable, less willing to pull up and move out to join a retraining program in preparation for a position perhaps inferior to their previous one. They do not come in a new, convenient portable model. To an important degree American employment is currently organized on the psychologically valid principle of successive promotions based on the accumulation of knowledge and experience. A man commits himself to a job and does his best, largely in the expectation that he will be elevated in time to a more responsible and remunerative position, not dismissed and forced to leave his home to enter a retraining program, in which he may begin on a par with younger workers.

The vision of the future implicit in much current employment analysis leaves little room for human beings. Machines are seen displacing workers (at varying rates, true) and the workers are relocated in turn by other machines in a steadily expanding economy. Such traditional human incentives and stabilizers as job security with regular promotions, or participation in the social activities of a particular community and advancement to community seniority and leadership, are sacrificed to the abstract value of economic progress through technology. Even occupational choice may be restricted as increasingly sophisticated vocational aptitude tests come into wider usage and worker placement is managed to an increasing degree by computers programmed to economic and technological criteria.

It is easy to project mechanized nightmares from technological trends. Communist China is the most horrific example of a society in which human values have in fact been subordinated to economic and technological values. A democratic society, however, is theoretically capable of defining its own values and subordinating technocracy to them. The Republican party, to a greater degree than the Democratic party, stresses the principle that conservation and extension of individual freedom, including the freedom of economic choice, properly takes precedence over the expansion of material welfare. Regardless of how one views the advance of technology, it is difficult to deny that it reduces job security; that it tends to reduce the number and profitability of small businesses; that it increases the efficiency of bureaucracies; that it affords new instrumentalities for the invasion of privacy and the observation and evaluation of individual lives; and finally, and undeniably, that it greatly expands the productivity and efficiency of the economy. Thus technological advance, as it is currently proceeding, contracts individual liberty, most particularly in the economic realm, but in the political and social realms as well, and at the same time makes theoretically possible a substantial increase in material welfare and comfort. Although the Republicans can hardly begin their campaign for majority approval by coming out against welfare and comfort, they should always be alert to the cost in human values of economic and technological progress. They should be always ready to act to safeguard individual freedom and privacy.

Furthermore, the Republicans cannot expect the Democrats to remain inactive. The radical left in the United States is attempting to use the advance of technology to justify radical changes in the structure of the American economy and society. Economists like Robert Theobald and povertarians like Michael Harrington assert that the new technology and the new poverty will necessitate vast expansion of the role of the federal government. The Administration currently rejects these arguments. The rejection, however, will not impress conservatives who have any awareness of the dynamics of Democratic liberalism. In foreign policy the Democrats are "liberal" until a crisis, when they often stiffen into a "conservative" rigidity. In domestic policy they are often conservative until a crisis. The new technology may well produce a job crisis in the future. The Republicans should not wait until it happens before they act. For in such a situation the

Democrats will not hesitate to act in ways offensive to Republicans.

One issue which is due to be engaged with increasing intensity over the next several years is reduction of the work week. Most Republicans who have so far considered the subject have recoiled in moralistic horror, as if the proposal represented a radical departure from existing practices. It is nothing of the sort. The work week already has been reduced from 66 hours in the mid-nineteenth century to 40 hours in the mid-twentieth. Further reductions are occurring now and will continue to occur. The question is whether the reductions will be adjusted to the development of automation or whether they will come primarily as a result of the strategic position of particular unions, such as the electricians in the intricately galvanized complex of New York City.

Republicans should make it conspicuously clear that work-week reduction, as well as promotion of small business, are central in their response to expanding technology and the problem of unemployment, and they should develop a program for the most humane and economic pattern of work-week reductions. In the highly competitive world economy, it is not realistic to advocate American deceleration in applying automation and other technology. The most constructive and conservative approach to the boon and problem of technology is to insist that its benefits be shared and that the national interest in maintaining full employment be served. Reductions in the work week should be made first as an immediate and localized complement to the introduction of job-reducing equipment. Thus the smallest businesses with the highest labor intensity and least ability to resist the demands of organized labor for shorter hours would not find their competitive position weakened by increased labor expenses—increases resulting in part from pressures raised by technological innovations in larger businesses. In any case Republicans should not equivocate on the basic point: the need for work-week reduction to increase the number of jobs in a situation of continuing technological progress. For the Republicans to allow the Democrats to pre-empt them on this issue would be not only economically reactionary but politically obtuse.

Complementary to the reduction of the work week, and explicitly linked with it in the Republican response to technology, should be an obdurate stand for the conservation of American's natural endowment. Increased leisure and vacation time will increase usage of America's national parks, beaches, and wilderness areas. Many of them are already so overcrowded that their essential natural values are lost. Such areas must be expanded and new areas must be set aside. Anyone who has seen the destruction of the redwoods in California, the onslaught of lumberers in the Cascade region in Washington, or the feverish negotiations of the steel mills for rights to the Indiana dunes— all as these areas are being considered by Congress as possible national parks—knows that this is a race against time and against opposition which strikes fast and resourcefully. Moreover, areas with natural assets in danger of permanent deformation or depletion, but not necessarily suitable for national parks, should also be protected. For example, it is intolerable that the irreplaceable farmland south of San Francisco be permanently lost through suburbanization for the temporary profit of California real-estate interests and that the hills of Western Kentucky be "skinned and decapitated" by strip-miners.

Opposition to such developments is not injurious to the free-enterprise system, but essential to its preservation. If free enterprise is allowed to damage irreparably and destroy irreplaceably, all for ephemeral profit—if it is allowed to exploit the nation's resources at will, polluting the country's atmosphere and its rivers, cluttering its beaches and its pastures, bulldozing away its richest soil—that system will so discredit itself that it will not ultimately survive.

Republicans, as conservatives, should take the lead in asserting the principle that in the use of the nation's resources and expansion of its technology the public interest must prevail. Because Republicans value private enterprise, they must ensure that it operates in the public interest. In the past, the party has often taken the lead in the field of conservation. This aspect of Republican tradition is supremely relevant today.

It is obvious that the future of the Republican party depends on its ability to capture the imagination of the nation's youth, overwhelmingly estranged by the Goldwater Presidential campaign and by the frenzied young conservative and Young Republican organizations. Contrary to the hopes of the radical left, American youth does not constitute a homogeneous class which could be organized into a coherent political movement. But young people nonetheless do share certain common interests which deserve the most urgent attention of the Republcan party as it develops programs for the future. Two key areas of youth concern are education and the military draft.

The draft is a feature of modern American life so familiar that most people have forgotten it represents a significant destruction of liberty and choice for millions of young men. It might receive more critical attention if most people did not simply and dully accept it as inevitable and necessary, and if its primary victims were not too young to be familiar with the rights and enjoyments of adult citizenship and too disorganized—like "the invisible poor"—to be heard in political debate.

Defense Secretary McNamara estimated at various times in 1965 that replacement of the draft by a professional incentive program would add an additional four[8] or twenty[9] billion dollars a year to the military budget; and he has given the obviously false impression that outright abolition is the only alternative to retention of the system as it is now. Republicans urged elimination of the draft in 1964, but without a full investigation of the real alternatives. Although military involvement in Vietnam is said to have made draft reform unrealistic, in fact it has exacerbated the inequities that the Selective Service System, with its multiple exemptions and capricious choices, inevitably brings. Republicans

[8] In answer to a question at a congressional hearing on the Defense budget on February 26, 1965, McNamara estimated $4 billion.

[9] In an interview with *This Week*, December 5, 1965, he said at least $20 billion. It is difficult to believe that the Vietnam war is solely responsible for the increase.

should follow up the initiatives of Congressman Curtis and former Senator Keating and sponsor a full-scale investigation of the possibilities for immediate reform and eventual elimination of at least the worst features of the present system. One clearly desirable change would give permanent exemptions to those who enlist in the Peace Corps or perform other low-paid services for their country, even if they fail to partake of the warrior mystique. In any case, further investigation is needed, and it is doubtful that the periodic Democratic inquiries, always conducted by the Pentagon, will come to any conclusions more adventurous than the usual two cheers for the status quo.

Draft reform should not be confused with disarmament. The inequities and inefficiencies of the present system, the high turn-over and the low morale, increase the expense and impair the military utility of the U. S. Army. A system which at least partly replaced the negative incentive of the draft with positive incentives for long-term enlistments would enhance the fighting capacity at the same time that it reduced the social burden of maintaining eternal vigilance over the volatile peace.

In few areas does the United States so exceed the rest of the countries of the world as in the quantitative availability of educational opportunities. No other country in the world approaches the United States in the proportion of its secondary-school graduates who attend college (50 percent) and no other country approaches the United States in per-capita spending on education.

The vast American investment in education has richly repaid itself. A recent study attributed 27 percent of the growth in the Gross National Product over the last fifty years to improvements in the quality of manpower. There is little reason why the investments of today should not bring a comparable economic return. But as important as the economic benefits will be the success of the schools in alleviating social problems, with significant political implications, which many educators long have assumed are not the province of the schools at all. Paramount is the matter of preparing Negroes for full integration into the society after a century of crippling privation. The primary agency for this process is the slum school, and it is in the slums that the American educational system is most seriously failing. There are inefficiencies, inadequacies, and distorted values elsewhere in the system, particularly in the South, but nowhere are they so incapacitating as the discrepancy between need and performance in the Negro ghettoes.

The programs of federal aid to secondary education submitted to Congress over the years before 1965 and regularly impaled on the issue of aid to parochial schools provided a fine example of the effects of the diffusion principle. These programs, if passed, would have had almost no significant effect on the schools that most need federal aid. The money would have provided temporary tax relief to the overburdened states. But its impact on specific, localized educational problems, particularly in the slums, and even its long-term impact on educational opportunity across the country, would have been negligible. In fact, by giving the false impression that the federal government was assuming important responsibilities in secondary education everywhere, these programs might have reduced the sense of responsibility of the states and localities where the major responsibility for education, practically and constitutionally, continues to reside. These federal programs were animated not by new educational problems of a national scope particularly suitable for federal treatment but by the financial problems of the states, which these programs nonetheless were completely inadequate ultimately to solve.

The federal contribution to the solution of American educational problems will always be secondary. Along with private individuals and foundations, the states and localities retain primary responsibility, and it is on these levels that there exist the greatest opportunities for productive initiative. On the local level, in relation to the slums, there is a need for the initiative and cooperation of Republicans for redrawing school districts to advance integration, for experimenting with new techniques designed to meet the special problems of slum children, and for developing programs to bring the best teachers, currently better paid in the suburbs, to slum schools. On the state level, the potentialities and challenges are equally great. James Bryant Conant has proposed creation of new regional interstate educational commissions for pooling of information and coordination of educational policies. Such commissions now exist principally for higher education. Dr. Conant called for a "bold new effort in cooperative federalism" to extend such commissions to lower-level education where diversity is less important. Educational policies collectively adopted or coordinated by the states themselves, which retain the primary responsibility, are likely to have a far greater impact than policies, however ambitious or enlightened, recommended by the federal government. Moreover such commissions should create new concern for local or statewide educational deficiencies previously unrecognized by the officials responsible, and foment among states a mutually critical and competitive attitude which can only benefit the overall cause of educational improvement.

Lyndon Johnson's Education Bill of 1965 at last shows a recognition that the chief need and justification for federal action, by the test of private, state, and local failure, is in the slums. Although the diffusion principle is not entirely circumvented (some of the wealthiest school districts in the country will be receiving funds), the bill nonetheless does represent a most desirable breakthrough, which in general should be critically supported by Republicans interested in maintaining a rational division of labor between the federal government and the states.

Another area where it is appropriate for the federal government to play an expanding role is in the provision of college scholarship aid. The Republican party during the Eisenhower Administration introduced one scholarship program, the Defense Education Act, which, with its emphasis on scientific and engineering skills, was designed to advance the military and economic benefits of education. Today, however, education is even more important in its role as a transmitter of intellectual and cultural values in a society with increased affluence and leisure time and with an aspiration for greatness.

Currently a considerable percentage of fully qualified high-school graduates, because of financial incapacity, never attend college, or attend colleges of their third or fourth choice. As a long-term objective Republicans should advocate a program of scholarship aid, perhaps limited at first to five hundred dollars a year, for any student admitted to an accredited college. For some students of lower-income families such assistance would mean the difference between college training or none; for students from families with slightly higher incomes, it would mean part relief from time- and study-consuming jobs or from the burden of post-graduation debts. For still others it would improve the choice of schools to the extent quality and price are commensurate. It would not bring about complete equality of educational opportunity on the university level, but it would bring America closer to this ideal than any other society. Because it would help the college by help-ing the student, in some cases it would free endowment monies for the improvement of teachers' salaries and capital plant, while keeping the federal government at arm's length. This goal of such a program is the creation, not of a welfare state but an Opportunity State.

The overall cost of the plan, if implemented in 1970, would be approximately four billion dollars annually. If the previous American experience with educational investment is an indication the program would quickly repay itself in an expanding GNP. But its primary value may come from its effects in enriching the lives of its beneficiaries in less measurable but no less important ways.

Such scholarship programs should be accompanied by tax incentives to encourage the support of private colleges. The trend toward bigger and more bureaucratic educational institutions is most acute among the great state universities. These leviathan public schools tend to be more similar to each other, more sus-ceptible to political influence, and less responsive to individual diversity than autonomous private universities. By supporting private colleges—perhaps through a rebate for taxpayers who contribute money to them—the Republicans would expand the variety of opportunities, and reduce the pressures for conformity in American education. The party should not have difficulty choos-ing between policies leading toward an educational system primarily designed to transmit technocratic values—to produce graduates ready to step submissively into preordained roles in a bureaucratic and technological society—and policies encouraging educational pluralism and diversity, designed to give maximum choice and opportunity to the free and self-reliant individual for his own fulfillment.

Today one quarter of all Americans are in school or college; ten years from now it will be one third.[1] Education is clearly a matter of deepest political importance. The American educational system, however impressive in magnitude and ambition, is nonetheless pervaded by obsolete and unnecessary bureaucratic customs and conventions, and by parochial and anachronistic attitudes. Republicans, because of their conservative disposition, will receive many invitations on the state, local, and national levels to defend the parasites of the status quo. But the status quo must change as the needs of the society change, and there is little about present practices which cannot be improved. Moreover, Republicans will receive continued appeals from the obscurantists who would attack the schools, colleges, and universities for their most indispensable quality, their intellectual freedom. The Republican gubernatorial candidate in New Jersey, Wayne Dumont, disgraced himself and his party in 1965 by making his primary campaign issue the refusal of the Democratic governor to intervene in the state university and compel the eviction of a young Marxist professor who during a "teach-in" expressed sympathy for the Vietcong. Such an issue is a confession of intellectual and political bankruptcy. Republicans, in the words of Dr. Conant, must "take education seriously."

In foreign policy partisan ideology is not as important as it is in domestic policy, or as important as national ideology. But the attempt over the last several years to discredit partisanship has reached the level of noisy if inarticulate clamor under this "consensus" Democratic administration. Although the intellectual level of the appeals for "national unity" rarely rises above a plaintive "stop bothering us" or "mind your own business," the

[1] Peter Drucker, *Harper's* (February, 1965).

attitude they express has inflicted important damage on our democratic processes and foreign policy. For the *absence* of a defined partisan role results not in bipartisanship, but in irresponsible and valueless partisanship, or the unreviewed, uncriticized conduct of foreign policy.

In order to employ our political institutions to the best advantage in the international arena, we must come to terms with the two-party reality. The provision of an important and positive role for the opposition will redound in more constructive criticism, more generous crisis cooperation, greater national unity, and a more effective foreign policy than the present attempt to deny almost any independent role at all for the Republicans.

Partisanship in American foreign policy has tended to vacillate from the apologetic to the obstructionist to the radical. There have been the tentative suggestions for marginal changes, familiar during the Eisenhower Administration, when the Democrats considered the President's prestige and popularity too formidable to challenge. There has been obstinate and uncreative obstruction, exemplified by myopic resistance on both sides of the aisle to the Kennedy and Eisenhower foreign-aid and trade-expansion bills. There have been the trumpeting demands for radical changes, such as adoption of a new isolationism, unilateral disarmament initiatives, disengagement in Europe, or preventive war. But no party in opposition has managed to develop a satisfactory rationale for the approach it has contingently adopted.

The incumbents have called for "bipartisanship" to neutralize the opposition. The opposition in turn has attacked or acquiesced more or less as political pressures indicated. Since the partisan approaches which have been employed successfully have not been articulated into a coherent party policy, there is no guide of authoritative precedent for new congressmen or other opposition leaders to follow. The result is that partisanship becomes haphazard and unsystematic and even the value of potentially useful partisan themes has been impaired by distortion and exaggeration.

Republicans have long been consistent in their reluctance to allow unchecked Executive control of foreign policy and have insisted on thorough legislative oversight. Constructive examples include the party's opposition to direct treasury or "back-door" financing of foreign aid, and the usual Republican skepticism toward "summit meetings" and other unorthodox diplomacy. A further extension of this principle of congressional review and worthy of the party's support, would be the creation of a senatorial committee to oversee the Central Intelligence Agency. This agency spends an estimated two billion dollars annually without any close accounting to the Congress.

The Republican desire for a check on the Executive has occasionally gone to undesirable extremes, as in the case of the proposed Bricker amendment, severely restricting the power of the President to conclude Executive agreements with foreign governments. If this bill had been enacted, it would have gravely hampered our diplomacy and overburdened the legislature. Another expression of this tendency, the chimerical McCarthyite assaults on the integrity of the State Department, represented partisanship gone berserk. However, these aberrations should not be allowed to discredit the underlying principle that executive conduct of foreign policy should be subject to the kind of close and constructively critical surveillance which the American Congress and two-party system can provide if it is responsibly managed. In fact, the political importance of foreign affairs combines now with the efficiency of administration news management to make such surveillance essential to meaningful democratic processes.

Principled partisan surveillance is also demanded by the nature of the international situation. In a period of rapid ideological obsolescence, when events are outpacing theories or outshouting them, there is a tendency—often decisive with the Democrats—to adopt an approach of unprincipled pragmatism in which problems are considered independently of each other and of the past. Secretary of State Dean Rusk once said we have 110 different foreign policies, or one for every country in the world; and a flexible approach is indeed preferable in a revolutionary period to the procrustean imposition of dogma. It is true that Republican principles themselves do not offer a significant guide to the problem of choosing the most promising design for a new submarine.

However the absence of principle also will have damaging consequences. Without a confident and programmatic commitment to its principles, the United States will find itself constantly acquiescing in the status quo or extemporizing when it changes. Events take control and impose on our diplomacy an expedient neutralism toward ideology and negligence toward principle. When totalitarian dictatorships emerge in the underdeveloped world, we find ourselves referring to "the necessity for centralized planning in primitive economies" or the need for political order. When a possible Communist threat arises in Latin America, we ignore all the principles of the inter-American system and land the Marines without telling them what to do.

Yet the United States has achieved the most durable democratic system in the world, the most powerful military establishment, and one of the most productive economies. We do not have to act in a diffident, fearful, or impulsive way. The Communists are militant in promoting and extending their system and contemptuous of law. Under such circumstances, ideological neutrality and expedient abandonment of principles are abdications which have the effect of serving the uneducated prejudices of the underdeveloped world, the ideological purposes of the Communists, and the lawless plans of aggressors. Although practical considerations will sometimes necessitate compromises, we must maintain and prosecute our commitments to such principles as democratic federalism, regulated free enterprise, and international legality, or they will become irrelevant.

In this connection two aspects of the proper role of the opposition emerge: first, though the Republican and Democratic parties are not so far apart that they possess radically different conceptions of the American role and purpose in the world, the two parties are distinctive enough to give significantly different emphases to various aspects of that role and purpose. One conspicuous example is that the Republicans attach considerably more importance to the conservation and promotion of private enterprise than do the Democrats. Republicans are apt to be more skeptical of Communist intentions, less hopeful about the negotiability of such cold-war issues as Berlin. These ideological tendencies lend important coloration to the views of the two parties toward the outside world. Republican principles cannot be applied directly and unmodified in international affairs but they can provide a valuable frame of reference which will influence policy differently than Democratic principles, such as they are.

Second, the opposition, just because it is not engaged in the daily conduct of foreign policy, is more likely to retain a comprehensive and far-sighted view informed by a concept of overall American objectives. In a Republican administration a natural receptivity toward ideological principles is balanced by the responsibility for day-to-day treatment of empirical problems. In the current situation, however, the Democrats' natural propensity toward expediency in foreign affairs is reinforced by their role as incumbents embroiled in ephemeral crises. In the Democratic administration the technical problems of the Atomic Energy Act eclipse the imperatives of alliance solidarity. The presence of Communists in Santo Domingo leads us to scrap the long-established principles of hemispheric conduct. We sacrifice ultimate goals to convenience. The Republicans can perform a supremely valuable function in continually drawing attention away from the transient fears and crises which can engulf policy to the ulterior principles which can enlighten it and give it coherence. But in both the domestic and foreign spheres, the Republicans must be specific and programmatic in application of their principles.

For the party to adopt such positions will require organizational and ideological reforms in some cases, but they do not have to be revolutionary. In the domestic sphere, the party can remain conservative, but it must become effectively, practically, constructively conservative to succeed. It cannot leave city government to the Democrats; it must engage the participation of the emergent political generation in improving government on all levels. It cannot be dogmatic about the role of the federal government. In areas where the state cannot or will not act, it must urge federal intervention, first through the provision of new incentives for private and state action, then, if necessary, through direct federal intervention. In the international sphere, the party should not attempt to reduce all problems to simple exercises in the containment of communism; it must develop programs which take into account all the intricate diversity of a modern world in which many nations, however irresponsibly, are trying to avoid cold-war entanglements. The crucial objective will be the development of an approach which, in fact rather than merely in proclamation, protects the essential American interests in the world and the best in the American heritage. The nation cannot afford, in a revolutionary time, to cling nostalgically to obsolescent social, political, and economic usages in the United States or to narrow ethnocentric concepts of international reality, while ignoring the very real threat to American interests and values posed, for instance, by the technological revolution and by the increasing immiseration of many of the overpopulated countries of the underdeveloped world. The party needs an ideological regeneration, and its progressives will have to show the way.

The Progressive
Republican

I N THE LAST election the progressive Republicans were emphatically vindicated in their assertions that a right-winger could not win. But they still have not demonstrated satisfactorily that they could win, or why they should. They still need a satisfactory ideological approach. If they can develop one and propagate is successfully, the party will be theirs because the right-wing approach has been demonstrated as a political disaster. Moreover, the party will be worth having, because it will have a means both to arouse its hard-core supporters, and to reach the millions who have left it. But if the progressives fail, the party will remain a lame and divided creature, incapable of offering national leadership or conducting a successful national campaign.

The progressive Republican can come up with many excuses for his ideological failure. There are the technical problems, the lack of money and staffing; there is the alienation of the intellectuals and the almost complete failure of the academic world to think in terms of the Republican ideological problem; there are the political pressures lending strong public support for Democratic programs; there is Democratic control of the Administration, structuring the issues and to an extent predetermining the feasible and responsible solutions; there is the hostility of many Republican magnates and financiers to new ideological departures; and there is, in the end, the feeling that the country is happy enough with things as they are and that progressive Republicans are satisfactorily occupied in revising, amending, reworking, and regulating the centralist overtures of the Democrats. These obstacles to change are undeniably formidable and in view of them it is indeed understandable that the progressive Republican does not make much of an effort to do anything new and venturesome.

For it is not as though there were something disreputable in the present approach of the progressive Republicans. Unlike their right-wing opponents, they are true to the party's traditions and to the nation's interests. Reasonable, responsible, and dedicated, they contribute valuably and constructively to the legislative process. Their deliberate skepticism toward new accretions of federal power for nebulous and indeterminate purposes is entirely justified and desirable, imposing on Democratic planners an otherwise unlikely deference toward the interests of the private economy and of state and local government. For example, it was the insistence of progressive, not right-wing Republicans, which caused the inclusion of an option for private insurance in the Medicare program. This option, by encouraging and partly subsidizing private programs, eliminated from Medicare all threat that, in itself, it could lead to socialized medicine. Moreover, the tendency of Progressive Republicans to support the Democratic Administration on the most crucial foreign-policy votes, like foreign aid and the Nuclear Test-Ban Treaty, shows a scale of priorities which appropriately elevates the national interest above partisan convenience. In fact, if the presently critical and revisionist attitude were enough to maintain progressive control of the party and to afford promise of national leadership in the future, the proponents of ideological reappraisal and regeneration would bear a heavy, though not insupportable, burden of proof, at least in political terms if not in terms of the national interest.

It is clear, however, that the present approach will neither give the progressives control of their own party nor afford promise of national leadership. It is grave political failure that constrains them to seek new approaches. It is their failure to maintain control of their party even against its most obtusely reactionary and jingoistic elements; it is their failure to fulfill their potentialities for conservative national leadership in an essentially conservative, because prevalently comfortable American society, whose traditional institutions and values are nonetheless faced by unprecedented forces of change and obsolescence; it is their failure to assert a memorable identity in the history of the time.

If the new responsibility of the progressive Republicans stems from their own failures, their opportunity stems from those of the Democrats. The Democratic failures are serious in many respects. But they are not cataclysmic or conspiratorial or likely to become so, and the opportunity they afford the Republicans thus is not obvious or easy. Right-wing attempts to magnify the Democratic failure, to misrepresent it as a catastrophe, could not substitute in 1964 for thoughtful and realistic critiques and persuasive alternatives. The people sensed empirically that Goldwater's frenzied visions of a coming debacle in the cold war and a gathering "fascism" in the United States were either theatrical or paranoid. The people know that the nation will likely survive under the Democrats and that the election of a Republican administration is not urgent, demanded by a mortal and immediate threat to the republic, misapprehended or mismanaged by the opposition.

The Republican party after Goldwater is burdened by a public distrust it has yet to dispel. Barring an unexpected Democratic collapse, the Republicans cannot win in 1968 without innovation, without a dramatic break from the past. They cannot win either by a compromise with reaction or by an incantation of moderate clichés. They must offer a telling critique of the Democrats and a distinct and appealing program of their own.

The prerequisites of revival are clear. The party must be willing to affront its right-wing zealots and provide imaginative programs for regeneration of the nation's metropolitan areas, where a steadily increasing proportion of the people live. And the party must provide enlightened and progressive leadership to win back the nation's growing ranks of young people, who, despite wild right-wing claims, were overwhelmingly alienated in 1964 and who, according to polls by Samuel Lubell and Louis Harris, are far more opposed than their elders to the theories of arch-conservatism. In appealing to these groups, the party must have a progressive candidate, preferably not associated with Goldwater in 1964. Republicans should not be driven to a compromise choice out of a misconceived notion that the progressives were disloyal then, for their reputed "disloyalty" will be one of their most important assets in appealing to an electorate which did not treat "loyal" Republicans very well in 1964.

It should not be supposed that there will be no risks in nominating a progressive in 1968. Right-wing Republicans, between calls for "unity", are talking about starting a third party in 1968 if an unacceptable candidate is nominated. It is possible that such a party, a Dixiecrat or national Conservative party, could win the states, except for Arizona, that the Republicans won in 1964. But otherwise it will be the Republicans who are reduced again to those Southern bastions.

The evidence of the Conservative party of New York in 1964 and 1965 and the Progressives and the Dixiecrats in 1948 do not give reason for Republicans to be alarmed by the prospect of a third party. Five out of the six New York Republican congressional incumbents who received a Conservative party endorsement were beaten, while several of the Republicans opposed by conservatives won by heavier margins than ever. The mayoralty campaign of William F. Buckley, Jr., designed to destroy John Lindsay in New York, actually took more votes from his Democratic opponent,[1] particularly among Irish and Italian Catholics who felt that the Democratic party had become too responsive to the demands of the Negro. Buckley, too, performed the service of dramatizing Lindsay's opposition to Goldwater. Truman was opposed in 1948 by both the Progressives and the Dixiecrats and won anyway. A third party now would give the right-wing its chance to show how many of those vaunted 27 million are really "dedicated conservatives," as they define the term, and how many are merely loyal Republicans. It would allow the Republican party itself to attend to the needs and interests of those who voted for Goldwater reluctantly, and also to the millions of Republicans who voted for Johnson, even while recognizing the President's very considerable flaws—flaws that ordinarily might have elected a Republican. Moreover, the party could provide a candidate who can reach the silent vote—not the white backlashers or the "underground" conservatives, but the 6 million Republicans who stayed home in 1964 or skipped the Presidential contest to vote for lower offices only, eloquently testifying to what *they* thought of the "choice." All this will require new approaches and personalities in 1968. If the extremists refuse to go along, they can be left behind. Only the Democrats will miss them.

The best hope of the Republican party today is the rapidly changing composition of the American electorate. The 1960 census figures indicate that by the 1968 election the average age of Americans will be approximately twenty-five, down eight years since 1960.[2] The huge generation, born after the war, will be graduating from schools and colleges in unprecedented numbers and into jobs of unprecedented average renumeration. Many of them will be making investments; a large proportion will be living in the suburbs and owning their own homes. Their ethnic self-consciousness will be tenuous; they will

[1] A poll by Samuel Lubell in the New York *World-Telegram and Sun* after the election showed the second choice of Buckley voters to be Democrat Abraham Beame, 7 to 5 over Lindsay.

[2] *Harper's* (February, 1965).

be neither impoverished nor unionized. Their dominant concerns will be education, employment, promotion, taxes, leisure facilities, health, foreign policy, and the improvement of the metropolitan environment. They will not be so susceptible to the nostalgic class and ethnic appeals of the Democrats, deriving from the forgotten conflicts and grievances of the 1930's. They will be unswayed by the ideological arguments for aggrandizement of government at the expense of the private-enterprise system on which their wealth and future opportunities depend. They will be interested in escaping the arbitrary harassment of expanding governmental and business bureaucracies. With more time and thus more time for politics, they will not follow reflexively a party line.

These voters will be more prosperous and better educated, their self-interest more conditioned by dispassion than any elec-torate in our history. They will epitomize a Republican dream: the free citizen, personally competent, socially concerned. A pro-gressive Republican party should become their natural home.

The generation that pioneered in the suburbs is being suc-ceeded by the generation that looks to the metropolis as a whole; they are a generation that engages the city with hope rather than resignation. They are demanding vitality from institutions their predecessors surrendeded to corruption and incompetence—the city halls of Louisville and New York, the statehouses of Wash-ington and Michigan. And their instrument very often is a re-formed and reforming Republican party.

But it is a measure of the recent failure of the party that in many cities and states, and nationally, the Republicans have ignored or affronted the new majority, and it is poised to opt for the Great Society. Its suburban forerunners first moved toward the Democrats in 1960, and in 1964 they voted overwhelmingly for Johnson. The Democrats, with the cooperation of the Repub-lican reactionaries, are moving to establish themselves within the changing electorate. The new electorate will not choose the Republicans unless the Republicans choose them, and the GOP too often has turned toward the past.

The Republican progressives are left with their potential and their opportunity. If the Republicans respond to the real problems of conservatism in a time of radical change, if they make a new ideological and political instrument, they can redeem the Republican heritage and win the new majority.

INDEX

A NOTE ABOUT THE AUTHORS

GEORGE F. GILDER was born in New York in 1939 and graduated from Harvard University in 1962. He was editor of *Advance Magazine* from 1960 to 1964. He has held a junior fellowship from the Council on Foreign Relations and is now an associate editor of *The New Leader*.

A native of Illinois, BRUCE K. CHAPMAN was born in 1940. He received a B.A. from Harvard University in 1962. He was publisher of *Advance Magazine*, of which he was a co-founder, from 1960 to 1964, and is now an editorial writer for the New York *Herald Tribune*.

A NOTE ON THE TYPE

The text of this book is set in Calendonia, a typeface designed by W(illiam) A(ddison) Dwiggins for the Mergenthaler Linotype Company in 1939. Dwiggins chose to call his new typeface Caledonia, the Roman name for Scotland, because it was inspired by the Scotch types cast about 1833 by Alexander Wilson & Son, Glasgow type founders. However there is a calligraphic quality about this face that is totally lacking in the Wilson types. Dwiggins referred to an even earlier typeface for this "liveliness of action"—one cut around 1790 by William Martin for the printer William Bulmer. Caledonia has more weight than the Martin letters, and the bottom finishing strokes (serifs) of the letters are cut straight across, without brackets, to make sharp angles with the upright stems, thus giving a "modern face" appearance.

W. A. Dwiggins (1880–1956) was born in Martinsville, Ohio, and studied art in Chicago. In 1904 he moved to Hingham, Massachusetts, where he built a solid reputation as a designer of advertisements and as a calligrapher. He began an association with the Mergenthaler Linotype Company in 1929 and over the next twenty-seven years designed a number of book types for that firm. Of special interest are the Metro series, Electra, Caledonia, Eldorado, and Falcon. In 1930 Dwiggins first became interested in marionettes and through the years made many important contributions to the art of puppetry and the design of marionettes.

Composed, printed, and bound by
The Haddon Craftsmen, Inc., Scranton, Pa.

Typography and binding design by Anita Karl

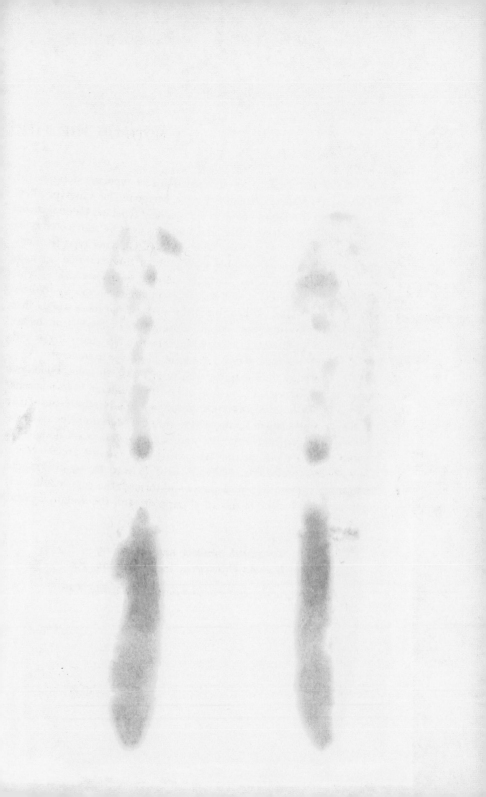

6/15/66